Taken for a ride: the electrobus pauses for the cameras on the day of the press launch in April 1906. Sitting inside the bus to the left of the driver is the brains behind the swindle, Dr Edward Ernest Lehwess.

A MOST DELIBERATE SWINDLE

HOW EDWARDIAN FRAUDSTERS PULLED THE PLUG ON THE ELECTRIC BUS AND LEFT OUR CITIES GASPING FOR BREATH

MICK HAMER

RedDoor

Published by RedDoor
www.reddoorpublishing.com

ISBN 978-1-910453-42-1

Cover design: Patrick Knowles
www.patrickknowlesdesign.com

Typesetting: Tutis Innovative E-Solutions Pte. Ltd

Print managed by Jellyfish Solutions Ltd

This book has its own website: www.mostdeliberateswindle.com. The website
has updates about the electrobus swindle, fuller information about the
sources used and a readers' forum for comments, queries and clarifications.
Any significant amendments will be incorporated in future editions.

To the unknown journalist
who first stumbled on the electrobus swindle

Contents

Contents

Introduction

I first came across the electrobus when I was learning to read. The only picture book in my parents' house was the *Pageant of the Century*, a chronological review of events in the first third of the 20th century, with big pictures and short captions.[1] It was not only a good way of learning to read, it was also a history lesson.

The editors of the *Pageant of the Century* had picked 25 photographs to illustrate the most important events of 1907. There was a dramatic shot of a church tower on the point of toppling over during the great earthquake that devastated Jamaica and killed 1000 people. There was the Kaiser reviewing the German battle fleet at Kiel. And there were the great and good in all their finery watching the racing at Ascot – and failing to spot the daring theft of the Ascot gold cup from a table in full view of the grandstand. Prominent among these momentous events was the debut of the electrobus.

Fast forward to 2007. By now I was a freelance journalist and casting around for story ideas, when I remembered the electrobus. The centenary was a topical peg and I knew exactly what the story was. Or at least I thought I did. It was a brave attempt to introduce environmentally benign transport in London, with clean and quiet buses. But it was doomed to fail. Vehicles that run off batteries, like the electrobus, have a fundamental drawback. Lead-acid batteries, which until recently were the most common type of battery, are heavy. Weight for weight, petrol packs far more power than a battery. So electric vehicles are heavy, slow and have a limited range. It was a contest that petrol would always win. And that, according to the received wisdom, was why the electrobus failed.[2]

All I needed to do was to find out a little bit more about these electrobuses and flesh out the story to make it come to life. My first surprise was how little there was in the obvious sources. The comprehensive two-volume *A History of London Transport*, for example, has four sentences about the electrobus – while devoting a lengthy passage to another electric bus that never carried a paying passenger.[3] It felt as though the electrobus had been airbrushed out of history.

After a bit more digging I came across a reference to the electrobus in an obscure journal. 'A certain amount of mystery appears to have surrounded the London Electrobus Company from its inception,' said the article, which went on to say that a Dr Lewis 'may have been responsible for some of the evident distrust with which the discriminating public have regarded the [electrobus] company'.[4] This struck a jarring note. It was at odds with everything that I had read about the electrobus and it implied that something dodgy had been going on. So what did happen to the electrobus? And who was the mysterious Dr Lewis?

Over the years journalists develop a nose for a story – a sixth sense that there is more to something than meets the eye. By now my journalistic nose was twitching – and I couldn't resist finding out more. After a bit more delving I discovered that 'Dr Lewis' was a German lawyer called not Lewis but Lehwess – Dr Edward Ernest Lehwess. The confusion over the names was easy enough to explain away: the name had been anglicised. But was there a better story here than the one I had expected? Finally, an old Foreign Office file confirmed that I was on the right track. In the margin of one sheet of paper a civil servant has added a handwritten warning about Lehwess: 'This man is a rogue.'[5]

Introduction

What started as a simple story about the history of technology had morphed into a fraud investigation. Every journalist loves a scoop. And I had one – even if it was a hundred years after the event. Fraud had killed off the electrobus, not any technical shortcomings. And the mastermind behind the fraud was Lehwess. The story appeared in the *Economist* in 2007 to coincide with the centenary of the first electrobuses hitting the streets of London.[6] But inevitably there was much more to the story than the magazine had space for.

Investigative journalism is not new to me. I have worked on several lengthy investigations. But this one was different, in two important ways. First, I had never worked on an exposé where all the participants were dead. The last person to have first-hand knowledge of the electrobus swindle died in 1986.[7] That meant there was no living person to nudge me in the right direction – or to obstruct my enquiries.

Second, almost all investigative stories are bankrolled by a newspaper or a television programme – for the very good reason that they are extremely time-consuming. From long experience I knew that freelancers should avoid investigative journalism unless they had a backer. The only tangible reward from pursuing this story would be to get at the truth. The task, it turned out, was far bigger than I anticipated. The mundane need to earn a living meant that the story frequently languished on the back burner for extended periods. The research – leafing through dusty files of old court cases, police notes, returns of long-forgotten companies and press clippings – had to be carried out in my spare time.

As I dug deeper, the story grew better and better. The trail led to an improbable series of thieves, cheats, blackmailers, swindlers, rogues and impostors. The cast of characters included the nephew of the Greek prime minister and his astrologer, a leading Scottish judge who took kickbacks, a music-hall artist who acted as

3

frontman for the swindle, a gunrunner, murky offshore companies, bent solicitors and accountants who could not be trusted to add up the pennies in a child's piggy bank. On top of fraud, bribery and blackmail, there was champagne, sex, juicy divorce cases, a drunken brawl and motoring derring-do. This was no longer a simple story about an electric bus.

For the most part there was little risk of these chancers being caught. Prosecutions for fraud were rare – partly because the London police didn't have a city-wide fraud squad until 1946 and partly because of a general assumption that thieves were drawn from the lower classes. Theft was a burglar making off with a bag marked swag not someone in a sharp suit plundering the life savings of parsons, publicans and postmistresses.[8]

The fraudsters were often in league with corrupt journalists. In the days before radio the printed word packed a powerful punch. Amateur dabblers in the Stock Exchange could easily be seduced by self-serving stockbrokers' circulars. For most people, the press was the only independent source of information.

This monopoly gave newspapers enormous power, which was often abused. Bribery was common and even the editors of respectable papers sometimes succumbed to the inducements they were offered.[9] On top of this, many papers carried unacknowledged 'advertorials' – seemingly independent articles that lauded the prospects of a particular company, but which had been paid for by the company and drafted by its public relations staff. Such was the prevailing culture of deceit that the foremost financial journalist of the day could write a bestseller explaining how to sift the truth from the lies in the financial press.[10]

When I started out in journalism the main tools of my trade – apart from a notebook and pencil – were still the Edwardian version of new technology, the telephone and the typewriter. It was easy to imagine being a reporter in an Edwardian newsroom. I instinctively felt at home there.

But if the work of an Edwardian newshound felt familiar, other features of the press were completely foreign. There was a genre of magazines known as 'reptile journals', published by fraudulent brokers and other dubious financial institutions.[11] These magazines are still a deceptive read. They contain a mixture of stories cut and pasted from respectable newspapers, outrageous puffs for dud shares that the publishers wanted to offload on to unsuspecting readers and, disconcertingly, the odd genuine piece of journalism. Their value lies not so much in the news they contain but in what they reveal about the activities of their proprietors. Many of the characters in the electrobus story published their own reptile journals.

Fortunately there was a counterbalance to all this misinformation. *Truth* and its splendid annual supplement the *Truth Cautionary List*, which by 1913 listed more than 750 swindlers and their con tricks, was a pretty reliable guide to the financial skulduggery of the era. Perhaps the closest parallel to *Truth*'s exposés in more modern times was the late Paul Foot's column in *Private Eye*.

Such were the twists and turns of the investigation that I frequently felt as if I was unravelling the plot of a complex whodunnit. As the investigation progressed one rogue led to another. Sometimes they were in an alliance, moving from one scam to another. Sometimes they cheated each other. The leading characters all had form. They all took part in similar scams, before, after and during the electrobus swindle. It was this pattern of behaviour that provided crucial confirmation of the swindle. It speaks volumes about the scoundrels behind the electrobus swindle that in an era when successful prosecutions for fraud were exceedingly rare, three of the central characters were jailed for other frauds or blackmail and two others fled the country when the authorities started to take an uncomfortably close interest in their activities. It wasn't credible to argue that the failure of the electrobus was the result of poor management, or some technological deficiencies: what did for it was fraud pure and simple.

However, there was equally little doubt that some of the more peripheral people in the story could have been innocents, who for a variety of reasons were sucked into a vortex of crime. The narrator of H G Wells' novel about fraud, *Tono-Bungay* – which was published when electrobuses were a familiar sight on the streets of London – is a good example of someone who became part of a swindle that was beyond his control, in his case because of misplaced family loyalty.

When I started out on this investigation the popular image of a swindler was one of a loveable rogue, an image doubtless influenced by capers like the Hollywood film *The Sting*, or the BBC Television series *Hustle*, one episode of which featured the ghostly presence of the infamous Edwardian confidence trickster James Whitaker Wright.[12]

It is a common misconception. One of the most prolific fraudsters of the era – who had a bit part in the electrobus swindle – was Ernest Terah Hooley. In a letter to Hooley's wife, one of the leading lawyers of the day described him as 'a charming man and I like him very much…I can well understand how he got his money from susceptible people.'[13]

On closer scrutiny the image of the loveable rogue, the aristocrat of the criminal classes, doesn't hold up. These swindlers hired burglars to steal embarrassing documents and strong-armed journalists to prevent them reporting company meetings. When the law eventually caught up with Hooley he adopted a belt and braces approach to justice. He engaged an eminent lawyer to defend him at the Old Bailey and he also enlisted a burly boxer to nobble the jurors who were trying his case.[14]

Hooley's close collaborator and notorious fraudster Horatio Bottomley also had recourse to heavyweight villains. Bottomley, a newspaper proprietor and sometime Liberal MP, had close dealings with some of characters in the electrobus story. His respectability was a veneer. Those who crossed Bottomley were threatened with violence or death. Was this simply bravado and bluster, or was there real menace behind his threats? A keen devotee of the sport of kings, Bottomley drew his muscle from the wrong side of the racetrack. His enforcers included Edward 'Eddie' Guerin, who had escaped from Devil's Island (he'd been caught blowing the safe of the American Express office in Paris and an ex-lover called Chicago May was charged with shooting him in a gangland squabble after his escape) and Darby Sabini, the leader of a gang of racecourse ruffians who was the model for Mr Colleoni in Graham Greene's novel *Brighton Rock*.[15]

It gradually dawned on me that there was a deeper explanation for the lack of coverage of the electrobus in the history books, beyond the stultifying effect of the libel laws. The conventional history of technology – from railways to computers – is a story of progress coupled with the heroic endeavours of the people developing the latest widgets. Financial chicanery doesn't fit comfortably into the accepted narrative, so with a few honourable exceptions successive authors have glossed over the bits that didn't fit. The result is a sanitised version of history.[16]

The electrobus story is more than a yarn about Edwardian fraud. It had far-reaching ramifications. A hundred years ago the future of transport technology hung in the balance: would the future belong to electricity, petrol or even steam? Today we are once again at an almost identical tipping point. This raises uncomfortable and difficult-to-answer questions. Did the electrobus swindle set back the prospects of electric vehicles for a century? Perhaps.

Buses were by far and away the most likely vehicles to have adopted battery power, because of their fixed routes and the predictable demands they consequently made on batteries. If battery power worked for buses then other vehicles might have followed suit. In the grand scheme of things, the failure of an electric bus may seem trivial, but it led ultimately to the failure of electric delivery vehicles. The result was a resounding victory for the internal combustion engine, which in turn established acceptable levels of noise and pollution. We still hear and breathe these consequences today.

Chapter 1

The First Electrobus

At noon on Wednesday 18 April 1906 a crowd of expectant correspondents from London's leading newspapers gathered at the Hotel Cecil in the Strand to view the new wonder of the age – the electrobus. This was a bus like no other. It was quiet. It was fume-free. And it was cheap. It promised to oust the dirty, noisy petrol bus that had recently started to belch out its fumes in the capital's streets.

The day was overcast, but pleasantly warm for mid-April.[1] The genial master of ceremonies was 55-year-old Philip Beachcroft, chairman of the newly formed London Electrobus Company, who invited Fleet Street's finest to take a ride on the new bus. This much-vaunted vision of the future was painted a gorgeous red and yellow with the word 'Electrobus' emblazoned in large letters along each side.[2]

The journalists who turned up for the grand launch had already been primed for the event. The editorial in that morning's *Times* fulminated at some length about the iniquities of the petrol bus.[3] In those days the *Times* editorials had the status of tablets freshly handed down from Mount Sinai and the Old Thunderer was on top form. 'The novelty is in several respects a highly unpleasant one...The motor-omnibus may be a very good thing in its way;

so is a factory chimney, and so is a pig. That fact does not entitle the owner of a factory chimney to poison the air at his own discretion.

'If a private citizen were to set up a petrol engine in his basement and allow its smoke to escape from a pipe at the top of his area railing, the police, we presume, would speedily have something to say to him. By what right does another private citizen do the same thing with a petrol engine mounted on wheels.' The reporters can have been in no doubt about the urgent need to contain the menace of the petrol vehicle. And here, by sheer good fortune, was the perfect solution – a completely green alternative that solved all the problems at a stroke: the electrobus.

The avuncular Beachcroft ushered the assembled scribblers on to the waiting electrobus, which set off along the Strand on a half-hour jaunt round central London. The electrobus performed splendidly, taking the steep climb up Ludgate Hill in its stride before silently gliding back to the Hotel Cecil.[4] There, over a lavish lunch, the bevy of reporters listened to the company's plans to clean up the city's streets and learnt that the company would be offering its shares to the public the following week.

The man who was promoting the company was introduced to the press as the Baron de Martigny, a slim, enigmatic young man of uncertain nationality, who spoke English with a vaguely North American accent but was also fluent in French, Russian and German.[5] It was de Martigny's job to sell the new company to the press and the investing public. He set about the task with aplomb. He stressed the electrobus's green credentials, telling one news agency reporter: 'Its advantages over the petrol vehicle are its speed, quietness, absence of vibration, cleanliness and lack of smell.'[6] The company, he told journalists, intended to put 300 electrobuses on the streets of London within a year.

The press handout spelled out in 18 bullet points the compelling advantages of the electrobus – and the disadvantages of its petrol-powered rival.[7] The electrobus was absolutely noiseless. There was no smell or smoke. There was none of the vibration caused by the snorting combustion engine. The electrobus had no clutch or gears, so it didn't jerk back into life after each stop to pick up passengers. At night, the electrobus had bright electric lights – like the modern electric trams that were replacing the old horse cars – and in striking contrast to the contemporary petrol bus, which like horse buses lit the interior of the vehicle with acetylene lamps. On gloomy winter days commuters found it hard to read their newspapers by the dim light of an acetylene lamp.

Naturally, the handout also stressed the dangers of petrol buses. Fuelled by an inflammable liquid, they could catch fire or explode. Today this claim may sound a bit far-fetched, but it was a real risk in Edwardian England. Only two days before the electrobus was unveiled to the press, the papers had reported a bus explosion in Scotland. The conductor evacuated the passengers promptly so no one was injured but the bus was reduced to scrap metal. During the course of 1906, 22 petrol buses caught fire in London.[8] Nor, said the handout, would the clean green buses mark their passage with a trail of dripping lubricating oil.

The electrobus would be far more reliable than the petrol bus and less prone to break down, because it had fewer moving parts. That meant electrobus drivers did not need to be part-time mechanics, because there would be no need to make running repairs. And finally, unlike the petrol bus motor, which idles when stopping to pick up passengers, the electrobus motor only works when the bus is moving, reducing wear and tear and saving energy.

Contemporary motor buses were extremely unreliable. At any one time a quarter of them were off the road for repairs and a broken-down bus was a common sight on city streets.[9] The week before, on Easter Monday when the bank holiday crowds packed the buses, one in ten broke down before they could finish their journey.[10] It was a point de Martigny seized on. 'The electrobus has none of the complicated machinery of its rival...There will be no disabled electrobuses at the side of the street. Our vehicle will not break down any more than the horsed omnibuses break down at present,' he told one news agency reporter.[11]

On top of all these advantages was the economic one – the central part of the claim of superiority. The chassis was simpler than the petrol bus so it would be cheaper to manufacture and according to the company the electrobus would also be cheaper to run than a petrol bus.

It was a textbook PR campaign and the company's efforts were rewarded with ecstatic press notices over the next 24 hours. The *Star*, a London evening paper, set the breathless tone: 'When the electrobus glided noiselessly out of the Hotel Cecil court this afternoon, giving forth no blue vapour and no smell, the people in the Strand stood almost aghast.'[12]

The next day's press notices were equally fulsome. Impressed by what they had seen, most journalists happily repeated the well-turned phrases from the press handouts emphasising the environmental advantages of an electric bus. 'Those who were privileged to ride in the electrobus yesterday,' wrote the correspondent from the *Daily Chronicle*, 'were struck by the absence of vibration. There was no jerk in starting and the car ran with remarkable smoothness. In contrast to the petrol omnibus there is neither smell nor smoke – an advantage which will be very generally appreciated.' A reporter for a San Francisco paper wrote that the bus 'ran as smoothly as a tramcar'. The *Standard* took a slightly different tack. It said that so far only the rich had been able to enjoy the comforts of a smooth-running electric car but 'now the London Electrobus Company are going to place this method of transit within reach of all'.[13]

The only slightly sour note had been struck a week earlier by the *Daily Mirror*. The electrobus needed approval from the police before it could carry paying passengers. A reporter from the *Mirror* had been on hand when police inspected the electrobus. 'Yesterday the much talked of electrobus made its first appearance on the streets. Its initial behaviour, to put it kindly, was not all it should be,' said the *Daily Mirror*, in an article under the ironic headline: 'Vehicle That Is to Conquer London Streets Towed to Scotland Yard'. The *Daily Mirror* reported that the electrobus had scarcely gone a dozen yards when it stalled, unable to move even an inch further. 'It was taken in tow by…a despised motor omnibus.'[14] The incident was easy enough to write off as teething troubles. What counted for most reporters was the highly successful press launch, which easily eclipsed the earlier glitch.

On Monday 23 April the London Electrobus Company launched its prospectus with adverts in the daily press. The company wanted £305 000 to finance its plans. Ordinary people now had a chance to be part of the electric revolution. All you needed was £1 to buy a stake in the inevitable profits. Investors had four days to apply for shares before the offer closed. Such was the enthusiasm for the electrobus that over the weekend before the offer officially opened shares were said to be changing hands at a premium of 25 per cent.[15]

The prospectus was glossy and lavishly illustrated. Superficially everything looked good. The board of directors had exactly the right mixture of expertise. This was a heavyweight board, oozing respectability and sporting some of the leading industrialists of the time. Beachcroft, the chairman, was also a director of the Electric Construction Company, the country's leading electrical engineering firm and supplier of electrical equipment to many of the nation's tramways as well as the electrobus company. John Musgrave was a director of Wilkinson Sword, a company famous for making razors and other steel products – with a sideline in assembling buses. Their credentials were impeccable.

Neither did the board lack experience in running buses. William Roberts was on the board of companies running motor buses in Birmingham, Edinburgh and London. Just three days before the prospectus was issued Roberts resigned as managing director of the London Motor Omnibus Company – one of the foremost operators of petrol buses in the capital – to throw in his lot with the London Electrobus Company.[16] Prospective investors might easily conclude that Roberts thought the electrobus was the shape of things to come. Certainly shares in the London Motor Omnibus Company fell sharply on the news of Roberts's resignation. Rounding off this group of men was young James Spencer Orr, promoter of the Edinburgh and District Motor Omnibus Company, which had been launched two months earlier. It was all very impressive. In April 1906 few people could foresee the eventual tribulations of the Edinburgh venture.

A lot was riding on the electrobus launch. If the London Electrobus Company succeeded in putting 300 buses on the streets of London it would challenge the supremacy of the petrol vehicle, which had begun to look as if it might supplant horse power.[17] At the beginning of 1905 there were only 20 motor buses in London. By the beginning of 1906 there were 230, still only a fraction of the number of horse buses. The London General Omnibus Company, the best-known bus company of its day, still mostly ran horse buses. In 1906 it had only 50 petrol buses on order, to be delivered at the leisurely rate of one a week.[18] The company chairman said it preferred to wait for reliable buses. 'Some of those now working on the streets will cause their proprietors to wish they had not embarked on so speculative an enterprise,' he said. Reporters attending the press launch of the electrobus were assured that the company would be running 40 of its cutting-edge buses in two months.[19]

The *Times* editorial had not been a one-off moan about the internal combustion engine. Petrol vehicles were widely reviled for their evil smells and noise. If the replacement of the horse by the internal combustion engine now seems inevitable, it didn't seem so at the time. The balance of power between electricity, steam power and petrol was on a knife-edge and the future of travel was up for grabs. *Tribune* considered the electrobus a 'dangerous rival to the petrol cars'. The *Evening News* concurred: it expected to see a 'keen fight'. The *Daily News* forecast: 'The doom of the petrol-driven omnibus is at hand.'[20] If the forecast was right, the repercussions would be felt around the world.

One of the chief selling points of the electrobus as far as the stock market was concerned was that it would be cheaper to run than the petrol bus. The prospectus claimed that running an electrobus would cost 9d or 10d a mile, compared to 11d a mile for running a petrol bus. The company's consulting electrical engineer, William Crampton, hammered home the point. The cost in the prospectus, he said, 'is in my opinion a fair and just estimate'.[21] The company's costs were fixed because it had fixed-price contracts for the maintenance of batteries and tyres. 'I have not the slightest hesitation in stating that I consider the superiority of electric bus traction for the Metropolis is in every way preferable to the petrol or steam motor.'

Prospective shareholders had to pay 1 shilling (5p) to apply for a £1 share, plus another 4 shillings when they were allotted a share. They could pay the balance of 15 shillings in easy stages spread over the coming months.* All they then had to do was to sit back and reap their profits from this exciting new technology. The public flocked to subscribe. Applications for shares flooded in to the city offices of the company's bankers with every one of the day's dozen postal deliveries. In the first 24 hours there had been applications for more than 120 000 shares and the share issue was well on the way to being fully subscribed. The London Electrobus Company would have all the money it wanted.

---

* Before 1971 the British pound was divided into pounds, shillings and pence. There were 20 shillings to the pound and 12 pence (d) to the shilling.

Yet one journalist who attended the press launch on Wednesday 18 April had remained stubbornly unconvinced. He was Stanley Spooner, the experienced but prickly editor of the *Automotor Journal*. The journal was one of the country's most authoritative motoring magazines and its fortunes were clearly linked to an expanding motor industry. Spooner, a keen proponent of petrol power, was extremely concerned about the threat the electrobus posed.[23] Over the weekend he launched a pre-emptive strike in an effort to scupper the next week's flotation.

On Saturday, he wrote to the major national newspapers arguing that battery power had failed before and would fail again. His killer point was that the cost of running an electrobus would be far higher than that of a petrol bus. Most papers did not publish the letter on Monday, to avoid upsetting advertisers, but Spooner's letter was widely published on Tuesday.[24] His claims were supported by John Stirling, the head of a firm that made petrol buses and which had built many of London's motor buses. The two men were clearly in cahoots. Stirling told every journalist who would listen that there had been many previous attempts to develop electric buses but they had all failed.[25]

On its own this challenge by the petrol partisans about the cost of running electrobuses meant relatively little. The electric enthusiasts responded by saying Spooner was exaggerating the cost of maintaining batteries, which was certainly true.[26] Claim and counter-claim were simply two sets of vested interests disputing figures with each other in the absence of hard facts. The electrobus was new technology and by definition did not have a track record.

But Spooner's intervention did prompt some journalists to take a more sceptical look at the flotation. Was there more to this share issue than met the eye?

Chapter 2

A Bogus Patent

The London Electrobus Company booked advertising space for the launch of its share issue in the major national papers. The large display adverts containing summaries of the prospectus were delivered to the papers over the weekend for insertion in Monday's editions. So both Spooner's critical letter and the prospectus were passed around Fleet Street's newsrooms on Sunday 22 April. The unspoken convention at the time was that 'a company prospectus is seldom subjected to outspoken criticism'.[1] It certainly wasn't fearless journalism, but it kept the advertising departments happy. With the exception of the *Daily Mirror*, which didn't have any advertising for the prospectus, the newspapers held back Spooner's letter for the following day.[2]

One journalist working the Sunday shift at the *Financial Times* picked up the prospectus and read it more closely to see what all the fuss was about. Something in the small print caught his eye. The company had agreed to buy from the Baron de Martigny a patent for the enormous sum of £20 000. This was something worth checking out.

The prospectus claimed that the hugely valuable patent was for a key technological breakthrough that would sweep all other buses off the road. 'The electrically-driven bus of the type of which this company has secured the monopoly,' said the prospectus, 'is protected by Letters Patent.' The cost of the patent was all the more extraordinary because the London Electrobus Company was only buying some extremely restricted rights to it.[3] The £20000 (equivalent to £8 million today) that the company was to pay gave it a monopoly for only seven years and only in London.[4]

The patent was exactly the sort of technological flim-flam that would bamboozle prospective investors. Many would believe what they read in the prospectus. More cautious investors might consult their bank managers or stockbrokers, but it was extremely unlikely that any high-street bank manager in Britain would have been able to check the relevance of a patent. It was easier for the *Financial Times*. The paper's city offices were barely a mile from the Patent Office.

On Monday morning the man from the *Financial Times* was standing in the drizzle in a side road off Chancery Lane waiting for the Patent Office to open. Promptly at 10 am the office opened its doors and the reporter went in and handed over 8d to buy a copy of the patent. It did not take him long to read the six-page document.

The patent, entitled 'Improvements in motor road vehicles', gave details of how a motor could be used to drive the rear axle of a vehicle. Although the patent had originally been taken out by the Compagnie Française de Voitures Electromobiles, a Parisian firm that made electric cars, the reporter quickly realised that it had nothing at all to do with electric traction.[5] The prospectus was seriously misleading. For all the relevance that this patent had to the London Electrobus Company, it could just as well have been a patent for a vacuum cleaner or a hair dryer. The *Financial Times* had a scoop.

With his curiosity aroused, the *Financial Times*'s journalist went back out into the damp morning air. This time he walked to Companies House, which was then based at Somerset House in the Strand, to check out the companies behind the electrobus. The *Financial Times* wasn't the only paper pursuing this line of enquiry.

For the city desk of the *Morning Leader* had also been intrigued by Spooner's letter and thought that this particular stock market flotation should be thoroughly checked out. The *Morning Leader* also sent a reporter to Companies House.

The two reporters both wanted to look at the files of the same two companies, the Motor Car Emporium, which was to supply the 300 electrobuses, and Securities Exchange, the company that was going to underwrite the share issue to the tune of £50 000. The files at Companies House soon yielded their secrets. Neither company seemed to have any real substance. The emporium's returns showed that it had a paid-up capital of just £7.[6] The file for Securities Exchange showed a company that was equally flimsy. It had a paid-up capital of £16 and was mortgaged to the hilt. Neither company, the reporters realised, could possibly fulfil the promises made in the electrobus prospectus.

The two journalists went back to their respective offices to file their stories. The weather had taken a decidedly unpleasant turn. Monday's drizzle had turned to sleet. The change in the weather could have been a metaphor for the fortunes of the London Electrobus Company. The stories in the *Financial Times* and the *Morning Leader* next morning, followed by the *Star* in the evening, were to have a devastating impact on the London Electrobus Company's attempt to raise money. The bogus patent was the *Financial Times*'s scoop.[7] The second headline on the *Financial Times*'s story neatly summed up the exposé. 'Problematical Patent Rights Backed by Penniless Syndicates'.

According to the *Financial Times*, the Motor Car Emporium had sold the rights to this patent on 12 April 1906 to 'a gentleman rejoicing in the euphonious name of Montague Jerome Ward (de) Martigny, who carries on business at 17 Cockspur Street S.W. under the style of the International Motor Traffic Syndicate'. A week later de Martigny sold on the London rights to the London Electrobus Company. Furthermore, said the *Financial Times*,

Chapter 2

the patent 'is not an electrical invention at all, but...merely a mechanical device having something to do with motor car axles'. What's more, the Baron de Martigny didn't even seem to own the rights to the patent. It wasn't his to sell. 'Now as a matter of fact,' typed the *Financial Times*'s man, with an understandable tone of triumph, 'no assignment [of the patent] has been registered at the Patent Office either to the Motor Car Emporium or to Mr Martigny or his syndicate.' The conclusion was obvious. The patent was no more than a device for ripping off investors for £20000. The London Electrobus Company's prospectus was worse than misleading: it verged on the fraudulent.

On close inspection, other parts of the prospectus turned out to be equally flaky. The Motor Car Emporium, for example, had agreed to assemble and supply 300 electrobuses from its base in Holland Park. The prospectus claimed that the London Electrobus Company had 'acquired a right to the delivery of 300 of such omnibuses within 12 months'. So how was this shell company with no assets to speak of going to supply £210000-worth of buses?

N° 3653   A.D. 1902

Date of Application, 12th Feb., 1902
Complete Specification Left, 11th Nov., 1902—Accepted, 8th Jan., 1903

PROVISIONAL SPECIFICATION.

"Improvements in Motor Road Vehicles".

(A communication from abroad by LA COMPAGNIE FRANÇAISE DE VOITURES ÉLECTROMOBILES, of Paris France, Manufacturers)

I, GEORGE BELOE ELLIS of the Firm of Mewburn, Ellis & Pryor of 70 & 72 Chancery Lane in the County of London, Chartered Patent Agents, do hereby declare the nature of this invention to be as follows:—

This invention relates to motor road vehicles, and more particularly to electri-
5   cally propelled motor vehicles, and its object is to improve and simplify the general construction thereof and to provide various improvements therein as

Figure 1 The pointless patent, a simple device designed to scam £20000 from investors in the London Electrobus Company.

20

'How the Motor Car Emporium is to finance this little deal the prospectus sayeth not,' said the *Financial Times*, 'and we confess ourselves unable to make good the deficiency.'

The underwriting arrangements were equally curious. The deal outlined in the prospectus was that if investment from the public in the London Electrobus Company fell short of £50000, the minimum the company needed to pay its promotion expenses *and* buy enough buses to operate a successful service, then Securities Exchange guaranteed to pay for any unclaimed shares.

'The files at Somerset House,' said the *Financial Times*, 'enable us to throw an interesting searchlight on a very bare skeleton.' In principle, the underwriting deal could land Securities Exchange with a bill for up to £50000. 'Here then is a pretty puzzle. How will the Securities Exchange,' asked the *Financial Times*, which was 'in debt to the tune of £600, take up £50000 shares in the London Electrobus Company?' The reporter from the *Morning Leader* came to strikingly similar conclusions. Securities Exchange was deep in debt.[8] 'In other words,' said the *Morning Leader*, 'the guarantee of 50000 electrobus shares undertaken by Securities Exchange Limited is not worth the paper it is written on.' It was not just the patent that was bogus, it was the underwriting too.

Over the next few days more details about the fraudulent flotation began to emerge as other newspapers followed up the story. Such was the sudden interest in the bogus patent among inquisitive investors – and journalists – that the Patent Office ran out of copies and had to order a reprint.[9]

It was time for a bit of door-stepping. The *Financial Times* sent a reporter to West London to visit the emporium's headquarters in Holland Park. Far from finding a substantial works gearing up to flood the capital's streets with electrobuses the reporter found 'merely an old stable yard with sundry appurtenances' next door to a pub. The yard had space for no more than 15 buses.[10]

Figure 2 The Motor Car Emporium's works: a former stables next door to a public house. The less-than-imposing entrance to the works can still be seen to the left of the old pub, which is now offices.

By Wednesday, midway through the four-day window for investing in electrobus shares, the press had turned. The story ceased to be the brilliant prospects for this new technology and started to be the crooked financing of the company's share issue. A trade magazine revealed that the consulting electrical engineer, who the prospectus claimed had carried out 'a detailed and practical examination' of the electrobus, had been appointed only the day before the press launch.[11]

Some of the criticisms were well wide of the mark, some were merely a rehash of Spooner's letter, but many hit uncomfortably close to home. In any case mud sticks. Instead of clamouring for shares, investors began clamouring for their money back. 'Very strong criticism of the London Electrobus venture has been heard on all sides,' wrote the *Daily Mirror*'s city editor, 'and those who have subscribed have in many cases sent in notices of withdrawal.' But getting their money back was not going to be easy – as the *Daily Mirror*'s cartoonist noted.[12]

By midweek Electrobus shares had dropped to a discount of 25 per cent. There was no point in paying the full price for shares from the company if you could buy them more cheaply on the Stock Exchange. The flood of applications quickly dried up.[13]

The normal practice was that shares would be allotted to successful applicants at the end of the period that the company

Figure 3 A lock-in: can there be any escape for the hapless electrobus shareholders? The investors' predicament as viewed by the *Daily Mirror*'s cartoonist in April 1906.

allowed for subscription, which in the case of the London Electrobus Company ended on Thursday 26 April. The four-day window for subscribing to the share offer was also a cooling-off period, during which prospective investors could withdraw.

However, with the press coverage becoming decidedly unsympathetic the London Electrobus Company cashed the cheques for 4 shillings as well as the initial 1-shilling deposits two days before the share issue closed.[14] People who had telegraphed the company to demand the return of their money before the end of the subscription period received a share certificate instead of a cheque.[15] The legality of this move was doubtful – it was certainly underhand – and it gave rise to widespread suspicion that the shareholders were being fleeced. The company promoters had taken the money and run. The newshounds of Fleet Street were hot on their heels. Who were these fleet-footed company promoters? The press tried to ferret out the truth. One financial magazine sifted the evidence and concluded that the Motor Car Emporium was behind the London Electrobus Company. From there the trail led back to a German lawyer called Dr Edward Ernest Lehwess. It was Lehwess, and not the enigmatic Baron de Martigny, who was the real promoter of the company.[16]

Lehwess had taken some pains to conceal any overt connection with the London Electrobus Company. He was not a director. He had no managerial position with the company and his name was conspicuously absent from the prospectus.

An enterprising reporter on the *Daily Mirror* whose coverage of the flotation had been consistently sceptical, door-stepped Lehwess at the London Electrobus Company offices on the south-west side of Trafalgar Square. The reporter effectively extracted an admission from Lehwess that he was the mastermind behind the electrobus by outing him as a company spokesman.

'We are quite satisfied with the way the public are taking up our shares,' Lehwess told the *Daily Mirror*. 'Applications have already far exceeded the minimum subscription.'[17]

The reporter also visited the newspaper's clippings library to check out Lehwess's back story. At the time all major papers maintained a clippings library, an indexed collection of press cuttings about the notable and notorious, and the *Daily Mirror*'s library was widely acknowledged to be one of the best on Fleet Street.[18]

The librarian handed over a fat file with a variety of press articles about Lehwess culled from society magazines and motoring journals as well as newspapers. Each of the cuttings was pasted to its own sheet of paper on which the librarians had written the date and the publication. Lehwess had already made headlines in an intriguing variety of contexts. The reporter leafed through the cuttings in the file. The majority of them were four-year-old articles about Lehwess's heroic endeavour to be the first to drive round the world. So when the *Daily Mirror*'s reporter wrote his piece for the following day's paper it dwelled at length on Lehwess's motoring exploits.[19]

However, the yarn about the pioneer motorist gave the article a respectable veneer, one that was unwarranted. The file contained other cuttings. It was easy to overlook the smallest one – a two-year-old news snippet from the *Daily Mirror* itself.[20] The 85-word item must have seemed inconsequential compared to all the meaty material about Lehwess's motoring feats. Yet it was perhaps the most pertinent cutting of all, because of the unflattering and revealing light that it cast on Lehwess's character. It was a report of a court case at the Old Bailey and Lehwess's conviction for trying to 'square' a police officer.

Chapter 3

The Lure of Siberian Gold

The newsreel cameras turned, the crowds cheered and with a message of 'God speed' from the Prince of Wales still ringing in his ears Dr Edward Ernest Lehwess set off from London's Hyde Park to drive around the world. Shortly after 10 am on 29 April 1902 a huge canary-yellow car with Lehwess at the wheel rolled majestically along Knightsbridge on its way to Southampton, Paris and Vladivostok, across America to New York and so back to London. There were ten passengers and an Irish terrier in the party. Something of the character of the expedition can be gleaned from the composition of the party. Not only was there a mechanic, who would be essential to keep the car going, but there was also a chef.[1] Was this was the greatest motoring adventure of its time? Or was it a junket? Or was there an underlying motive – the lure of Siberian gold?

Lehwess was born in 1872 into a wealthy land-owning family in Sophienthal, some 45 miles east of Berlin. His father died when he was an infant leaving his mother Jenny to bring him up alone. After going to school in France and Germany, Lehwess went on to study law at Zurich University. Along the way he learnt to speak three languages fluently, French, German and English. As a student he was keenly interested in motoring and claimed that as a child he had ridden in the first car in Berlin when it drove through

Figure 4 Dr Edward Lehwess pictured behind his desk for the society magazine *Candid Friend* in 1902.

the Brandenburg Gate under the watchful eye of the old Kaiser, Wilhelm I.[2]

Lehwess arrived in England in early 1896 and quickly became known as an expert in international law and more specifically the rights of princes – the subject of his thesis.[3] As a new and interesting character on the London scene, he attracted the attention of social reformers Beatrice and Sidney Webb and gained an entrée to their circle of friends, attending meetings and going to country house parties. The young Lehwess was full of himself and making the most of the social whirl. Contemporary photographs portray a shortish man with a neatly trimmed goatee beard, a twinkle in his eye and a slightly podgy face, betraying a well-developed taste for the good life.[4]

After one country house party George Bernard Shaw hints in a letter to his future wife that Lehwess may be suffering from the conviviality – or other excesses – of the previous evening. 'I have slept most prosaically and am the better of it. Did Lehwess – well, I shall see what *he* looks like' before observing him going down to breakfast: 'Ha, there goes Lehwess, looking immensely satisfied with himself.'[5]

Away from these mildly leftward-leaning gatherings Lehwess was also becoming something of a celebrity in motoring circles. He was one of the earliest members of the Automobile Club of Great Britain (which became the Royal Automobile Club in 1907) and was frequently to be found at club dinners and motoring events both in Britain and on the continent. To launch its automobile show at Richmond Park in June 1899 the Automobile Club organised a drive for invited members from its clubhouse in central London to Richmond Park to witness the opening of the show by the Prince of Wales, who would become Edward VII in 1901. Some of the most prominent members of motoring society took part in the drive, including John Douglas-Scott-Montagu MP, later Lord Montagu of Beaulieu, and Alfred Harmsworth, who owned the *Daily Mail*. Lehwess was among the first of this select group to arrive.[6]

Three months later Lehwess announced an audacious plan to drive 8000 miles from Pekin (Beijing) to London. The details of this epic journey appeared exclusively in Harmsworth's *Daily Mail*.[7] In an age when technological advances seemed to be abolishing geographical barriers, Lehwess's adventure captured the public imagination. The story spread around the world, reported even in countries that weren't anywhere near the route. The scheme also betrayed a telling streak of self-delusion in Lehwess. A month after the drive to Richmond – a trip of less than 10 miles – Lehwess took part in a motoring version of the Tour de France, an endurance trial that covered almost 1400 miles. Half the field failed to finish – including Lehwess, who didn't even complete the first of the seven stages.[8]

Although Lehwess claimed to have spent six months preparing his Asian expedition the details were sketchy. His idea was to drive north from Pekin across the Gobi Desert to the Russian border, turn left when he reached the new trans-Siberian railway and follow the tracks west across Russia. The journey would take about three months.

It was a preposterous plan. There were few paved roads outside Europe and quite where Lehwess expected to find petrol in Manchuria or Siberia is unclear. When confronted with these criticisms Lehwess was blithely dismissive. 'I have been…told that my needs for fuel, water and provisions will of themselves make the trip impossible.' His critics, he told the *Daily Mail*, were speaking 'without knowledge of any kind. I do not mind what people say. I mean to carry out my plans and there is an end to it.'[9]

The story died a death with the turn of the century. By the summer of 1900 China was in the grip of the anti-Western Boxer uprising and travel in the country was unsafe. When an American journalist enquired about progress that year Lehwess said that he had been compelled to postpone the journey until the spring of 1901 because of problems completing the necessary arrangements. 'It is manifest that the scheme is so impossible that the postponement will necessarily be an indefinite one,' reported the journalist.[10]

Undeterred, Lehwess resurrected the scheme towards the end of 1901. This time he told the *Evening News* – which was also owned by Harmsworth – that he planned to drive from Paris to Vladivostok.[11] A car was being built in Paris especially for the trip. This time the plans for the expedition seemed more realistic. Lehwess, who according to the *Evening News* was 'one of the most expert and enthusiastic automobilists of the day', told the paper that 'elaborate arrangements will be made for depots of petrol at various points along the route'.

The story aroused the interest of Frank Harris, who edited the society magazine *Candid Friend*. Today Harris is best known for his four-volume autobiography, which scandalised polite society and was so sexually explicit that it had to be published in Paris.[12] Harris was a larger-than-life figure who strutted the literary stage of Victorian and Edwardian England. He was born in Ireland in 1856 and went to America to make his fortune. On his return to Britain, at the age of 28, he became editor of the *Evening News*. He was a friend of Oscar Wilde and helped him financially and he was also close to George Bernard Shaw.

Harris went on to edit two of the most prestigious literary magazines in the country, first the *Fortnightly Review* and then the *Saturday Review*, where his circle of contributors included Shaw, Joseph Conrad and a budding new author, H G Wells. These years were the high point of his literary career.[13] By the time he was editing *Candid Friend* his star was on the wane: the magazine's turgid formula of paragraphs about the doings of dukes and pictures of society celebs exhibits little of his earlier editorial flair.

Harris spotted the article about Lehwess in his old paper and saw potential in the trip. Not only was Harris a keen motorist but being rather down on his luck at the time he was also continually casting around for ways to make money. He saw in this marathon journey an opportunity to indulge his interest in motoring and a chance to bring off a financial coup and clear his mounting debts.

For there was another side to Harris. He might have been an important London literary figure but he was also close to two of the most infamous con men of the age: Ernest Terah Hooley, a financier and serial bankrupt, and the sometime newspaper proprietor Horatio Bottomley. On at least one occasion Harris acted as Hooley's fixer, paying off a blackmailer.[14] Harris also dabbled in a bit of blackmail on his own account. Although H G Wells thought 'he was far too loud and vain…to be a proper scoundrel there were times when the shortage of money seems to have steered him towards more unorthodox methods of raising funds'.[15]

Towards the end of 1901 Lehwess and Harris held several meetings to finalise the details of the expedition, probably in the magazine's offices in Henrietta Street, just off Covent Garden.[16] With the magazine's financial backing Lehwess and Harris upped the stakes. No longer was this going to be a drive from Paris to the Pacific. Instead, 'the famous motorist', as the *Daily Mail* called Lehwess, was embarking on a far greater undertaking. He aimed to be the first to drive around the world.[17]

Six weeks after the *Evening News* article *Candid Friend* announced that it was sponsoring the drive and putting up much of the finance. 'Round the world on a motor-car – *The Candid Friend* expedition,' trumpeted the headline emblazoned across the magazine's cover.[18] Naturally the expedition would now start in London, the city where its sponsor was based. From there the route went on to Paris, Berlin, St Petersburg and either Pekin or Vladivostok before crossing the Pacific, driving across the United States and returning to England.

With the sponsorship of *Candid Friend* in the bag Lehwess went to Paris in December to inspect progress on his new car. 'Car' doesn't adequately describe the huge vehicle, one of the most luxurious ever built. It could sleep four, with bunks as plush as those in a first-class railway carriage. In addition to spare parts and a tent for the rest of the party to sleep in, the car had storage space for fishing tackle and rifles – both for hunting game and fending off brigands.[19] The cost was eyewatering. At £3000, it cost as much as ten of the neat three-bedroom terraced houses currently being built in London suburbs like Chiswick.[20]

Plainly satisfied with the work, Lehwess and some friends went to the Théâtre du Châtelet to see the enormously successful stage production of Jules Verne's *Around the World in Eighty Days*. Afterwards the party adjourned to Maxim's, the famous belle époque restaurant, where over a convivial meal they decided to name the car Passe-Partout after Phileas Fogg's faithful valet. They liked the idea so much they celebrated with another bottle of Pommery.[21]

Over the next few months the intrepid automobilists became the toast of Paris. The expedition may have been financed in London, but it was a French car that was going to achieve the feat of driving around the world and the cream of French society feted the travellers. Lehwess and his co-driver enjoyed their celebrity status to the full, dining out in the French capital's best hotels and restaurants in the company of princes and nobility as well as opera stars such as Dame Nellie Melba.[22]

Candid Friend trumpeted the great new adventure in three successive issues, followed in the New Year by an article about the expedition written by Lehwess himself. In the article Lehwess claimed he was a naturalised Englishman. This was a lie. And it would not be the last one.

Most accounts of the round-the-world trip present it as a ground-breaking motoring adventure, reflecting the contemporary press coverage.[23] But the trip had an important underlying commercial motive, which only occasionally surfaced in newspaper reports. Lehwess told an American reporter that Asiatic Russia was the focus of his interests. He elaborated on this point in his article in *Candid Friend*. He was, he said, an 'ardent student of political economy' and that 'we know nothing of the great mineral riches [of Siberia]' and in particular of the great gold belt that runs from Siberia to Patagonia. Harris's biographer shrewdly observed that the scheme had more to it than met the eye. 'Dr Lehwess was to go forth, sponsored by the *Candid Friend*, and return bearing tidings of gold, corn and fruit, which Harris, and perhaps he, would reap.'[24]

It was only once the expedition was underway that the detailed itinerary emerged, mentioning for the first time a significant diversion through the Siberian town of Nerchinsk.[25] Nerchinsk was the new Klondyke and Siberian gold was the financial speculation of the moment, a speculation that was inextricably linked with Hooley. In 1900 Hooley had set up the Siberian Goldfields Development Company Ltd, which had a nominal capital of an impressive £1 million, to exploit the gold mines of Asiatic Russia. Frank Harris loyally puffed the shares in *Candid Friend*.[26]

The company claimed to have a concession to mine gold in Nerchinsk. But Hooley's plans suffered a body blow when the Imperial Russian government denied that the company had a concession. Hooley had been bankrupted two years earlier so he operated the company through a series of nominees including his wife.[27] This didn't fool the Russian government, which said it would never grant a concession to Hooley's company because the 'origin and composition and the action of its board, does not offer sufficient guarantees of its standing'.[28]

Nevertheless Hooley continued to offload shares in the company wherever he could – which would eventually lead to a prosecution for fraud. He later wrote disarmingly of the Siberian Goldfields Development Company: 'I don't know that it ever paid any dividends, but it used to provide unending comfort to people who like to look at a handsome piece of scrip.'[29]

Now that Hooley's claim to the gold had proved false Lehwess plainly hoped to exploit the Nerchinsk concession. Six weeks before the party left London, he registered an offshore company in Guernsey, specifically to pursue his interests in the gold mines. Criticism of offshore companies is nothing new. Guernsey registrations were widely condemned at the time because of the island's lax rules and secrecy. 'Companies whose promoters have fraudulent intent can be registered with insignificant cost,' complained the *Statist*, which carried out a major exposé. Guernsey had become a refuge for 'shady company promoters' with 'fraudulent aims'. 'Many outside registered companies in Guernsey…have been of very – shall we say? – peculiar character.'[30] It was a description that certainly fitted the Asiatic Banking and Trading Corporation.

This £1-million company had extraordinary ambitions. Working hand-in-glove with a Berlin-registered subsidiary of the same name, the Asiatic Bank aimed 'to develop the resources of and turn to account any lands in any part of the world'. The company intended to exploit mines, oil and timber and to achieve these aims it was to build new towns with their own gas works and power stations. The company had seven shareholders. They included Lehwess, his mother Jenny and John Sutherland Harvey, the proprietor of *Candid Friend*.[31]

Figure 5 Dr Edward Lehwess behind the wheel of his huge motor car, Passe-Partout, posing for photographs in Hyde Park on 29 April 1902 before setting off to drive around the world.

Passe-Partout excited a lot of public interest and was exhibited at the motor show held in Islington in April 1902. The Prince of Wales, the future George V, was among the visitors and he was clearly very taken with it. He made a close inspection of the car and talked to Lehwess at length about its workings. One particularly unusual feature of the car was its use of pneumatic tyres: most heavy vehicles of the time had solid rubber tyres which were less comfortable but much more reliable. The prince wished the adventurous traveller every success.[32]

There were two cars in the party, Passe-Partout, with its powerful 25 horsepower engine, and a smaller car made by Argyll, a Scottish car manufacturer, which had joined the tour to publicise the reliability of the company's products. The party set off from Hyde Park Corner on 29 April 1902, posing for photos and the newsreel cameras, which filmed Lehwess in Passe-Partout 'running at high speed on Rotten Row'.

Passe-Partout had only travelled 25 miles or so before one of its pneumatic tyres exploded with a loud bang. 'It is a sad end to a brilliant car,' said Frederick Aflalo, an experienced traveller who was one of the party, adding melodramatically: 'Let us die quickly and be done with it.'[33] The party adjourned for a long lunch at the Angel Hotel in nearby Guildford, which may have helped to soothe Aflalo's nerves, while the newsreel cameras recorded the tyre being repaired.[34]

The party set off again in the late afternoon and reached the nearby town of Farnham in time for dinner. They had travelled some 38 miles from central London – a journey that then took about 90 minutes by train. Progress remained on the leisurely side and it took four days to reach Paris, where the expedition stopped for more repairs to Passe-Partout's tyres.

Some of the party, including Aflalo, deserted in Paris, giving up the expedition as a bad job. Lehwess himself slipped quietly back to London, where a journalist spotted him 'renewing his acquaintance with those of whom only a few days ago he had taken a long farewell'.[35] He returned to the French capital and there the party stayed for six weeks, watching the horse racing at Longchamps and resuming the series of opulent dinners that had begun a month earlier when he collected Passe-Partout from the factory in Paris.

The expedition set off again in mid-June. Shortly after reaching the German border near Metz, at a place called Lorry, Passe-Partout ran over and killed a pet cat. The travellers were compelled to leave the village in some haste as a crowd of irate women and children hurled a barrage of sticks and stones at the deadly vehicle. The party reached Berlin towards the end of the month, 12 days after leaving Paris. And there the travellers stopped for another two months to enjoy the social whirl of the German capital.

The constant delays exasperated H Percy Kennard, a writer and Russian expert, who was chronicling the expedition's progress and sending regular despatches to the motoring press in Britain. The expedition, he wrote, was failing to show the superiority of the automobile over the railway. It wasn't just quicker to take the train, he said, it would be quicker to walk. 'The expedition has many objects,' he wrote sarcastically. 'One is to show the possibilities of automobilism.' What was demonstrated 'beyond dispute [was] the immense staying power of…our automobile – this power being especially marked in towns like Berlin and Paris'.[36]

According to Kennard, the reason for the Berlin delay was the need to negotiate permits to enter Russia. But that was only part of the story. By early August *Candid Friend*, the expedition's sponsor, was on the point of going bust. The magazine had fought off an attempt to close it in February but had less luck when its printers demanded payment in May.[37] The last issue was published on 9 August 1902, which was a severe blow to the expedition's finances.

The party resumed the journey east on 1 September. Although Lehwess was still sanguine about success, many were less certain.

'It is when they reach the trackless deserts and encounter "roads" where cyclists have shouldered their machines that the real struggles will begin,' wrote the motoring correspondent of the *Manchester Guardian*.[38]

His prediction was unerringly accurate. After an eight-day stay in Warsaw, where the party was royally feted with another seemingly unending round of celebratory dinners, Passe-Partout set off for the Russian capital of St Petersburg. The roads got steadily worse. Progress was correspondingly slower, as the heavy car regularly sank up to its axles on soft surfaces. The travellers often had to round up men and horses from local villages to help put their mechanical monster back on whatever the local semblance of a track was. On one occasion they gave up on the impassable main road and struck out across a ploughed field. At some point, the car's vital toolbox fell off and was lost on the road. The party arrived in St Petersburg towards the end of September, where they stopped again for a fresh round of banquets and outings.[39] Russian hospitality, wrote Lehwess in a despatch to the French motoring press, was legendary. Certainly Lehwess's fondness for fine dining and immediate gratification seemed to trump the lure of Siberian gold.[40]

With the Russian winter approaching, the expedition was plainly in trouble. The clearest sign of this was when Lehwess laid off his chef and sent him back to England.[41] The final words of Kennard's next despatch were 'to be continued'.[42] But it was his last despatch. Winter was closing in and the prospect of Siberian gold was fast receding. Lehwess abandoned the journey, leaving the world's most expensive car stuck in a snowdrift near Nijni Novgorod, nearly 4000 miles short of the gold mines of Nerchinsk.

The news took some time to filter back to London. But Lehwess was ready with a cover story. He wired the London papers to say that Passe-Partout had been 'laid up' and was not going to continue the journey. Lehwess had gone back to Moscow. The spin he put on this change of plan – to distract attention from the expedition's failure – was that he had met a 'young Moscow lady in Berlin and promised to come back and marry her'.[43]

Back in England Lehwess sold Passe-Partout to a London motor dealer and business associate called Charlie Friswell, who went to Russia to reclaim the car. With the aid of local peasants and some horses, Friswell dug the car out of the frozen snow and carted it off to the nearest railway station, where it was put on a train and taken back to England.[44] In April 1903 it was once again exhibited at the motor show in Islington's Agricultural Hall. It was then converted into a minibus and last seen two years later carrying shooting parties around the New Forest.[45]

And what happened to the eastern promise of Siberian gold? Nerchinsk never saw a gold rush to rival the Klondyke and the elusive crock of gold remained buried. Lehwess soon tired of the embraces of his Moscow lady and returned to Britain to try his hand at selling motor vehicles to the masses.

Chapter 4

Two Criminal Convictions

At 10.30 am on 10 May 1904 Frank Froest turned up at the plush Albermarle Hotel in Mayfair. With his elegant silk hat and patent leather shoes Froest looked every bit the prosperous country gentleman, perhaps visiting friends in London. The appearance was deceptive. Froest was one of the most senior officers in Scotland Yard's criminal investigation department, a detective with a well-earned reputation for bringing confidence tricksters to justice.[1] In his pocket, Chief Inspector Froest had a warrant for the arrest of Ernest Terah Hooley, who lived and worked in a suite of rooms at the hotel.

Hooley was in his dressing gown still having breakfast when the inspector called. He finished eating and dressed. While the police waited for him they seized a number of documents from his safe. Then they took him to Bow Street police station in a horse-drawn four-wheeler. Meanwhile, in a carefully synchronised swoop, police arrested Hooley's friend and close colleague Harry Lawson at his offices. Later that afternoon both men appeared before the Bow Street magistrates charged with fraud.[2]

The arrest of two of the foremost financiers of the day was headline news and set in train a series of momentous events. The image of Hooley as the man with the Midas touch would be irrevocably tarnished. For Lawson, one of the pioneers of the nascent motor industry, arrest would lead to a year's hard labour. Lawson's enforced absence created a vacuum at a crucial stage of the motor industry's development. The void was quickly filled by Dr Edward Lehwess, and the monopoly he established paved the way for the electrobus venture.

Lawson, a maverick motoring promoter and fraudster, was Lehwess's role model, rival and sometime collaborator. Relations between the two men were clearly cordial. Lehwess was often to be found at motoring events organised by Lawson, along with other prominent motorists who were Lawson's business associates.[3] Lawson had been a key figure in the development of the bicycle industry in the late 19th century. He helped to invent the modern bicycle and claimed that investors had made millions from his efforts.[4] As the growth in cycling gave way to a boom in motoring Lawson was in pole position, poised to extract as much money as he could from the new technology.

Lawson was already the leading figure in motoring when Lehwess arrived in England. His greatest claim to fame was organising the 'emancipation run' from London to Brighton in November 1896, an event that celebrated the passing of the Locomotives on Highways Act, which effectively legalised the use of motor cars on the public highway. Today the veteran car run is an annual event, commemorating the original run and ensuring Lawson a place in the pantheon of motoring mythology.[5]

On paper the London-to-Brighton run was organised by the Motor Car Club. Although some respectable motorists were associated with the club, especially in its early days, it was little more than a way of promoting products made by the largely fraudulent enterprises in Lawson's financial empire.[6] The club went into decline after the Automobile Club – a genuine motorists' club – was established in 1897.

Lawson's big idea was to create a monopoly in the manufacture of motor vehicles by buying up suitable patents. He claimed that these patents gave his companies a 'master patent', which entitled him to a royalty on every car used on British roads.[7] For a few years the threat of confiscation of infringing cars kept the fictional idea of a master patent intact until a series of legal actions by disgruntled motorists caused the scheme to fall apart.[8]

Lehwess, like Lawson, was also attracted by the prospect of almost limitless profits that could be made from cornering the lucrative market in motor vehicles. At the time France, and to a lesser extent Germany, were the world's leaders in automotive technology. Lehwess, with his extensive continental contacts and fluent languages, was ideally placed to exploit this opportunity. He set up an importing agency called the Automobile Association.[9] The name was a deliberate nod to Lawson's Motor Car Club, implying as it did some semi-benevolent mutual organisation. However, unlike Lawson's club, the Automobile Association didn't even have the veneer of membership.

In its first two years, the Automobile Association was very active and threatened to eclipse Lawson's companies as the major source of motor vehicles. At the London motor show of September 1898 the association's stand had the largest collection of vehicles, dwarfing the display put on by Lawson's companies.[10] The scale of operations was such that Lehwess must have done a deal with Lawson and paid royalties on the cars he sold.[11] However, the Automobile Association's star soon dimmed and it went into liquidation following a boardroom bust-up.[12] Lehwess turned his attention to his plan to drive around the world.[13]

Shortly after the arrests of Hooley and Lawson the police received a tip-off that a car in West London was using false number plates. Since the beginning of 1904 motor vehicles had to be licensed and to carry number plates so they could be identified. The car belonged to the Motor Car Emporium, which had replaced the Automobile Association as Lehwess's operating company.[14]

The police kept an eye on the emporium's premises. They saw a car with a number plate that showed it had been registered in Leeds. However, when the police checked with their colleagues in Leeds they found that the number had never been issued.[15] A few days later James Yellen, a 44-year-old police sergeant, saw a different car with the same number plate emerging from the emporium's yard and being taken for a test drive.

The driver took the car for a spin then returned and motored round the corner to be met by Lehwess, who was waiting for him outside the handsome semi-detached Victorian villa in Holland Park Avenue where he lived with his mother.[16] Yellen followed on foot – the villa was only six or seven minutes' walk from the emporium's yard. He found Lehwess talking to the car driver, a good-looking young American.

Yellen asked Lehwess about the number plates. Lehwess produced a bravura display of ducking and diving worthy of any second-hand car salesman. He initially denied that the car belonged to him but then changed his tune and said that if Yellen accompanied him back to the emporium he would show him the car's licence. Yellen agreed. A little later the policeman called at the emporium's offices where he found Lehwess. Lehwess then said he couldn't find the key to the drawer where the licence was kept. He then changed his story again, admitting that the car didn't have a British licence and finally said the car's number was an old French one.

At this point Lehwess pulled a sovereign out of his pocket and said to Yellen:

'Take this and say nothing about the matter.'

'No thank you,' the police officer replied firmly.

Lehwess then followed Yellen around the premises trying to press the gold coin on him, wheedling and imploring him to forget all about it. Yellen continued to refuse. 'I don't do business in that way,' he said.

Three men, the emporium's manager, the American and Lehwess, found themselves arraigned before the West London magistrates. The American was Leonard K Clark, an enthusiastic motorist and a director of Provincial Carriers, a parcel delivery company that Lehwess had a stake in. Provincial Carriers operated out of a large garage near Victoria – a garage destined to play an important part in the electrobus story.[17] All three men were charged with 'fraudulently allowing a false identification mark to be used on a motor car', while Lehwess also faced the considerably more serious charge of 'wickedly and corruptly' trying to bribe a policeman, a charge that could attract a prison sentence.

This was the first time any motorist had been prosecuted for failing to display a number plate.[18] The emporium's manager was fined. The unfortunate American – who probably had no idea that the car had false number plates – was also fined.[19] Lehwess was sent to the Old Bailey for trial. He left court with the words of the prosecutor ringing in his ears. 'Motorists were rich people, and it would be a serious matter if it was thought they could evade the act by making money payments to police officers.'

His appearance at the Old Bailey was something of an anticlimax. At the previous hearing the national newspapers relied on reporters from local papers to supply copy for their stories. At least one Fleet Street paper organised its own coverage at the Old Bailey – anticipating a juicy tale to tickle the public's fancy.[20] The reporters were in for a disappointment. Instead of a lengthy trial, Lehwess pleaded guilty to minimise any damaging publicity and in the hope of avoiding a prison sentence. He was fined £50 for attempting to bribe a policeman. He had managed to stay out of jail but his efforts to avoid damaging publicity were only partially successful and a newspaper clipping was soon winging its way to the Automobile Club.

The fallout wasn't long coming. Lehwess had joined the Automobile Club in July 1898 less than a year after the club was founded and he had played a prominent part in many of the club's events. The club now decided that Lehwess's conduct damaged the good name of motoring and suspended his membership indefinitely.[21] Most members would have taken the hint and resigned. But not Lehwess. Instead he suffered the ignominy of being expelled from the club in December 1905.[22]

The conviction and its consequences were a watershed for Lehwess. Before his trial at the Old Bailey Lehwess had been a keen, almost compulsive, self-promoter, someone who enjoyed celebrity and assiduously courted publicity in the gossip columns. After his conviction he became much more reticent and began constructing elaborate stratagems to avoid having his name overtly linked to his business dealings.

Lawson would not be so lucky. The origins of his prosecution went back to Hooley's bankruptcy in 1898. The official receiver, the government official who investigated the bankruptcy, believed that Hooley and Lawson had defrauded shareholders in a tyre company and thought the pair should be prosecuted.[23] But nothing happened.

Hooley had too many influential friends. He hobnobbed with royalty, was on good terms with the press – he routinely bribed editors to ensure favourable comment on his stock market flotations – and he was friendly with a whole raft of the titled gentry, people whose names made decorative additions to the boards of Hooley's companies. These directors were derisively referred to in financial circles as guinea pigs because they would sell their title and reputation for a guinea, although most of them were paid a lot more.[24]

These friends in high places made a prosecution 'one of exceptional importance and difficulty,' according to the government's treasury solicitor.[25] Hooley left people in no doubt that he would name names. A prosecution would 'have witnessed such a parade of titled dabblers in finance as the most ardent lover of mud throwing and mirror breaking could desire. Now that Mr Hooley is to be left severely alone by the criminal lawyers,' commented one newspaper, 'no august names will be endangered'.[26]

This narrow escape didn't deter Hooley and Lawson. Maybe they took comfort in the observation of the novelist Anthony Trollope on an earlier generation of swindlers: 'When a man's frauds have been enormous there is a certain safety in their very diversity and proportions.'[27]

They continued their scams, foisting dud shares in worthless companies on to gullible victims. One of these was a wealthy publican. Hooley told him that a client had fallen on hard times and needed to sell his valuable shares in the Siberian Goldfields Development Company. The publican handed over a cheque for £3000 made out to Hooley's 'distressed client'. It never seems to have occurred to him to ask why if the deal was so good Hooley did not keep it for himself.[28]

Hooley then alerted the publican to another unmissable opportunity, the Electric Tramways Construction and Maintenance Company. This was one of Lawson's companies. The publican wrote another cheque for £1500. The pair continued to suck him dry. Every few weeks there was a new cover story, another company and still more astoundingly cheap shares.

In the autumn the electric tramways company held a lavish dinner at the Hotel Cecil in the Strand. The chairman, reading a speech written by Lawson, announced that the company had £100 000 in the bank and that it would pay an immediate dividend. The event was widely reported in the financial press, including a five-column piece in the *Statist*, a reputable financial magazine.[29] The claim was to prove Lawson's undoing.

When the dividend failed to materialise the publican asked his solicitor to investigate.[30] The solicitor uncovered a web of deceit. The electric tramways company had no money and Hooley did not even have a valid mining concession in Siberia. All in all the publican had been taken for £26 000.[31]

The police were called in and Froest headed the investigation. Froest had one of the shrewdest minds at Scotland Yard and had already successfully brought a number of high-profile criminals to justice, including the infamous Victorian fraudster Jabez Balfour. He would rise to become head of the criminal investigation department and after retiring he became a noted writer of detective thrillers.

Froest methodically built up his case. The distressed client who urgently needed to get rid of his Siberian gold shares turned out to be Hooley's personal secretary. The publican's cheque had been paid into the bank account of Annie Hooley – Hooley's wife. The article that appeared in the *Statist* had been paid for by the company. It had cost £21.[32] The paper trail led back to Lawson, who had not only written the chairman's speech, but also signed the cheque to pay the *Statist*.

This time the director of public prosecutions decided to prosecute. What had changed? It was all to do with the victim. This was a simple swindle, involving a pair of con men and a publican. There was little risk of those titled and influential members of the gentry having their good names sullied in the courts.

After a 13-day trial at the Old Bailey the jury found Hooley and Lawson not guilty of fraud but they found Lawson guilty of publishing false information about the Electric Tramways Construction and Maintenance Company. He was sentenced to 12 months' hard labour. Although only one swindler had been jailed no noble names had been mired by the court process and the government was pleased with the result. The treasury solicitor wrote to Scotland Yard to praise 'the tact, intelligence and industry' that Froest and his colleagues had displayed during the investigation.[33]

Lawson's discomfiture was Lehwess's opportunity and he seized it with both hands. He had observed Hooley and Lawson's methods at close quarters and quickly grasped that real money could be made by promoting companies – especially if the promoters were not too fastidious about observing the law. It was the first step on a slippery slope. Before his bribery conviction Lehwess had been a bit of a chancer, a slightly dodgy second-hand car salesman. Now he moved into company promotion, calculating that his legal training would enable him to avoid ending up in the dock at the Old Bailey.

In the early days of the motor industry both Lawson and Lehwess dealt principally in motor cars. But as the industry evolved, both men switched their attention to commercial vehicles. There was hard commercial logic behind the move from cars to buses.

There are no reliable figures for the number of commercial vehicles in Britain at that time. The total number of vehicles on the road, including private cars, was doubling every two to three years and the number of commercial vehicles was also expanding exponentially.[34] Private cars were still largely playthings for the rich and commercial vehicles were potentially far more profitable.[35] A car might sell for £100 to £200: a bus would sell for three to five times this amount with commensurately larger profits.

The London bus market in particular was potentially very lucrative and the obvious target for the new technology. The horse buses of the two main bus companies carried around 300 million passengers a year, not far short of the 400 million passengers who travelled by tram. Lawson made several attempts to gain a toehold in this market. One of his motor buses began running a service in the London suburbs in late 1902.[36] The service lasted a year, but it was a sign of things to come. By the summer of 1903 two major London bus companies were negotiating to buy motor buses from Lawson.[37]

Lehwess was working on parallel lines, hoping to create his own monopoly in commercial vehicles. When he was driving from Paris to Berlin, on his way to the gold mines of Nerchinsk, Lehwess made an unscheduled detour to Bielefeld, where the vehicle manufacturer Dürkopp had a large factory.[38] He was particularly interested in the chassis that the company produced for buses and lorries.[39] In May 1903 he announced plans to put 500 German motor buses on the streets of London.

He publicised his scheme by driving a bus behind a column of athletic stockbrokers taking part in the first of what would become the annual Stock Exchange walk from London to Brighton – in part because the event was guaranteed to attract press attention and partly to demonstrate the bus to the assembled financiers. However, the strolling stockbrokers were unimpressed and if Lehwess had hoped to attract an investor, he failed. There was no rush to finance the scheme. The German bus invasion of London fizzled out.[40]

After these false starts the motor bus boom finally took off in London in a big way in 1905 and 1906. The established horse-bus operators were naturally keen to keep a close eye on developments. The London Road Car Company, the second-largest bus operator in the capital, engaged press clippings agencies to monitor the proliferation of new companies and retained a financial analyst to provide it with confidential reports.[41]

The motor bus craze, warned the London Road Car Company's analyst, was uncannily reminiscent of the 19th-century railway boom. The public had been seduced by the glamour of new technology. Practically all these new concerns were promoted by companies that supplied motor buses, like the Motor Car Emporium. Company promoters were taking advantage of investors in much the same way as the swindling railway promoters had in the 19th century who, as Trollope put it, made their fortunes not by constructing railways 'but by the floating of the railway shares'.[42]

The motor bus boom attracted more than its fair share of sharks becoming, as one observer shrewdly pointed out, 'the happy hunting ground [for] the derelicts of the company promoting world'.[43] Furthermore, when the new companies raised money from the public the promoters pocketed an extortionate share of it. Many of the promotions bore the hallmarks of a rip-off, reported the analyst, who pointed out that among the people backing these promotions 'the same names occur with suggestive frequency'. One of the names that occurred with very suggestive frequency was Edward Ernest Lehwess.

Lawson's hopes of cornering the commercial vehicle market were stymied by his imprisonment. He lost his appeal at the end of January 1905, exactly when the boom was taking off. While Lawson was doing hard labour, Lehwess did a series of deals with the jailed financier's companies, which were controlled by Lawson's associates. Lawson clearly sanctioned these deals, because they continued after his release from prison.[44]

Partly as a result of these deals the Motor Car Emporium secured a near monopoly in the supply of buses and goods vehicles. A succession of stories in the trade press detailed the emporium's progress. There were new buses, parcels vans, a mobile advertising hoarding, an ambulance and a beer delivery wagon.[45]

Throughout the boom years of 1905 and 1906 anyone who wanted a lorry or bus invariably had to deal with the Motor Car Emporium.[46] It was always a flaky company. Its lack of capital meant that it could easily go bankrupt. But despite having no assets to speak of the business was phenomenally profitable. By the end of July 1907 the emporium's turnover in the previous 18 months was £145 000 of which £50 000 was profit.[47] It was on this foundation that Lehwess would construct the electrobus promotion.

Chapter 5

A Most Deliberate Swindle

Such was the stink created by the flotation of the London Electrobus Company that a rumour went round the City that the scam was the brainchild of Ernest Terah Hooley, the notorious company promoter. Hooley felt he had to counter this unfounded slur on his character. 'I shall be extremely obliged if you will deny the story in the most emphatic terms,' he told the *Daily Mirror*.[1] Despite his links with Lehwess there is no evidence that he had any part in the electrobus swindle.

In less than two weeks since the flotation the fortunes of the London Electrobus Company had been transformed. The share price plummeted. By 1 May 1906 partly paid electrobus shares, which had already cost investors 5 shillings, were worth just 3d.[2] The hapless shareholders, who had paid only a quarter of the cost of the shares, were legally liable to pay the balance of 15 shillings per share in full. 'The shares are valueless,' one City insider told the *Daily Mirror*. 'The only way to get rid of them is to pay people to take the responsibility off your hands.'[3]

In a desperate attempt to shore up the company's position, Herbert Rowbottom, the London Electrobus Company secretary, wrote to shareholders saying that the press criticisms about the cost of running electric buses were 'entirely unjustified'.[4] He enclosed a two-page report from a well-respected electrical engineer, who gave details of trials that he had carried out on the electrobus. The electrical design was very good, the engineer wrote, and the bus was 'an eminently practical carriage'. He backed the company's claims about the advantages of electric vehicles over their petrol rival and said that the cost of maintaining the batteries would be 3d a mile, half the amount Spooner had claimed. 'I have every confidence that your electric omnibus will have a great success,' he concluded.[5]

The *Daily Mail* and the *Daily Mirror* took the lead in urging shareholders to go to court to get their money back on the grounds that the company had issued a false prospectus.[6] A firm of City solicitors, acting on behalf of a number of aggrieved investors, issued a writ against the London Electrobus Company demanding that the contracts should be revoked and the shareholders' money returned. Two other firms of solicitors joined in as the demands for refunds snowballed. On 3 May a High Court judge froze the electrobus bank accounts, ordering the company not to touch the shareholders' money.[7]

On 7 May the *Daily Mirror* trumpeted the success of its campaign to force the company to return shareholders' money after the company announced that shareholders would be given the opportunity to withdraw.[8]

Despite the success of the shareholders' legal actions the *Financial Times* hadn't given up on the story. The newsdesk sent reporters to door-step key people connected with the electrobus. One went to the battery supplier, but drew a blank. He was quite above board – and he even had a valid patent for his novel design of battery.[9] The reporter who went to check out the London Electrobus Company's headquarters had rather better luck.

The company's HQ was in a sturdy block of stone-built Victorian offices on the south-west side of Trafalgar Square.[10] But here the impressive stage management that had characterised the launch faltered. A firm with the ambitions of the London

Electrobus Company could be expected to have an imposing suite of offices, with the very latest telephones and typewriters. The *Financial Times* found no sign of the London Electrobus Company, not even a brass plate with the company name on it. Instead the name on the office door was Improved Electric Traction Ltd, a previously obscure company and one that was not mentioned in the prospectus.[11] 'There is, however, another syndicate of significant similarity,' sharing the premises, observed the *Financial Times*, 'and that is the International Motor Traffic Syndicate' – which according to the prospectus was de Martigny's trading name.

It was all very peculiar. The *Financial Times*'s reporter retraced his steps across Trafalgar Square and on to Somerset House in the Strand. What was Improved Electric Traction? And who was behind it? Once in Companies House the journalist looked up the file and found that the company had been registered that March by John Neely, the same solicitor who registered the London Electrobus Company in April and the solicitor of the Motor Car Emporium.

By another curious coincidence, Improved Electric Traction was set up to pursue a business deal with William Roberts, who was a director of the London Electrobus Company. The *Financial Times* wondered about the connections between the Motor Car Emporium, Lehwess and Roberts. 'It would be interesting to know…whether Dr Edward Ernest Lehwess is associated with him [Roberts] in this enterprise and to what extent.'[12] The paper also noticed that one of the directors of the Motor Car Emporium, the company supplying the electrobuses, was Ernest Rowbottom, 'presumably some relation of Mr Herbert James Rowbottom, the secretary of the London Electrobus Company'. The *Financial Times*'s conjecture was spot on. The two Rowbottoms were brothers.[13]

There was undoubtedly more to the electrobus story than met the eye and a feeding frenzy developed as one journalist after another dug around to see what they could uncover. One financial magazine spelled out the facts for its readers. Before the London Electrobus Company could run a single bus, it had to pay £20 000 for a pointless patent, £8500 to de Martigny for promotion expenses and a further £2500 to Securities Exchange for the bogus underwriting. The magazine calculated that Lehwess and his cronies could pocket the first £31 000 of any money the public invested. Only when public subscriptions exceeded this amount would there be any money left to buy electrobuses – and that would have to be paid to Lehwess's Motor Car Emporium.[14]

The revelations forced two members of the electrobus board to resign, including Orr, who finally seemed to have realised that he had been duped.[15] The wheels were starting to come off the electric bus.

The company's formal offer to aggrieved shareholders, when it came the following week, was an astonishing 'climb down', said the city editor of the *Daily Mirror*.[16] The three-page circular came within a whisker of admitting that the company had lied about the patent. The patent did not specifically relate to electric buses and the claim to have a monopoly on electric buses 'cannot be substantiated'. 'An expert opinion had now been obtained as to the validity of the patent and such opinion is unfavourable,' admitted the circular. The company also now conceded that cashing cheques before the end of the subscription period was probably unlawful.[17]

Despite this, the circular urged shareholders to keep faith with the electrobus. It enclosed yet more reports by two more electrical engineers.[18] Both largely supported the prospects of the electrobus and one made the entirely reasonable point that electric buses were more likely to succeed than electric cabs, because there was always the danger of cabbies picking up fares when their batteries were almost exhausted and getting stranded some way from the charging station. But the bottom line was that investors could have their money back if they felt they had been misled. In a series of court cases the London Electrobus Company was forced to refund more than a thousand shareholders.[19]

On 1 June the board announced that the company had exceeded the minimum share subscription of £50 000 – by just 119 shares. But even this wasn't what it seemed. The vast majority of individual shareholders – about 90 per cent – had taken their refunds. A few small shareholders unwisely paid heed to the electrobus company's blandishments, kept faith and continued to hold their shares. Among them were Mary Price, a teacher from Chesterfield, Sam Sheldon, a barman at the Railway Tavern in Diss, and Conrad Skinner, a pensioner from Uxbridge who was hoping to make his old age slightly more comfortable. Each of them had raided their nest eggs and invested £5 in the London Electrobus Company. None would ever see their money again.

The company's share register shows that one of the larger remaining shareholders was Edward Ernest Lehwess, 'a gentleman', who held 750 shares. But his holdings were dwarfed by the 38 000 shares held by Securities Exchange, which clearly could not pay for anything like this number.[20]

Despite its impressive sounding name Securities Exchange was far from being a respectable financial institution. It was a 'bucket shop', a disparaging term for companies that palmed off worthless or non-existent shares on gullible punters at extortionate prices.[21] Bucket shops also often operated a complex system for betting on the movement of share prices. The system may have been complex, but the scam was as simple as it was merciless. For the owners of a bucket shop the gamble was a case of 'heads we win, tails you lose'.[22]

The nearest modern equivalent of a bucket shop would be a boiler room. Bucket shops lured in 'suckers' with the promise of instant riches. 'Increase your income,' ran one typical circular directed at gullible gentlefolk. 'Why rest content with five per cent interest on your invested capital when you can obtain a handsome fortnightly dividend of sums of £10 and upwards invested in absolute safety and your capital guaranteed against loss.'[23]

The man behind Securities Exchange was William Longman, an 'outside broker' – a stockbroker who was not a member of the Stock Exchange and someone who worked on the fringes of the respectable financial world. Longman, who was 35 when the electrobus company was floated, had made his money by marrying astutely. His wife was a wealthy widow, 14 years older than him. The widow's wealth helped Longman to finance his career in the City and he used her money to set up Securities Exchange in 1902.

Longman was exposed as a bucket-shop keeper in the *Critic*, a magazine that had a long-running campaign to expose the iniquities of these operations.[24] Longman tried to gag the *Critic*'s editor Henry Hess by threatening him with a libel action. Hess had a reckless indifference to such threats and refused to shut up. 'I earnestly warn my readers to have nothing to do with this bucket-shop, or with any of its recommendations.'[25] Thus goaded, Longman went to court.

The ensuing court case did nothing to help Longman's reputation. The Lord Chief Justice, who heard the case, said that the use of the pejorative term bucket shop was tantamount to calling Longman a swindler. The jury, which clearly took the judge's words to heart, decided that Longman had been libelled but awarded him a derisory farthing in damages.[26] It was a moral victory for the *Critic*, effectively confirming that Longman was indeed a swindler.

Small wonder that the London Electrobus Company was condemned in one magazine as 'a farcical concern' largely created for the benefit of Lehwess and Longman.[27] Despite the appalling publicity the company remained outwardly optimistic. At its first meeting at the end of August the chairman announced that the share issue had raised £50 000 and that on the strength of this the company had ordered 30 electrobuses, ten of which would shortly be delivered to the company's garage near Victoria.[28] The company also announced that it would be seeking permission for its shares to be officially traded on the Stock Exchange.[29]

The application to allow trading in electrobus shares annoyed those investors who felt they had been duped. Two of them wrote to the Stock Exchange to say they had been misled by false and fraudulent statements in the prospectus. The company was 'a most deliberate swindle', concluded one of them and the Stock Exchange should not aid and abet the swindle by allowing traders to deal in electrobus shares.[30]

Certainly the leading luminaries at the Stock Exchange were not impressed. The company was in a curious position, commented the Stock Exchange's secretary, with measured understatement. The company had set a minimum subscription of £50 000. By the end of the year after all the court actions had worked their way through the legal system only 46 841 shares had been issued. So it had been allowed to start up in business even though it had failed to raise its minimum subscription. [31]

Rather grudgingly the Stock Exchange did eventually grant the electrobus company's application, swayed perhaps by the fact that Securities Exchange no longer held its block of 38 000 shares. The list of shareholders that the electrobus company sent to the Stock Exchange showed that a block of 25 000 shares had now been taken by a financial institution.[32] And what was the name of this welcome new benefactor? The Asiatic Banking and Trading Corporation, of Guernsey, the bank Lehwess had founded just before he set off to drive around the world.

But there was some good news for Longman. His bucket shop was in hock to his wife Rebecca, who had provided the finance to set up Securities Exchange. Now she was becoming increasingly keen to see her money returned – not the least because of her husband's pursuit of younger women. Rebecca took a dim view of it when Longman took a protracted holiday in Monte Carlo with one mistress, which jeopardised his main source of finance.[33]

The 'underwriting' fee that Securities Exchange collected from the London Electrobus Company share issue enabled him to pay off his wife's loan.[34]

The flotation was riddled with sharp practice. Why, for example, were the bogus patent rights restricted to London? The answer lies in the registration of seven other electrobus companies, covering Birmingham, Liverpool and other places.[35] If the patent was worth £20000 in London then how much would it be worth in Birmingham? And in Liverpool? And Glasgow? This had the makings of an extremely lucrative sideline. But despite the praiseworthy efforts of journalists to expose its shortcomings it took years for many of the more curious details to become public.

Official confirmation of who was behind the financial fiasco of the electrobus share issue emerged a year later. The London Road Car Company had ordered 51 petrol buses from the emporium but the emporium had failed to deliver. The London Road Car Company sued and bankrupted the emporium. Because of the suspicious circumstances surrounding the bankruptcy, the official receiver investigated and confirmed that the real promoter of the London Electrobus Company was the Motor Car Emporium. De Martigny was simply the emporium's stooge. And nowhere in the official receiver's illuminating report is there any mention of the company having paid anything for any patent.[36] The main beneficiaries of the electrobus promotion, as a few inquisitive reporters rightly suspected at the time, were Lehwess and the Motor Car Emporium – in which the two chief shareholders were Lehwess and his mother Jenny.

Who then was the mysterious de Martigny? It has taken a century for the final pieces of the jigsaw to fall into place – after the recent release of documents by the National Archives. The answer would surely have brought a knowing smile to the lips of the *Financial Times*'s unknown journalist. For the Baron – or Count as he was sometimes styled – was not to be found in *Debrett's* or in any other directory of nobility. It was a stage name. De Martigny was a Canadian music hall artist. He was born Montague Jerome Ward in Montreal in 1873 and adopted the 'de Martigny' suffix as part of his stage act.[37]

Until recently he had been living in theatrical digs in London's Waterloo Road.[38] So the Baron's ancestral home amounted to no more than a single room in a South London tenement, which he shared with his wife, a music hall singer.[39] His financial expertise consisted of managing stage acts, such as the Russian Imperial Troupe of singers and dancers. Under de Martigny's management the Russian Imperial Troupe appeared at such prestigious venues as the Gaiety Theatre, Oldham, and the Star Palace of Varieties, Barrow-in-Furness.[40] In Oldham the troupe was top of the bill. 'The Russian Imperial Troupe, in their picturesque costumes, have furnished a capital entertainment as vocalists and dancers,' reported the *Era*. But that was about as good as it got. Mostly the troupe was a supporting novelty act on the provincial music hall circuit.

Chapter 6

The Dress Rehearsal

'It was a scandalous arrangement,' said Mr Justice Ridley, who demanded an explanation. The scandal was a secret deal between Dr Edward Lehwess and Norman Doran Macdonald, a director of a bus company in the Scottish capital of Edinburgh. Lehwess had been giving Macdonald a backhander of £10 for every bus the company ordered from the Motor Car Emporium. The Edinburgh shareholders had been kept in the dark about this kickback and even Macdonald's fellow directors were unaware of it. Or at least they said they were.[1] And the arrangement was all the more scandalous because Macdonald was so eminently respectable: not only was he chairman of the Scottish Automobile Club he was also Scotland's leading criminal lawyer and a senior judge.

The Edinburgh and District Motor Omnibus Company and the London Electrobus Company were just two of the new operators spawned during the motor bus boom of 1905 and 1906. Many towns saw their first motor bus during these years.

The Edinburgh and District Motor Omnibus Company was floated on the London Stock Exchange in February 1906. There are close parallels between the flotation of the Edinburgh company and that of the electrobus company two months later. The cast of characters was similar and in both cases the Motor Car Emporium was supplying the buses. The Edinburgh flotation was effectively a dress rehearsal for the electrobus share offer.[2]

In the event the public wasn't very enthusiastic about the profits to be made from running motor buses in Edinburgh. The city already had an efficient tram network, and the flotation raised only £28 500, only slightly more than its minimum subscription and well short of its target of £200 000.[3] Nevertheless some 700 small investors put money into the company. The second largest shareholder, with a holding of £500, was George Bernard Shaw, who was probably inveigled into investing by Lehwess.[4] All of these shareholders would get their fingers badly burned.

The promoter of the Edinburgh company, at least on paper, was Captain James Spencer Orr, soon to become a director of the London Electrobus Company. A company promoter was a sort of financial midwife, someone who would retain experts to advise on a company's prospects and prepare the all-important prospectus to attract investors. In return the promoter received a hefty fee, which in the case of the Edinburgh company was £6500. Today the company promoter's role would normally be taken by a major investment bank. An Edwardian promoter plainly required a lot of financial experience. Neither Orr nor the Baron de Martigny fitted the bill. Orr was 23 years old and a captain in the City of London Yeomanry – a unit of the territorial army. He was already in financial difficulties and would soon become bankrupt.[5] Orr, like de Martigny, was merely a dummy for the real promoters.

So who were these anonymous men? One clue was in the shares that the company handed out in return for help promoting the company. Aside from Orr, there were two significant beneficiaries of these shares: Lehwess and one Hyman Herman.[6] Herman was the chief clerk of Securities Exchange and the true owner of these shares was William Longman.[7] The Edinburgh and District Motor Omnibus Company was yet another Lehwess and Longman production, one of many company promotions that these two rogues foisted on the public.

After the lukewarm response to its share offer the Edinburgh company reduced its order for buses from 150 to 30 in line with its smaller capital.[8] It paid the Motor Car Emporium £12 000 but twelve months later had little to show for it. The emporium had delivered only 16 buses, five of which worked and four that might work if a lot was spent on them. The other seven had been assembled from incompatible components made by several different manufacturers and were condemned by engineers as unfit for public use.[9]

The shareholders were becoming increasingly restless and there was talk of suing the Motor Car Emporium. A year after the flotation matters came to a head at a series of stormy shareholders' meetings. Most of the London-based newspapers ignored the travails of a provincial bus company, largely leaving coverage to the Scottish papers and a reptile journal that was putting the squeeze on Lehwess and Longman.[10]

The first of the meetings was held in London on 20 March 1907. The directors wanted to put the company into voluntary liquidation, which would forestall any moves to take the emporium to court. The shareholders were naturally eager to quiz the board of directors. Apart from a few excursions the Edinburgh and District Motor Omnibus Company had not operated a single bus route. Now the directors claimed that the company couldn't pay its creditors. Where had all the money gone?

The move to put the company into voluntary liquidation alarmed some of the more worldly-wise shareholders, including one with a seasoned eye for a scam – Alfred Mayhew. Mayhew, a retired colonel in the Indian Army, was one of the good guys in this sorry saga. His mission in life was to clean up sleaze in the City of London. 'I served 27 years in India, which I found to be a pretty bad place,' he later said. 'But when I returned to London I found it to be a sink of iniquity – and I determined to do all I could to expose…the rascals who rob the widow and the orphan.'[11]

Mayhew hoped to set up a League for the Protection of Shareholders, in which shareholders would use their mutual strength to protect themselves against shady financiers. The launch of the league and its attempts to expose 'rotten or fraudulent concerns' were reported in the press, but Mayhew's efforts to clean up the City were stillborn, partly because the old soldier died not long after this publicity.[12]

Voluntary liquidation was often tantamount to a cover-up. When a company was insolvent the courts could order compulsory liquidation, where the liquidator was generally the Board of Trade's official receiver, someone of unimpeachable independence, whose enquiries would often reveal any wrongdoing behind a company's failure. But compulsory liquidation was rare. More than 18 000 companies went bust while Edward VII was on the throne but barely 1000 were the subject of compulsory liquidation.[13] The others opted for voluntary liquidation, often hole-in-the-corner affairs where, as Mayhew put it, the directors 'have arranged all the details so as to secure a quiet burial of the concern, without the formality of an inquest'.[14]

The tactic Mayhew and his associates adopted was to buy small stakes in companies they suspected were dodgy, such as the Edinburgh company.[15] These stakes gave them the right to ask awkward questions at company meetings and the legal status to ask the courts to intervene to protect shareholders.

In the run up to the Edinburgh company's March meeting Mayhew asked shareholders to back his call for a probe to discover where the money had gone. Longman moved swiftly to head off this danger. The week before the meeting Herman, Longman's sidekick, wrote to shareholders pledging his support for the thorough investigation Mayhew was demanding and asking them to entrust him with their proxy votes. Many who could not attend the meeting did.

When the meeting opened, the shareholders were taken aback to discover that none of the directors had turned up to face the music. The chairman of the *Edinburgh Evening News*, the local man on the board, claimed to have resigned long ago. William Roberts, who was the company's chairman as well as being a director of the London Electrobus Company, suddenly found that his business as an estate agent in Birmingham required his immediate attention. Instead a burly man with an immaculate handlebar moustache announced in a vaguely Australian accent that he was chairing the meeting on behalf of the directors.[16]

The beefy stand-in was 54-year-old Charlie Hogg, a man who lived in some style in a 19-room mansion near Horsham in Sussex.[17] Hogg was a familiar face in the City of London, a persuasive orator with a reputation for being able to cajole even the most recalcitrant shareholders into acting against their own best interests.[18] He was naturally much sought-after by shady company promoters like Lehwess and Longman when they were in a tight corner. Hogg would later be jailed for diverting cash from a mining company into his own pocket. 'No one acquainted with Hogg's career,' commented the *Financial Times* in a succinct character reference, 'will consider that the sentence of 12 months' imprisonment…is at all a heavy one.'[19]

At the beginning of the meeting shareholders were dumbfounded to hear that Herman had changed his mind about an investigation, and that he now supported voluntary liquidation and would use all the proxy votes he had garnered to support Hogg. The meeting was packed – and not just with shareholders. A large and vocal group of the promoters' supporters shouted down anyone who spoke in favour of an investigation. In the end the shareholders, overwhelmed by this turn of events, agreed to voluntary liquidation.[20]

Two weeks later the shareholders met again to confirm the original decision. Macdonald seems to have been pricked by his conscience, because this time he turned up – although he sat in the body of the hall and not on the platform. According to reports, the meeting was of a 'lively character'. Hogg was continually interrupted and shareholders struggled to make themselves heard as different factions shouted each other down.[21]

Mayhew called for an investigation of the company's affairs, to be carried out by a committee of shareholders, instead of voluntary liquidation. Hogg became increasingly tense as the meeting spiralled out of his control. When Macdonald rose to speak in support of an investigation, Hogg lost it. 'The affairs of the company would not be safe in their hands, I decline to put the resolution,' he shouted. Pointing at Mayhew's supporters he thundered: 'You can go to court if you like. This meeting is now closed.' And with that he stormed out.[22]

Macdonald sat down and wrote to the *Scotsman*, vigorously dissociating himself from Hogg and saying he was anxious that the company's affairs should be investigated and that he was making these points when the meeting broke up.[23] Macdonald had turned King's evidence. In letters to the pro-investigation faction Macdonald blew the whistle on the promoters' plot. He said that Hogg and his chosen liquidator were stooges.[24] They were planning a 'hole in the corner' sale of assets, where the buses would be sold off for a few hundred pounds and then used to run a bus service in the south of England. Mayhew went to court and had the sale stopped.

However, the shareholders' rebellion fizzled out after it lost the support of a major creditor and the company went tamely into voluntary liquidation.[25] Hogg's liquidator sold the buses for a knock-down price to a company that was a front for Harry Lawson, who was by now out of jail.[26] By early September the fire sale was over and the money it raised was swallowed up by the expenses of the liquidation. There was no money left for shareholders, so George Bernard Shaw never saw his £500 again.

The shareholders did not get their day in court until 1909, long after all the money had vanished. The shareholders, led by Mayhew, sued the directors for issuing a false prospectus. Mayhew told the court that he was induced to buy his shares by the statement in the prospectus that the company had 'secured the delivery of 150 buses', adding that he later came to the conclusion 'that the company was a swindle'.[27] The claim was slightly disingenuous: Mayhew had only bought his stake in the company because he had a shrewd idea that it was dodgy.

Mayhew and the other shareholders won their case in the High Court, although the verdict was overturned by the Appeal Court. Mayhew's real success was in exposing the financial skulduggery behind the promotion and revealing Macdonald's kickback. There can be little doubt that most deals like this were destined to remain hidden for ever. Only a legal action launched by disgruntled Edinburgh shareholders had brought this one into the open.[28]

Even after the judge demanded an explanation Macdonald maintained his silence. He didn't even send a lawyer to proffer an excuse. He continued his damage limitation strategy in the Appeal Court. He was the only director who didn't appeal because he would have 'great difficulty in contesting that part of the case'.[29]

The strategy was partially successful. The reporting of this sensational deal was curiously erratic and smacks either of excessively nervous libel lawyers or an establishment cover-up. Neither the *Financial Times* nor the *Financial News* mentioned the backhander. It was left to the *Scotsman*, the *Times* and the *Manchester Guardian* to name and shame Macdonald.[30]

Mr Justice Ridley never got the explanation he wanted. And the story about the kickback survives only in a few yellowing press clippings.[31]

Chapter 7

Post Office Motors

By 1906 Frank Harris was down on his luck. His finances were often precarious, the result of an extravagant lifestyle coupled with a sporadic income. He had spent the money that he earned from editing his friend Winston Churchill's biography of his father Randolph, and he was now on the look-out for fresh ways of making money. His finances worsened significantly after he lost his latest job editing a motoring magazine and with his debts mounting he was living at a secret address to avoid his creditors.[1] He still had a keen interest in motoring and one of his speculative ideas was to replace the Royal Mail's parcels coaches with modern motor vans.[2] And he knew exactly who to talk to about motor vans – Edward Lehwess. Dr Lehwess's Motor Car Emporium enjoyed a near-monopoly in the supply of commercial vehicles.

The two men had remained on good terms after Lehwess's failed attempt to drive around the world. When *Candid Friend* closed, Harris tried to raise financial backing for a glossy high-society motoring magazine, but the scheme was stillborn.[3] What emerged from the wreckage of the project was a new magazine – the *Motorist and Traveller*. It was financed by the Dunlop Tyre Company and its job was to promote the company's tyres.[4] Harris became the editor at a handsome salary of £500 a year and one of the few regular advertisers, apart from Dunlop, was Lehwess's Motor Car

Emporium.[5] The magazine was not a success and Dunlop sacked Harris around the beginning of 1906.

Harris's idea wasn't entirely original. The Post Office still used horse-drawn mail coaches to take parcels from London to suburban post offices and it had recently replaced the night mail coach from London to Brighton with two motor vans.[6] It was a sign of things to come. Harris acquired an option to take over a number of parcels contracts from the Post Office and raised nearly £4000 to pursue the scheme, mostly from friends and acquaintances. Within days of losing his job at the *Motorist and Traveller* he registered a new company, the Motor Coach Syndicate.[7]

In June 1906 Harris went to Paris to inspect potential vehicles. While there is no doubting Harris's enthusiasm for motoring, he did not have any engineering expertise. Given Lehwess's extensive contacts in the French motor vehicle industry it is highly likely that he set up this trip for Harris and may well have accompanied him. After the fiasco of the electrobus flotation he was also in France around the same time, developing his latest money-making scheme – taximeters.[8]

The syndicate certainly helped to ease Harris's financial woes in the short term, paying him generously for newspaper articles that he had written – presumably puffs about the potential of motor vehicles to replace horses for postal work. He received £60 for writing an article for the *Times* in August, followed shortly after by a further £150 for writing articles in other unspecified papers and magazines.[9] Of course, Harris would not have been the first journalist to have exaggerated his expenses or falsified his financial claims. But there doesn't seem to have been a corresponding flood of publicity about postal vans in the *Times* or elsewhere.

Harris the journalist did not stay out of work for long. By the end of the summer he had found a new job as literary editor of *John Bull*, a news magazine founded by Horatio Bottomley, who had just become an MP in the Liberal landslide at the general election of 1906. The magazine, which was partly financed by Bottomley's old friend Hooley, was proud of its distinguished catch, trumpeting the appointment of 'our brilliant literary and dramatic critic'.[10]

Harris's trip to Paris to examine suitable vehicles came to nothing. So while Lehwess was casting around for ways of breathing new life into the electrobus swindle, he did a deal with Harris to take over the mail van scheme. Lehwess renewed the options, which were close to expiring, and used the syndicate to promote an entirely new company – the National Motor Mail Coach Company – which would raise the money to finance the scheme by offering its shares to the public.

What emerged from this manoeuvring was a scaled-down version of the electrobus flotation. The company was seeking £100 000. Its handsomely illustrated prospectus, printed in colour and featuring a fleet of vans with 'Royal Mail', a crown and the letters 'ER' emblazoned on the side, was issued in May 1907.[11] The company, wrote *John Bull* in a short notice that was almost certainly inspired by Harris, 'takes over some valuable contracts from the General Post Office. It seems a promising proposition.'[12]

The magazine was taken to task over this plug by one of its feistier readers. Bottomley's magazine had established a reputation as a fearless exposer of City sleaze, largely by attacking well-known bucket shops. The reputation was only partly justified. Most of its attacks simply repeated exposés that had already been published elsewhere but they attracted readers and distracted attention from Bottomley's own get-rich-quick schemes. The reader warned that *John Bull* was misleading its readers. 'The company is not putting the whole facts clearly before the public and I trust you will advise your readers to go slow.'[13] The fearless *John Bull* published the letter – but not until three weeks after the share offer had closed.

The mail coach company's directors may have seemed impressive to casual readers of the prospectus, but for the most part they were the usual guinea pigs, hired for their distinguished names rather than their financial expertise. The minimum subscription was set at £35 000, the amount needed to pay the initial expenses and buy enough vans to give the company a reasonable start in life. In the event, the investing public displayed a marked lack of interest.

Like the electrobus flotation the share issue was underwritten and the underwriter was left holding some 20 000 unsold shares. The underwriter, who doubled as the company promoter, was Herbert Webb, who had previously been the manager of Provincial Carriers, the parcels delivery company with the garage in Victoria. Webb was not a wealthy man. As a promoter he was simply a convenient front for Lehwess, rather like Orr in Edinburgh and de Martigny in London, because Lehwess wanted to conceal his links with this promotion.[14] As an underwriter he subcontracted his liabilities.

The chief subcontractor was Securities Exchange, Longman's bucket shop, which took 12 000 of the unsold shares. After his initial foray as an underwriter in the electrobus share issue Longman was honing his underwriting technique. He adapted the bucket-shop keeper's principle of 'heads I win, tails you lose' to underwriting. If a flotation was successful then Longman would pocket his commission. But if the share offer failed and he was left holding unwanted shares, Longman welshed on the deal. He defaulted on a series of similar underwriting deals in a career that spanned more than two decades.[15]

Most of the remaining shares were taken up by a previously unknown enterprise called the Modern Traffic Development Corporation. Despite its grand name, the corporation had a paid-up capital of just £7. The sole director was Captain Edward Locock, who joined the board of several companies in the Lehwess network around this time and who was plainly a trusted friend. The corporation too was a front for Lehwess – although naturally his name did not appear on the file at Companies House. The only other official named in the file was the company secretary. She was Lehwess's typist.[16]

In the normal course of events the National Motor Mail Coach Company could have been expected to go into voluntary liquidation after the failure of its share issue. Once the shareholders' cheques had been cashed, a compliant liquidator would then allow Lehwess and Longman to pocket a substantial part of the money, leaving nothing for the shareholders.

It was a common type of deception. For the Edwardian company promoter, failure was often more profitable than launching a successful company. It was a well-worn path, as one observer later pointed out: 'A prospectus was issued making the most extravagant claims for the business, shares were allotted and deposits collected. The company would then mysteriously fail, leaving the unfortunate shareholders in the lurch.'[17]

This time things were slightly different. Sir Martin Conway, the chairman of the mail coach company, was an explorer of some note and not a typical guinea-pig director. He may have been hired for his title, but he had scruples and he was concerned to see that everything was done properly. He refused to cash the investors' cheques if the underwriters failed to pay their share.

Of course, there was never any question of the underwriters paying up. They had neither the intention nor the means to pay for their shares. Instead Lehwess and Locock pulled off a sleight-of-hand worthy of a music-hall magician. First, the audience was shown the money. The Modern Traffic Development Corporation wrote four cheques totalling £1350 as a down payment on its share of the underwriting. The money duly appeared in the National Motor Mail Coach Company's bank account. Conway still wavered. The clincher for him was when Locock turned up at a board meeting brandishing a wodge of banknotes.[18] With Conway's acquiescence the company cashed the investors' cheques.

The second part of the conjuring trick was to make the money vanish. The only reason that the Modern Traffic Development Corporation could issue the all-important cheques was because Lehwess had paid enough to cover them into the corporation's bank account. Once the shareholders' cheques had been cashed the National Motor Mail Coach Company returned the money to Lehwess – with interest – writing him a cheque for £2000. So the money-go-round started with Lehwess, who paid money into Locock's company, which in turn passed it on to the National Motor Mail Coach Company, where it whistled back to Lehwess – gathering a bonus of £650 on the way.[19]

Thereafter, the Modern Traffic Development Corporation, which operated out of Locock's offices in Covent Garden, only ever existed on paper. When Companies House eventually got round to asking Locock for the corporation's annual return – a frequently overlooked legal requirement – Locock wrote back saying 'this company had carried on no business of any kind for the last two years approximately, the cause being its entire absence of assets.

'I now beg to ask you whether it is necessary under the circumstances I have set forth above for the return to be made, and in case it should be necessary, how is the 5/- stamp [5 shilling] you allude to, to be paid when there are no assets of any kind?' The correspondence then ceased. The next letter from Companies House was returned marked 'gone away'.[20]

In September 1907 the National Motor Mail Coach Company found that the underwriters were not going to pay up for their shares. Consequently the company did not have enough money to take over the Post Office contracts or to buy a fleet of motor vans and start its business. The directors – Conway seems to have stopped playing an active part – decided that the company should be put into voluntary liquidation.

Although the flotation had flopped there had been a significant take-up by relatively low-paid postal workers, who appreciated the logic of replacing horses with motor vans, people like Joanna Pouncy, a 53-year-old sub-postmistress in Dorchester. But these small shareholders were unlikely to cause any trouble: they could not afford to throw good money after bad by hiring expensive lawyers and going to court. So there was every prospect that Lehwess, Longman and the others would be able to divide the spoils between them.

They reckoned without a deeply affronted retired naval commander, who gathered together a group of similarly disgruntled shareholders. They took the company to court, arguing that they should get their money back because the share subscriptions had failed to exceed the minimum threshold – because the underwriting was phoney.[21] The court agreed: and appointed its own liquidator to ensure that the shareholders were not cheated out of their money.[22]

The liquidator confirmed that Webb was a stooge and that the real promoter of the company was Lehwess. He forced Lehwess to pay back some of the money he owed.[23] It was a result of sorts for the shareholders. In May 1910, some three years after she had paid £5 for her shares, Pouncy received a cheque for £2 16s (£2.80). It was followed in November by another for £1 5s (£1.25).[24]

Chapter 8

A Transatlantic Con

In the summer of 1906 both Lehwess and Longman embarked on transatlantic voyages. The two men were visiting America with an eye to new business. Lehwess hoped to sell French technology to New York – the taximeters he had acquired on his recent visit to France – and Longman was prospecting for treasure in the Sierra Madre. Both men were also scouting around for a source of top-quality, reliable batteries so that they could re-energise the electrobus swindle.

It was natural that Longman and Lehwess should look west for a new battery supplier. Thomas Edison had repeatedly, if optimistically, announced the perfection of the storage battery and the United States was known to be a world leader in electric cars.[1] The original electrobus battery had been an untested design. The plates were made of a lead paste mixed with horse hair. The sulphuric acid in the battery dissolved the hair, giving the plates a sponge-like texture, which increased their surface area while reducing their weight.

This technique produced a lighter and more powerful battery, but at the expense of weakening the plates. A battery had to be rugged if it was to withstand the bumps and jolts generated by a bus with solid rubber tyres travelling over rough roads. The catastrophic failure of a plate might easily have been the reason why the prototype electrobus had broken down when it was being inspected by Scotland Yard. Furthermore, the battery's inventor had been taken aback by all the bad publicity. It was not good for his brainchild to be best known for its association with a swindle.[2]

Not only would an American battery be a credible power source for the electrobus but there was also the added bonus that Americans were almost entirely unaware of the unsavoury details lurking in the bus's background. For although the American papers had covered the launch of the electrobus, and carried a widely syndicated column commenting on 'electrobus' being a word that was new to *Webster's Dictionary*, no hint of any wrongdoing had reached the papers stateside.[3] Anyone on the other side of the Atlantic who knew about the electrobus swindle would have had to have been an assiduous reader of the British press.

Meanwhile, Lehwess's other problem was what to do with the electrobus garage while he and Longman worked out how to relaunch the company to their mutual benefit. In March 1906, just before the electrobus company had made its share offer, Lehwess had taken over the lease of a large garage in Horseferry Road, not far from Victoria Station, after Provincial Carriers moved out. The garage was earmarked as the electrobus charging station, a place where a large fleet of buses could be housed and maintained and their batteries recharged.[4]

The failure of the flotation left Lehwess holding the lease on the garage – and nothing to put in it but a solitary electrobus. So in May 1906 he moved another bus company into the garage. This was called Reliance Motor Transit. It too was a Lehwess and Longman enterprise, one of a number of small and ephemeral companies the pair promoted.[5]

Reliance Motor Transit paid the rent on the Horseferry Road garage – to Lehwess. It also paid the rates and started to refurbish the premises.[6] It even shared a telephone number with the electrobus company. The one thing it didn't do was to run any buses. The money behind Reliance Motor Transit came from an extremely wealthy Austrian-born gunrunner called Louis Spitzel, who had been convinced by Lehwess that there was money to be made by getting in on the ground floor of the motor bus boom.

Spitzel, who was said to have a personal fortune of £2 million, was scarcely a blameless character – and therefore an ideal mark for a confidence trickster. Originally a diamond merchant, he went bankrupt in Australia. He then did a vanishing act, leaving his creditors to whistle for their money. Four years later he surfaced in Shanghai, where he developed a new career as an arms dealer. Said to be the man who introduced the first Maxim gun into China, Spitzel became the largest supplier of arms to the Chinese government and the right-hand man of General Li Hung Chang, one of the most powerful figures at the Chinese court. China backed Russia in the Russo-Japanese war of 1904–05 and much of Spitzel's fortune came from running the Japanese blockade of Port Arthur to supply the Russians.[7]

When Spitzel died in Austria early in September 1906 the company lost its only source of finance. The Reliance company did the corporate equivalent of a moonlight flit. It disappeared from the Horseferry Road garage leaving behind unpaid bills.[8] Spitzel's heirs and executors believed he had been taken for a ride and accused Lehwess of fraud. The subsequent court cases neatly illustrate the difficulty that flawed characters have in recovering money after a con trick. Spitzel's heirs forced Lehwess to compensate the estate, in return for dropping all accusations of fraud. In the meantime the ensuing publicity following Spitzel's death reached the ears of his creditors in Australia. They sued his estate and got their money back.[9] In the end it was Spitzel's estate that lost the most.

In June, barely a month after the collapse of the electrobus flotation, Longman sailed to America, taking a first-class cabin on a liner bound for New York. His ultimate destination was Mexico's silver-mining region where he spent several weeks before returning to the United States, although he was also keeping a sharp look-out for suitable battery suppliers.[10] Not long after, the Mexican Smelting Corporation was registered in London. This shadowy new company had no capital and its only activity was to relieve a naive clergyman of £10000, which earned the promoter 12 months in jail.[11] The exact link with Longman isn't clear – maybe Longman had been at least partly paid for his services with shares – but Securities Exchange was soon trying to offload the company's shares through adverts in the financial press. 'Mexican Smelting Corporation Limited. Preference shares in this company for sale. What offers?'[12]

Lehwess was also off on his travels. While Longman made his way to America Lehwess went to France to acquire some taximeters, devices that automatically calculated cab fares. Ironically, the point of these devices was to combat fraud – to prevent cab drivers overcharging. Lehwess set sail from Southampton for New York in September. While the remaining shareholders in the London Electrobus Company nursed their losses, Lehwess travelled first class on the *Kronprinz Wilhelm*, one of the most luxurious liners on the North Atlantic run.

The German ship briefly held the Blue Riband for the fastest crossing of the Atlantic and it was one of the world's most technologically advanced liners – a veritable showcase for the latest in electrical devices. It was one of the first ships to have a Marconi telegraph, electric central heating and dozens of electric motors that worked everything from cranes to the ship's watertight doors.

Lehwess arrived in New York towards the end of September, carrying a letter from the London Electrobus Company giving him authority to negotiate a deal with a suitable battery supplier. He gave American reporters an embellished account of his visit, saying he wanted to buy batteries 'for a big London concern now running electric omnibuses'. This was his first visit to the

United States and aside from searching for batteries he was also trying to persuade the city to buy eight French taxis fitted with taximeters that he had imported. His contact at the New York Transportation Company was an old friend. The 27-year-old superintendent was none other than Leonard K Clark, the man who had been with Lehwess when he was caught using a false number plate two years earlier.[13] Their discussions were evidently productive and Lehwess registered a new company in New York to sell taximeters.[14]

By now Lehwess and Longman had narrowed their search for the perfect battery. Over the next month Lehwess held a series of meetings with Commodore Charles Gould, the 62-year-old head of the American Gould Storage Battery Corporation, both at Gould's New York offices just up the street from Grand Central Station and at the corporation's factory near Buffalo. The Gould Storage Battery Corporation, which had a capital of $5 million, was one of the world's leading battery manufacturers and it specialised in rugged heavy-duty batteries for use in transport. Not only did many of the electric cars, vans and trains in the United States use Gould batteries, so did the United States Navy.[15]

Lehwess told Gould that the electric bus was a sure-fire winner, given the right batteries. He also outlined his other interests in commercial vehicles and promised Gould that the burgeoning British market was just waiting for the advanced technology of the Gould battery.

Lehwess and Longman had done their homework well. Gould had taken out patents to protect his innovative technology in the United States – and in Britain. Lehwess, who had a number of patents in his own name, knew that Gould's British patent rights would lapse if the batteries were not manufactured in Britain.[16] It was a useful lever in the negotiations. Lehwess offered to solve Gould's patent problem by setting up a company in England to sell and manufacture Gould batteries.

The two men edged towards a deal. Lehwess would register a British company to manufacture Gould batteries and pay £25 000 into the company's bank account. In return Gould would grant the British company a licence to manufacture and sell batteries made to the Gould patents. In return for this licence Gould was to receive just over half the shares in the British company, giving him nominal control of it. The rest of the shares would be held by Lehwess and his associates. The final part of the deal was that Gould would ship 15 sets of batteries to England and help to train the electrobus engineers on how to get the best out of them.

On paper this was a very good deal for Gould. It opened up the prospect of being able to sell his batteries throughout the British Empire as well as protecting his British patents – and all for the cost of a few batteries. However, Gould was a shrewd and cautious businessman – the commodore title was an honorific handle from the New York Yacht Club, where he indulged his passion for sailing. He demanded a token of good faith.

He stipulated that Lehwess must pay $10 000 (then worth just over £2000) into a New York bank account as a guarantee. When it was confirmed that Lehwess had set up the British company and paid the £25 000 into it, Gould would ship the batteries across the Atlantic and release the guarantee money.[17]

Lehwess returned to England in November and duly registered a new company, the Gould Storage Battery Company. He then wired Gould to tell him that the new company had been set up as agreed.

On 30 November Gould sent a telegram to Lehwess:

'Do I understand £25 000 in cash has been paid in?'

'All shares issued cash,' wired back Lehwess.[18]

On the strength of this assurance Gould allowed Lehwess to retrieve the money he had deposited in New York. There was just one problem with this categorical assurance. It was a lie.

The Gould Storage Battery Company had been registered at Companies House ten days before this exchange of telegrams.[19] Just over half the shares in the company were indeed registered in Charles Gould's name. But there the agreement started to unravel. There was only one director, and that was Lehwess's trusted friend Captain Locock. The rest of the company's shares were held by the captain and the Asiatic Bank. The company had issued 21 000 shares, but only 100 of the £1 shares had been paid for in cash. In return for this modest investment Lehwess now had batteries worth several thousand pounds.

In his meetings with Gould, Lehwess had deliberately concealed the fact that he owned almost all the shares in the London Electrobus Company. Nor had he owned up to the fact that the Asiatic Bank only existed on paper. It would take more than a year before Gould found out that he had been deceived.

The day after receiving Lehwess's telegram Gould carried out his side of the bargain and shipped the batteries to England accompanied by his most experienced electrical engineer, Rufus Chamberlain. Chamberlain was one of the key figures in the development of the Gould battery and the inventor credited with several of Gould's patents. His job was to troubleshoot any technical snags, such as the best charging regime for the batteries, so that over-charging did not shorten the battery life.[20]

For the next few weeks Chamberlain and the engineers at the electrobus garage in Horseferry Road worked hard to ensure the smooth working of the bus. By early January the electrobus was becoming a regular sight on the city's streets, carrying a dozen or more people in experimental trips around the capital before finally gaining Scotland Yard's approval to carry paying passengers.[21]

His job done, Chamberlain sailed back to New York in mid-January. The cross-Atlantic collaboration continued. Three weeks after Chamberlain arrived home the imposingly tall figure of Ernest Rowbottom, the 34-year-old general manager of the

London Electrobus Company, walked down the first-class gangway of the White Star liner *Majestic* and set foot in New York for the first time. He had $350 of company money in his wallet to cover his expenses while he learnt first hand how to get the best out of the Gould batteries.[22]

Rowbottom was a pivotal figure in the early part of electrobus story. Before becoming general manager of the London Electrobus Company, he had been the general manager of the Motor Car Emporium. Rowbottom was also a director of Improved Electric Traction, the shadowy company occupying the London Electrobus Company's offices when the reporter from the *Financial Times* came calling.

Lehwess had anticipated that the emporium was likely to have a limited life. So two years before it became bankrupt he registered a new company, which would lie dormant until he needed it.[23] In January 1907 he brought this new company to life, renaming it the Electric Van Wagon and Omnibus Company. This was the company that was now going to supply electrobuses. It was based in Locock's Covent Garden offices and the directors included Lehwess, Locock and Rowbottom.[24]

Rowbottom is an ambiguous character in the electrobus story. He was an insider and in a position to know about the dubious financing. Did he turn a blind eye to all this? He certainly had an incentive. He had a well-paid position, which was fortunate given that he had a wife, a mistress and two families to support. Or was he too taken in by Lehwess's plausible patter? He undoubtedly had considerable faith in the future of the electric vehicle. A journalist who knew him well gave him a glowing character reference, describing him as 'a rare one for work'.[25] Whatever he may have suspected, or known, Rowbottom tried hard to make the electrobus a practical proposition.

Over in New York Chamberlain and Rowbottom were able to report the substantial progress they had made to Gould. The electrobus was performing well and the new company that was going to make the electrobus would be displaying a large selection of buses and other vehicles at the forthcoming Commercial Vehicle Exhibition in London, all powered by Gould batteries.[26] The electrobus engineers were competent. Lehwess had shown Chamberlain the electrobus company's share register as proof of the venture's financial integrity. Everything seemed hunky dory. But Chamberlain was an electrical engineer, not a financial expert, and he was blissfully unaware of all the behind-the-scenes chicanery.

While the engineers were hard at work Lehwess set about creating a seductive new image for the London Electrobus Company. The contract with the Baron de Martigny was cancelled and the bogus patent had vanished. A new company was going to make the electrobus, in place of the emporium, which was now a busted flush. This was all part of the essential window dressing. To cap it all, the electrobus company now boasted an impressive new garage and charging station.

The public relaunch of the electrobus was set for 21 February 1907. From time to time the sun poked through the clouds, making it a pleasant enough day to take a trip in an open-top bus. At 11 am an expectant throng of journalists drawn mostly from the trade press gathered in front of the London Electrobus Company's offices in Trafalgar Square.[27]

'Will you come for a ride in an electrobus,' said John Musgrave, the company's genial new chairman, 'and judge for yourself of its comfort and convenience.'[28] Powered by a Gould battery slung beneath the vehicle, the bus glided along to the garage at Victoria, so that journalists could inspect the new arrangements for charging the batteries. The electrobus then set off on a route that took them past the Houses of Parliament, up the Strand and along Fleet Street, where most of Britain's major newspapers had their offices, past the Stock Exchange – where the vehicle drew cheers from bystanders – and back to the Hotel Cecil for lunch.

'The 'bus itself is well constructed, elegantly upholstered, admirably lighted, and, with the exception of the musical rhythm of the motors, runs silently. There is no noisome smell [and] no danger to clothes from oil,' wrote one reporter in a paean of praise doubtless penned during the post-prandial afterglow.[29]

Chapter 9

A Fresh Start

At 7.30 am on the morning of 15 July 1907 the first electrobus to carry paying passengers set off from Victoria Station on the 35-minute journey to Liverpool Street. It was a glorious summer's day and by noon the temperature topped 77 °F in central London – perfect for a ride on an open-top bus. The company's fleet of six electrobuses did 'a roaring trade' reported the newspapers.

The electrobus is 'the aristocrat among public conveyances,' wrote an enthusiastic reporter from the *Daily Express*. It 'has exceedingly good manners for it makes no noise and under no pretence will bump its clients around'. With its plush fittings, said the *Daily Express*, the bus resembled a private electric brougham, the deluxe carriage of the day.[1]

In Victoria Street people stood and stared, amazed by the silent passage of the electrobus. At Liverpool Street a police constable said, in a tone of admiration, 'they seemed to be going very smoothly'. And a driver from the competing Vanguard company grudgingly conceded that a passing electrobus 'seemed to be going all right'.[2]

'We claim that the electrobus – without smell, noise, vibration and oil-dropping is the ideal means of traction for the town,' declared Ernest Rowbottom, the company's general manager. 'We are running a service of six vehicles from Victoria station to Liverpool Street – a distance of nearly four miles.'

'We shall soon have fifty electrobuses and a service [every] six minutes in various parts of London,' said Rowbottom. No one seemed to notice or if they did no one seemed concerned that the company had made a strikingly similar claim the previous year.

Compared with the fanfare that had accompanied the flotation of the company, coverage of the launch of the bus service was muted. The previous year's misleading prospectus had left its mark. Not many of Fleet Street's newsdesks thought it worth sending a reporter to cover the opening day even though the route took the electrobuses past the windows of all the newspaper offices in Fleet Street. Most newsdesks thought the beautifully warm weather on St Swithin's Day, with the promise of a sweltering summer to come – false as it turned out – was more newsworthy. The *Daily News,* the first to cover the start of the service, didn't send its reporter until the following day.

The coverage in the trade press and provincial papers was better and more timely. Their verdict was almost unequivocal. The electrobuses were 'high in public favour', 'incomparably superior to the petrol-propelled variety' and doing 'a very good trade'. 'Other things being equal,' one reporter predicted, 'the electrically propelled bus will inevitably drive the petrol vehicle off the streets.'[3]

Most of the press took the relaunch at face value. There was no financial angle to the story, no disgruntled shareholders asking for their money back. For most reporters the only story was the pleasing silence of the buses. Almost the only sour note came from Stanley Spooner's *Automotor Journal,* which still carped about the electrobus's economics. The electrobus would not be able to compete with motor buses, it claimed. It must have been placed on the road 'from philanthropic motives...so long as the ordinary gullible investor is not called on to pay the piper nothing but praise is due to the introduction of such a form of public travel'.[4] But even Spooner had to concede that the electrobuses were popular: 'The public were not slow to avail themselves of their comfort and easy travelling.'

The paradox at the heart of the electrobus story is that although the company was crooked the buses themselves were well engineered and well managed. The close collaboration between Gould and the electrobus engineers had paid dividends. In many ways the behind-the-scenes operation was every bit as impressive as the buses themselves. Everyone who saw the new garage admired the slick battery-charging operation. It was a tribute to Rowbottom's managerial skills and the efforts of Gould's engineers.[5]

The electrobus garage and charging station was on the corner of Horseferry Road and Earl Street, now called Marsham Street.[6] Each electrobus made several trips from Victoria to Liverpool Street in the morning before returning to the garage at lunchtime and swapping their batteries for fresh ones. After the morning shift the drivers drove their buses in through the Earl Street entrance and up a ramp, stopping the bus over a hydraulic lift.

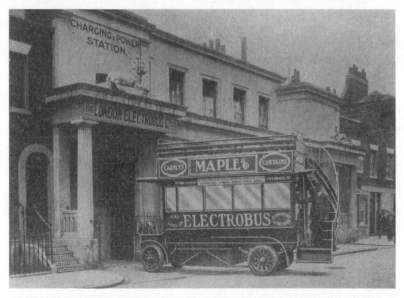

Figure 6 An electrobus entering the company's garage and charging station in Earl Street (now called Marsham Street). A photo taken at the start of operations in July 1907.

The garage staff pushed a trolley under the bus, raised the lift, released the bolts securing the battery, dropped the exhausted battery on to the trolley and replaced it with a fresh one. The old battery was then sent off for recharging. The whole process took around three minutes, after which the electrobus drove off the ramp out of the garage and back into Horseferry Road. Ten minutes later the bus was ready and waiting to pick up passengers at Victoria Station.

In the summer of 1907 the auguries for the electrobus were favourable. The sight of the first electrobuses plying their trade on the streets of the capital prompted a fresh flurry of protest about the shortcomings of the motor bus. Discontent about traffic noise and pollution had been simmering since the beginning of the motor bus boom. Questions were asked in Parliament after Sir James Dewar, an eminent chemist and the inventor of the vacuum flask, fulminated about the dangers of the noxious fumes produced by the exhausts of petrol vehicles. Herbert Gladstone, the home secretary, agreed to look into it.[7]

Towards the end of 1906 Sir Theodore Martin, a Scottish poet and author of the official biography of Queen Victoria's consort Prince Albert, chaired a protest meeting of the Street Noise Abatement Committee at the Medical Society of London. 'Motor omnibuses,' suggested one speaker, 'ought to run underground in main drains, like other nuisances.'[8] The next month London's local councils held a day-long conference 'to consider the evils and annoyance arising from motor vehicles' and decided to send a deputation to Gladstone.[9]

Although the bus wasn't the only source of noise and pollution it was one of the most visible and the easiest target because of its fixed routes. By July 1907 there were nearly a thousand motor buses in the capital. The Home Office received a continual stream of complaints and demands for a curb on these unwelcome juggernauts.[10]

Figure 7 Swapping batteries: a fresh battery on the hydraulic lift, ready to be raised and bolted on to the underside of the bus. It took three minutes to change batteries. As pictured by the *Electrician* in 1907.

In London buses were licensed by the Metropolitan Police, which in turn was responsible to the Home Office. The civil servants in the Home Office, who plainly didn't live close to a motor bus route, were dismissive of the protests and tended to trivialise those who complained. When Sidney Colvin, an eminent art critic, wrote to the *Times* about bus noise Home Office officials were sniffy: 'Mr Colvin is an artistic person no doubt of keen sensibility.'[11] But there were plenty of people who thought Colvin was right. 'The noise of these machines has turned all the leading thoroughfares into veritable pandemoniums,' agreed one influential magazine.[12]

As a friend of the late Queen, Martin enjoyed unfettered access to the letters column of the *Times*. 'I can endure no longer the misery caused by the incessant roar and rattle and pestilential atmosphere and dust diffused by these monstrous vehicles,' he wrote. The din and smell of the buses had forced him to leave his house in Kensington's Onslow Gardens and stay in his country home in rural Wales.[13]

However, Martin's complaints did not meet with an altogether sympathetic hearing. The police could order buses off the road if they were emitting 'excessive noise or the undue emission of noxious fumes'. But the government did not want to stifle the emerging motor industry. The Home Office and the police were at one on the need for restraint in enforcing the law. Sir Edward Henry, the commissioner of police at Scotland Yard, spelled out the official attitude in a letter to the Home Office. The police, wrote Henry, should be wary of interfering to avoid hampering this young and important industry.[14] The police attitude amounted to 'torpid indifference', snorted Martin.[15] Home Office officials disagreed. The air of complacency was unmistakable. It was, said an official, a 'reasonable policy'.

In the meantime Martin had been persuaded to become president of the Street Noise Abatement Committee, part of the Betterment of London Association. This was an unwise decision that would seriously damage the cause of the anti-noise campaign, although Martin wasn't to know it.

The man behind the anti-noise committee was Thomas Bowden Green, a notorious swindler who preyed on the respectable and elderly, enlisting their support for one or other of his 'philanthropic' enterprises. To Bowden Green these charities were cash cows. He was rather less interested in the causes he espoused and rather more interested in generating a healthy income for himself. Bowden Green organised a petition calling on the home secretary to clamp down on motor buses. A considerable number of artists, lawyers, MPs and eminent citizens of all kinds signed the petition. One of the few who refused was George Bernard Shaw. While he sympathised with the call for cleaner, quieter buses – possibly mindful of his investment in Edinburgh but more likely because he found cruelty to horses compelled to pull heavy buses repugnant – he thought motor buses were 'cheap, swift, clean, humane, interesting and pleasant'.[16]

When the home secretary eventually agreed to receive a deputation Martin, who by now had turned 90, headed it. The deputation included Bowden Green. Martin told Gladstone that he had lived in Onslow Square for 50 years and he hoped to die there, but his death might be accelerated by these detestable motor buses. There was, he said, 'a mass of carriages of an unprecedented size, of an unprecedented weight, making a horrible noise, shaking houses and making it impossible for any person either to enjoy his house during the day or to get his sleep at night'. Gladstone was dismissive, claiming the government was powerless to act.[17]

Gladstone, a Liberal politician and youngest son of the former prime minister William Gladstone, may not have felt much sympathy for the well-heeled and Conservative-inclined voters of Kensington. But rather more importantly, both Gladstone and his civil servants were keenly aware of Bowden Green's notoriety.

Before the Betterment of London Association became interested in motor buses it ran a long-standing campaign to clamp down on street musicians, and in particular barrel organs. *Truth*, that scourge of the disreputable, had repeatedly exposed Bowden Green as the man behind a series of bogus charities and he had been a fixture in the *Truth Cautionary List* since it was first published in 1903.[18] Malcolm Delevingne, the home secretary's private secretary, was an assiduous reader of *Truth*. He decided to enquire more deeply. He wrote to the Charity Organisation Society, which then had an informal role overseeing charities, saying that he had heard that Bowden Green was a bogus philanthropist. Back came the reply: 'you have been rightly informed – we know Mr Thomas Bowden Green extremely well'.

The Charity Organisation Society went on to give chapter and verse on Bowden Green's varied career: from National Thrift, where he adapted Samuel Smiles's doctrine of fighting poverty through self-help to one of fighting poverty through helping himself, to his role as trustee for a trade union during the London dock strike of 1889 where he 'retained a very thrifty hold upon the trust funds'. In more recent years, continued the letter, he had set up the Betterment of London Association. At this point the letter in the Home Office files has a note in Delevingne's hand: '*Truth* knows all about this.'[19]

The force of the arguments against motor buses put forward by Martin and the others was blunted by their association with Bowden Green. The brush-off for the Betterment of London Association was scarcely surprising. 'On the whole I doubt if they are as much nuisance as barrel organs,' wrote a Home Office official.[20]

Outside London, local councils rather than the police licensed bus services and they were not so susceptible to being leant on by the Home Office. Many councils adopted a much more robust attitude to noisy buses than the Metropolitan Police. A few refused to license them at all. In Manchester a new service of motor buses attracted a storm of protest, mainly from influential citizens living alongside bus routes. A petition signed by 155 residents came up with a familiar list of complaints including 'the appalling noise and the most obnoxious smell'. The motor bus, residents complained, was an 'imperfect, barbarous and retrogressive invention' which would injure the flowers in front gardens. The council withdrew the company's bus licences – forcing it into liquidation after just six months.[21]

Nevertheless, the London police began to take a tougher line on substandard buses during 1906. This change of attitude followed a truly horrific bus crash. A Vanguard motor bus was taking a party of firemen from the village of Orpington on the outskirts of London to Brighton for a day out beside the sea. At the top of a steep hill at Handcross, some 18 miles north of Brighton, the brakes failed and the bus ran out of control down the hill before smashing into an oak tree at 40 miles per hour. There were 36 people on the bus; ten of them died.

'Handcross Hill Horror' was the headline in the *Westminster Gazette*, which added that this ghastly calamity was the worst 'in the history of the new mode of locomotion'. The disaster was unparalleled, agreed the *Daily News*.[22] The accident was a wake-up call for the government and prompted some serious soul-searching. In the aftermath of the tragedy experts were quick to point to the shortcomings of the bus. It wasn't just safety that was the problem, but noise and pollution too. One widely quoted expert said that four-fifths of motor buses would be on the scrapheap within two years, adding that it was time that the regulations were stricter and properly enforced.[23]

Until the Handcross disaster the police attitude had been one of forbearance to an experimental form of transport. After the accident, the police began to clamp down on the worst offenders. Constables started ordering dangerous and substandard buses off the road, prompting accusations by the bus industry of police persecution. Some idea of the scale of the problem can be gleaned from figures provided by Sir Edward Henry, Scotland Yard's chief commissioner. There were around 1000 motor buses on the roads of the capital during 1907, the year after the Handcross crash. That year, the police made 8500 reports of buses being unfit to be on the road. Nearly 5000 of the reports were for excessive noise.[24] On average, every bus in London was ordered off the road every six weeks and had to be repaired before it could resume normal service.

As the police stepped up their efforts to control petrol buses, so the companies fought back. Evading regulations is nothing new. Today defeat device software can cheat pollution controls by detecting when a vehicle is being tested and cleaning up the exhaust during the test. A century ago the defeat device was sawdust. In London, Scotland Yard had to approve each new type of bus before it was licensed to carry passengers. The police could refuse to approve a bus if it was too noisy. It became common practice even among respectable operators to fill the gearbox with sawdust to deaden the noise during the police inspection.[25] Once the bus was licensed the operators dispensed with the sawdust and took their chances with the bobbies on the beat.

By the summer the motor bus industry was in crisis. Apart from the constant stream of protests about noise and fumes, many buses were unusable either because the police had ordered them off the road or because they had broken down. On top of that the motor bus was proving ruinously expensive to run. To many people it seemed that the motor bus boom was heading for bust.

The expense of running the early motor buses was hitting investors where it hurt most – in their wallets. Shareholders in the older bus companies who had enjoyed a steady flow of income in the days of horse power now saw their dividends drying up. Both the London General and the London Road Car Company, which had been highly profitable in the days of horse power, posted losses in the first half of 1907. The value of their shares plummeted by an average of 70 per cent in two years.[26] About four out of ten buses belonging to Vanguard, the third largest operator of motor buses in London, were off the road awaiting repairs.[27]

In July, just five days after the electrobuses started running, London's fourth largest motor bus company collapsed. One source ascribed the collapse to the 'energetic harrying by the police'. The company itself blamed the high cost of running its buses, which it put at 1s 6d per mile – some 80 per cent higher than the figure Spooner claimed was the cost of running a motor bus. To add to the irony, the company's motor buses were made by John Stirling, the man who together with Spooner had led the chorus of claims about the prohibitive running costs of electric buses.[28]

Suddenly the explosive growth in the number of motor buses was thrown into reverse. The London General announced that it was withdrawing its motor buses on one route from Oxford Circus to the suburbs and replacing them with old-fashioned three-horsed omnibuses. The horse-drawn buses were not much slower – 5 to 6 miles per hour instead of 6 to 8 miles per hour for the motor bus – and they were almost guaranteed to reach their destination.[29] In the long run they were cheaper. It was a straw in the wind for the *Economist*, which predicted that the horse would see off the motor vehicle, just as it had survived the coming of the steam engine.

'The public, which rushed with such luckless enthusiasm to invest in motor-bus companies and motor-cab companies, has had a severe lesson…when we read the statement made at the meeting of the London General Omnibus Company by Mr Henry Hicks, the deputy chairman, that no motor omnibus has yet been invented that can be made to pay,' commented the *Economist*.[30] Hicks's sentiments echoed through the popular press: 'Motor Omnibuses. Can they pay?' asked the *Daily Mail*.

Within the space of a few weeks three smaller London bus companies and one in Birmingham also scrapped their motor buses and brought back horse power.[31] In July and August 1907 more than a hundred of London's motor buses – around one in eight – were scrapped. Even the normally loyal proponents of petrol power in the trade press were forced to admit 'the temporary failure of the motor bus'.[32] The head of the London County Council's trams – the main opposition for the motor bus – was even more optimistic. In a few years, he allegedly said, motor buses would only be seen in museums.[33]

The bus companies weren't alone in having second thoughts. Many well-to-do people who had scrapped their carriages and converted their coachmen into chauffeurs were now reverting to the old ways. There was, said the *Economist* with a hint of wishful thinking, an increase in demand for horses.

A week after the first electrobuses began carrying passengers a deputation of 17 inner London councils went to see Sir Edward Henry, the commissioner of police at Scotland Yard, urging him to clamp down on the buses that created 'such a terrible noise and such a terrible nuisance'. The commissioner argued against tougher action and expressed his optimism about a new type of noiseless bus: the electrobus.[34]

The disarray in the bus industry was the perfect opportunity for the electrobus. Few people were better placed to appreciate the shortcomings of the motor bus than the man behind the electrobus company. After all, Lehwess had sold many of these buses. The London Electrobus Company now had a chance to establish itself as a major London bus company. The only thing holding it back was a lack of finance. Its only real source of capital was the rump of some 200 small shareholders who between them owned some 7500 shares.

On paper Lehwess, Longman and their nominees held the majority of the electrobus shares. But this was all smoke and mirrors. The pair were taking money out of the company – in promotion expenses, underwriting fees and advance payments for buses – as fast as the instalments on their shares became due.[35]

Despite Ernest Rowbottom's claim that the company would have 50 electrobuses by the end of 1907 there was just one new electrobus. In the meantime the number of motor buses began to creep up again. Despite continued doubts about whether the motor bus would ever prove economic, a steady increase in the price of fodder helped to keep the companies interested in the new technology.[36] The window of opportunity for the electrobus was beginning to close.

Chapter 10

A Brawl in The Edgware Road

The evening's celebrations came to an abrupt end with the arrival of the bill. Dr Edward Ernest Lehwess refused point blank to pay it. His dining companion Captain Edward Locock weighed in. Fuelled by four hours of serious carousing, the captain called the restaurant owner a thief and put his boot through the restaurant window, shattering the midnight calm of the Edgware Road and attracting the attention of a passing bobby on the beat. It was the signal for the outbreak of hostilities. Lehwess and Locock were soon in engaged in a pitched battle with the restaurant staff. When the police eventually gained entry they found a scene of devastation. Broken bottles, glasses, vases and crockery littered the dining room floor. And the piano stool, with only two surviving legs, lay useless on the floor.[1]

The day of 9 September 1907 was pleasantly warm, one of those days that makes you think summer still has a little something left in it. Lehwess drove to Locock's offices in Covent Garden to put the final touches to the registration of a new company. It was to be called the International Motor Traffic Syndicate Limited – the original syndicate had not been incorporated – and would join equally impressive sounding concerns, such as the Guernsey-based Asiatic Banking and Trading Corporation, as a substantial shareholder in the much talked about London Electrobus Company.

Figure 8 Captain Edward Locock at the wheel of his car in 1902.
A *Candid Friend* photograph.

The electrobuses had quickly captured the public imagination.
By September 1907 the buses had all the makings of being a nice
little earner – although there were some doubts about exactly who
would be reaping the profit. They were silent, clean and reliable and
without the tangle of overhead wires that characterised the electric
trams. They were the original green machines, buses powered by
batteries alone – and obviously superior in most respects to the
smelly, noisy and widely loathed petrol buses.

Although Lehwess controlled the London Electrobus
Company anyone wanting to know more about the people behind
the company would be hard pushed to find irrefutable documentary
evidence. His shares were mostly held in the names of nominees
and he had set up a complex network of companies to disguise his
connections with the company. Locock was already a director of
several of these companies and now he was a founding subscriber

of the new International Motor Traffic Syndicate, the latest strand in this web of deception.

Three people met that September day in the offices Locock rented on the second floor of Bedford Chambers, a gracious red-brick building on the north side of Covent Garden with offices above the arcades occupied by the market's fruit and vegetable merchants. At the centre of the group was Lehwess, the ebullient German lawyer. By his own admission an egotistical man, the 35-year-old Lehwess was in the prime of life and brimming over with schemes for making money.

Locock, a 40-year-old stockbroker, was to all appearances a more conventional British military figure who could have stepped straight from the pages of the *Boy's Own Paper*. He was the son of a diplomat in the Foreign Office and had served in the British army in West Africa, rising to the rank of captain before malaria and rheumatic fever forced him to retire. Locock and Lehwess shared an interest in motoring. With his military bearing and neat moustache, the gallant captain cut a dashing figure. Locock was a member of the London Stock Exchange and a figure of some considerable wealth. He once landed in Vancouver with $2500 in banknotes in his wallet, according to immigration officials who made a record of passengers' spending money.[2]

What did not quite fit the clean-cut image was Locock's reputation as a lothario. His wife, who was nine years younger than him, was an acknowledged beauty who had graced the cover of the society magazine *Candid Friend*.[3] She was as dashing a character as her husband. She shared his interest in motoring – she had her own car – and was a keen amateur jockey. But love-rat Locock, as today's tabloids would dub him, carried on a series of affairs with a string of women, before, during and after their marriage.[4]

The third person in the Covent Garden offices that day was 22-year-old Rose Sawer, an accomplished typist who was the daughter of an Essex stockbroker. Sawer became company secretary of the

International Motor Traffic Syndicate – a position which seems to have been a job share with Locock. The job was not all they shared for Sawer was Locock's current mistress. The two of them had a three-year affair, meeting up at the discreetly comfortable Tollard Royal Hotel in Holborn, where they signed the register as Mr and Mrs Sewell.[5]

Locock and Sawer's personal and business activities were closely intertwined. They were also partners in the Hilda Ainslie Typing and Translation Agency, which for a time shared offices with the International Motor Traffic Syndicate. The proprietor of the agency – who you might assume was Miss Hilda Ainslie – was a fictitious person, created out of a combination of the pair's middle names: Rose Hilda Sawer and Edward Ainslie Locock.[6]

The trio put the finishing touches to the application and sent the papers off to Companies House. Locock and Sawer had both signed the official forms. But one name was absent – Edward Ernest Lehwess. Although his name didn't appear on the application his fingerprints were all over it. The syndicate was, as he was later compelled to admit in court, 'my trading name'.[7] Now it was time to celebrate a good day's work. Locock and Lehwess, accompanied by two women, motored to the Edgware Road and parked outside the Oxford Restaurant around 7.30 pm. The newspaper reports of the subsequent fracas do not reveal the identity of the two women but Rose Sawer was likely to have been one of them.

While the Oxford Restaurant wasn't quite in the same class as top-drawer institutions like Simpson's in the Strand or Romano's, the food was good and it attracted a well-heeled clientele.[8] Beside its exotic Italian fare the Oxford Restaurant had the added attraction of private dining rooms where, as was later suggested in court, all the party's appetites could be discreetly satisfied.

Lehwess and Locock hired an upstairs room with a piano and the party adjourned for an aperitif, returning to the restaurant around an hour later to enjoy the comforts of their private dining room. Locock sent a waiter out for wine and the party sat down to an elaborate five-course meal – hors d'oeuvres, followed by Dover soles, a whole Surrey chicken, risottos, ices and finally coffee – all washed down with liberal quantities of burgundy and champagne to judge from the empty bottles that were later thrown around the dining room. Dinner over, the soirée continued with parlour songs around the piano.

The bill arrived shortly before midnight. Lehwess took one look at the bottom line, £2 5s (£2.25), and refused to pay. (The equivalent in today's money would be around £215.*) Locock went downstairs to sort things out with the restaurant's owner, Enrico Colatto. Locock argued that the bill should be less than half that amount. Surely, he suggested, there had been some mistake. There had not, insisted Colatto. The party had been pushing the boat out and had ordered expensive extras that were not included in the fixed-price menu. With an unpleasant row brewing the women left the restaurant and sat in the motor car parked outside and waited.

Back upstairs in the dining room Colatto politely asked the gentlemen a second time to pay. It was closing time and his staff, who slept above the restaurant, wanted to go to bed, he said. The 'gentlemen' were intransigent. They leant back in their chairs, said they were extremely comfortable and were quite happy to stay there until morning. If Colatto wanted his money he could sue them.

Colatto had taken the precaution of locking the front door to prevent the pair doing a runner. Now he threatened to call the police – a move that swiftly caused events to spiral out of control. Locock put his foot through the restaurant window, allegedly to draw the waiting ladies' attention to their plight. Colatto caught hold of Locock to prevent him breaking any more windows. Locock kicked Colatto in the shins and escaped from his grasp.

---

* This figure is calculated from the Retail Price Index. There are several ways of comparing inflation and all give very different answers: see www.measuringworth.com.

Chapter 10

Lehwess then lost it in a big way and started throwing glasses, vases, flower pots and anything else that came to hand.

A 25-year-old Italian waiter, Bertolini Giovanni, rushed upstairs to help Colatto, picking up a poker from the fireplace and hitting both Locock and Lehwess with it. The brawl soon became a free-for-all. Two female staff stood screaming with fright, but the rest of the half-a-dozen staff joined in with gusto. Locock felt a rush of air near his ear as a champagne bottle flew past his head before hitting the wall and shattering. Colatto smashed the piano stool over Lehwess's head, breaking two of its legs.

Another small but feisty waiter tried to hit Locock over the head with an empty Burgundy bottle. Locock punched him violently in the stomach. The force of the blow propelled the waiter backwards into the ladies' toilet. Locock rushed downstairs in an attempt to reach the sanctuary of the car outside, but found the front door locked. Seconds later, another wine bottle flew through the air narrowly missing his head and splintering the woodwork.

Soon afterwards Lehwess emerged from the dining room with blood streaming down his face and sat on the stairs beside Locock who was sweating profusely. Outnumbered and exhausted it was time to throw in the towel. Whispering in German, Locock told Lehwess they were in no condition to defend themselves and suggested they should pay the bill and get out. Lehwess would not hear of it. Visibly pale Locock asked if he could have a glass of water. Colatto brought him one and Locock paid up – without telling Lehwess.

At this point the police arrived in force. The ladies in the motor car told them there was a fight going on. One constable knocked on the restaurant door but a 'foreign voice' refused to let him in. When the police finally got inside they found a scene of chaos. Giving evidence later, one officer described the mayhem: 'The room was in great disorder. The music stool was broken and a portion of it was missing. A chair was overturned, a flowerpot was broken on the floor and broken pieces of glass were about the room and on the staircase.'

When Lehwess and Locock finally escaped outside they found a cordon of police holding back a large crowd of passers-by who had been attracted by the disturbance. That would have been the end of the incident but for Lehwess, who grabbed hold of Giovanni as he left the restaurant and handed him over to the police insisting he should be prosecuted for assault. Colatto ducked out of the way and sought refuge in his restaurant.

Being bested in a brawl with Italian waiters was a blow to Lehwess's self-esteem. Deeply affronted by his loss of face, Lehwess mounted a prosecution against Colatto and Giovanni. The ensuing court case was the talk of the town and made for sensational newspaper headlines. To *Lloyd's Weekly News* it was like a scene from one of the new silent movies. 'WILD WEST END FIGHT. Bottles and Flower Pots Fly in an Italian Restaurant.' While the *Daily Mirror* had 'RESTAURANT FREE FIGHT. Gentlemen's Objection to Their Bill Leads to Extraordinary Midnight Scenes.' Most of the national newspapers carried lengthy reports of the trial. The story was a riveting read and a welcome diversion from the more sobering fare of the army's new airship and the news of the Quebec bridge collapse, which killed 75 workers building the bridge.

The trial opened the following day at Marylebone police court, before Alfred Chichele Plowden, a magistrate known to reporters on the local papers as 'the court jester', because of his sardonic interjections. Despite the light-hearted tone of the newspaper reporting – and Plowden's comments – the case was deadly serious. Lehwess, who was mounting a private prosecution, had secured the services of Richard Muir, the most feared and forensic prosecutor of his day. Three years later Muir would secure the conviction of Dr Crippen. If convicted, Colatto and Giovanni could face a spell in prison.

Predictably, both parties blamed each other for the violence. Locock said Colatto fought like 'a tiger' and Giovanni behaved like

Chapter 10

'a madman'. Lehwess corroborated the captain's story. Both men denied any aggression and Locock claimed that he and the doctor were 'quite sober', which seems highly unlikely.

For his part Colatto said he had been very polite and denied threatening to murder his customers. Giovanni said he had gone upstairs to restore order when one of the gentlemen 'flew' at him. He defended himself 'with a poker about the size of my little finger'.

'The smallest poker this world contains,' observed Plowden, who was clearly enjoying the case.

The trial entered a second day. Muir began by suggesting a motive for the restaurant's allegedly excessive bill. He said the private room might have been used for 'some improper purpose' – and this explained why Colatto thought he could get away with overcharging.

On the second day, Lehwess attended court with his head wrapped theatrically in a bandage and a plaster on his nose. Muir had a decidedly modern view of evidence.[9] He believed eyewitness accounts were generally unreliable and preferred hard physical evidence. He called Lehwess's doctor, Louis Macrory, who had a practice in Battersea, to give medical evidence about the severity of Lehwess's wounds.

Macrory said Lehwess had a one-inch long wound on the bridge of his nose, two similar wounds on his head and a large bruise on his right shoulder blade caused by a blunt instrument. 'Had Dr Lehwess not been a strong man,' said Macrory, 'he would have sustained a fractured head and contusion and concussion of the brain.'

'You mean by a strong man, a thick skull?' asked Plowden.

The medical evidence was not quite all that it seemed. What Macrory did not tell the court was that his relationship with Lehwess was not simply one of doctor and patient. The two men also enjoyed a close business relationship. They were two of the seven founding shareholders in the Asiatic Banking and Trading Corporation, an investment that might prove very profitable if the

102

London Electrobus Company took off in a big way, because the bank held a large stake in the company.[10]

The trial resumed in early October, when the case came to an untimely end – at least as far as the nation's newspaper readers were concerned. With the case due to last several more days and further graphic details eagerly anticipated a number of Fleet Street papers sent their own reporters to cover the case, rather than relying on copy provided by reporters from the local papers.

However, the lawyers had done a deal. Muir knew the prosecution was looking increasingly preposterous and the case was going nowhere. There was also a mounting risk that the longer the case went on the more likely it was that the identity of the 'two ladies' might be disclosed. Indeed they might even have been called to give evidence, in which case they would have had some difficult questions to answer about what exactly they were doing in a private dining room alone with two gentlemen.

The sense of disappointment among Fleet Street's finest was palpable. 'The sensational case of alleged assault at a West-end restaurant came to a sudden end today by a full apology being tendered and accepted by the plaintiffs,' mourned the reporter from the *Evening News*.[11]

Muir had told Lehwess and Locock to swallow their pride and accept a face-saving apology. It had all been an unfortunate misunderstanding and Giovanni was now prepared to admit injuring Lehwess.[12]

'What was it that transformed this little elysium in the Edgware Road into a pandemonium of passion and violence? It was all to be found in a little bill,' mused Plowden, who welcomed the settlement as a saving of time and money. 'From an early stage,' he added, 'I formed the impression that there were faults and loss of temper on both sides.'

The newspaper reports suggest that Muir had to lean on Lehwess to accept the settlement. For Lehwess was not one to give up. He had a vindictive streak and was prone to embark on lengthy legal battles when a more prudent man would have swallowed his pride. He displayed a reckless indifference to the consequences of all the publicity surrounding the Edgware Road brawl. His was an unusual name and it wouldn't be long before it rang a bell with someone on a national newspaper. The next logical step would be to check him out in the clippings libraries. And that could easily have spelled disaster for the next round of the electrobus swindle.

Chapter 11

Enter the Black Prince

In its first six months of operation the electrobus had exceeded all expectations, said the *Financier*, in its report on the London Electrobus Company's first general meeting, held in November 1907. This spin was repeated in all the main financial papers, which carried extensive first-hand accounts of events at the meeting. These strikingly similar reports were not quite what they seemed, however. They were all paid-for advertorials, a practice that was rife in the Edwardian era. The original press handout, complete with apparently impromptu 'hear hears' and 'laughter', survives in the National Archives.[1]

One magazine excelled itself. *Motor Finance* published its verbatim report of the meeting in an issue that went to the printers before the meeting took place.[2] *Motor Finance* was run by the latest partner in the electrobus swindle – Edward 'Teddy' Beall, a solicitor and publisher, convicted fraudster and blackmailer. Some people in the City believed Beall was the model for Charles Augustus Milverton – the master blackmailer of the Sherlock Holmes story – although there are more convincing candidates.[3]

Very few people knew Beall was behind *Motor Finance* because he hid his connection behind a smokescreen of fronts and false names. Even the office staff didn't know his real name.[4] By the autumn of 1907 Beall was playing an active part in the electrobus swindle. So perhaps *Motor Finance*'s scoop was not so surprising.

Chapter 11

With his handlebar moustache and trademark cigarette Teddy Beall was known in the City as the 'black prince'. Every day in the 1880s and 1890s he would travel to and from his office in the City in a magnificent coach pulled by four beautiful high-stepping black horses, driven by a coachman and accompanied by two liveried footmen with their arms folded in front of them. A casual bystander might have thought this vision of opulence was some visiting foreign dignitary or maybe a freeman of the City of London exercising an arcane ancient right. It was not.[5]

The young Beall was one of the sights of the Victorian City of London. People would stop and turn their heads in astonishment as the debonair young man in the tall hat and frock coat faced with silk walked along the pavement. A chain-smoker and *bon viveur* Beall was one of the City's most colourful characters who, one reporter commented, led a 'luxurious life with a pronounced predilection for its epicurean factors'.[6]

Beall's activites – both legitimate and otherwise – were plainly very lucrative. Reputed to be a millionaire, by the 1890s he lived in considerable style in a palatial mansion near Maidenhead, waited on by 20 liveried servants. In the country Beall played the part of a country squire. In the City he was a shark, a fraudulent company promoter.[7]

Beall was born in Cheltenham in 1852. His first brush with the law came early, when at the age of 27 two cheques he cashed at the South Kensington Co-operative Society bounced. He escaped prosecution for fraud only because his father-in-law, the Co-op's managing director, pledged to pay the debt.[8]

Beall had a shrewd legal mind and was said to know company and criminal law better than anyone else in the City. But from almost the very beginning he was a wrong'un. He promoted a series of shady companies, ran bucket shops to offload the shares and puffed the shares in his sham financial papers, such as the *Financial Critic* and later the *Financial Gazette*.[9] Beall gained notoriety as a 'company wrecker', someone who would use his magazines to ruin a company with bad publicity. Beall would either profit from the tumbling share price by taking a 'bear position' – betting that the price would fall – or the company could avoid this disastrous turmoil by paying Beall hush money.[10] Either way Beall stood to profit handsomely.

For a long time Beall was closely linked with fellow shyster Hooley. As a solicitor he often persuaded his wealthy clients to invest in Hooley's overpriced companies, skimming off a secret commission from Hooley of a shilling for each share he sold. Relations between the two men cooled when Hooley was made bankrupt. At the inquiry into Hooley's high-profile bankruptcy, the official receiver wanted to know why Hooley had paid several large cheques to Beall. Hooley's explanation was that Beall was blackmailing him. Hooley, plainly something of an authority on the subject, said Beall was one of 'the three worst blackmailers in London'.[11]

The wheels finally came off Beall's elegant carriage after he promoted the London and Scottish Banking and Discount Corporation, or Beall's bogus bank as it quickly became known. The *Financial Times* was alive to the scam from the moment the bank's prospectus began to circulate. 'Our advice to those who may receive copies of this precious prospectus is…to put it in the wastepaper basket. It will come in handy for lighting the fire and thereby will be more profitable than it is likely to be to the holders of shares.'[12]

Despite this damning verdict some investors were impressed, perhaps by the bank's Lombard Street address or perhaps by the circulation with the prospectus of a pamphlet on *Banks and Banking*, an apparently erudite publication written, it turned out, by an undischarged bankrupt.[13] By puffing the bank in his reptile journals, Beall ensnared unwary investors.[14] But the bank did little business; it was no more than a conduit for enriching Beall. He had two accounts at the bank. They were both overdrawn.[15] He also took £5000 out of the business for promoting the bank and a further £2000 in 'travelling expenses'. There were no receipts for these expenses, which doubtless helped to pay for his elegant carriage.

No one at the bank had any grounding in banking. The closest thing the bank had to a financial expert was a Greek man, whose relatives were in banking in Constantinople. The Greek's own City expertise amounted to selling Balkan cigarettes and Turkish delight in a shop in Fenchurch Street.[16]

The directors had no control over the bank. They were paid around a guinea and a half to attend weekly board meetings and took their orders from the bank's solicitor – Beall. According to one director, the board meetings were events where one signed the odd sheet of paper – usually without reading it – and apart from that the sessions consisted of 'champagne, whisky and soda and very good cigars'. His story was confirmed by a commissionaire, whose job was to supervise the removal of the empties.[17]

The bank's failure to produce any accounts led to increasing unrest among its shareholders. Matters came to a head at a shareholders' meeting held in Edinburgh at the end of 1894. Beall knew that dissident shareholders intended to force the bank to be wound up in the hope of recovering some of their money. What followed was a text-book example of packing a meeting. In the run up to the meeting the bank's secretary, a man called Baker, travelled to Glasgow. There he hired 18 men from a boarding house, promising them 10 shillings each and their train fare to Edinburgh to attend the bank's meeting.

The evening before the meeting Baker held a dress rehearsal, a vital necessity, because the occupants of a Glasgow boarding house were not drawn from the moneyed classes normally found at shareholders' meetings.[18] He told the men they were 'shareholders pro tem' in the London and Scottish bank and their job was to act as 'claquers', to voice appreciative 'hear hears' whenever the directors spoke and to shout down any dissident voices – and of course vote for the board. Packing meetings in this way was a tactic used extensively by Beall and other shysters of the era.[19]

At the meeting Baker was on the door with orders to bar the press. All shareholders had to produce evidence of their holdings – except the Glasgow boys, who were nodded through. The vetting broke down when there was a scuffle at the door during which at least one reporter succeeded in gaining entry. It was a stormy meeting, with the largely Scottish shareholders denouncing the bank as a gross swindle – although the precise words were sadly too fruity to be recorded in a Victorian newspaper. 'It was like Bedlam,' said one of the more polite shareholders.[20]

Beall tried to head off the dissidents with a set of accounts which showed the bank holding assets worth £40000. On the strength of these the bank would pay a dividend of a staggering 125 per cent, he said. But the accounts had been falsified. The bank was losing money and its assets consisted of shares in Beall's other companies. None of the share certificates was worth the paper it was printed on. The meeting decided, on a show of hands, not to wind up the company – the majority was provided by the temporary shareholders from Glasgow. The genuine shareholders went to court to challenge the decision.[21]

When the case came to court everyone connected with the bank either vanished or was ill. Most of the directors resigned. Beall, who had taken the precaution of removing the bank's books from the safe, was also now providentially ill and compelled to take the sea air in Brighton. The secretary, who had been the doorkeeper at the meeting, couldn't be found. The court decided to wind up the bank.[22]

'Beall's Bank Busted' declared the *Financial Times*, whose headline writers relished the alliterative potential of the bogus bank. The *Financial Times* didn't mince its words about Beall, describing him as 'a notorious swindler' and 'a fraudulent solicitor'.

At first it seemed as though the authorities were not going to prosecute, just as they were initially reluctant to prosecute Hooley and Lawson. But after a shareholder successfully sued Beall for money he had invested, the judge was so appalled by Beall's chicanery that he sent the trial papers to the director of public prosecutions.[23]

In June 1899 Beall, carrying a light fashionable overcoat over his arm, appeared at the Mansion House in the City of London charged with fraud – fleecing the public to the tune of £29000 on the strength of a false prospectus. After a 14-day preliminary hearing Beall was sent for trial at the Old Bailey. He had one last stroke to pull. He hired Richard Muir as junior counsel for the defence, not because he was noted for his abilities in defence, but because this prevented the prosecution from using Muir's forensic skills. This was not enough to save him and Beall was convicted and sentenced to four years in prison. He fainted when the sentence was handed down. 'The conviction of Beall,' commented the *Financial Times*, removes 'that clever rogue from our midst'.[24] Beall was struck off as a solicitor and celebrated the first days of the new century in a cell at Parkhurst.[25]

Beall emerged from prison in October 1902[26] and promptly changed his name by deed poll to Edward Boyle. He teamed up with an accountant called James Merchant, who had worked on one of Beall's reptile journals before Beall was jailed. The two men ran a bucket shop called Clement and Hayes, in an office off the Strand.[27] The clerical staff knew Beall as Clement, while Merchant was called James Hayes. In his other offices – and he normally kept three or four of them within easy walking distance of each other – Beall was Boyle, or sometimes Boyd. The police, who kept Beall under surveillance for several years, later said that he had not done an honest day's work since he came out of prison.[28]

The burgeoning motor industry was the speculation of the moment and Beall set up a series of fly-by-night companies to make motor vehicles and tar-spraying concerns that promised to make dustless roads, concealing his connection with these companies with a series of false names.[29] His interest in motoring was complemented by his latest reptile journal, *Motor Finance*, a weekly magazine that first limped off the presses in December 1906. Apart from a couple of genuine adverts in its early issues, including one from Dunlop, all the advertisers were companies in the Beall group, either motor manufacturers or tar sprayers.

Clearly, advertising revenue was never going to fund *Motor Finance*. The magazine's real purpose was blackmail. The basic technique hadn't changed since the days when Beall was blackmailing Hooley. The way Hooley told the story, two articles would be drafted about a company. One was a hatchet job; the other would praise its prospects. An emissary would then be sent to the company with proofs of both articles. He would explain that the article praising the company would cost a sizeable sum of money – the other one was free. In the days when Hooley was rolling in money he was a regular source of income for blackmailers like Beall.[30]

Beall had been honing his technique for decades. The target was usually a company that was slightly dodgy or in financial difficulties. If his timing was good, and a shareholders' meeting or some other sensitive event in the company's calendar was looming, then the directors of even respectable companies would often conclude that it was worth paying up just to avoid the bad publicity. Less respectable outfits were much more vulnerable to blackmail.

For the first half of 1907 *Motor Finance* published a series of well-founded exposés, which were mostly written by Beall's partner Merchant. There was an amusing satirical piece about a motoring ace called Sedge and his six-cylinder 'Rapier' car. The target was the motoring pioneer Selwyn Edge and his six-cylinder Napier car. It was a well-judged target. Edge had been a close colleague of Lawson and *Motor Finance* decried the plan to offer shares in his Napier car firm as a truly 'lawsonian prospectus'.[31]

The companies associated with Lehwess and Longman were the subject of similarly well-judged and accurate attacks. In February

Chapter 11

the Edinburgh and District Motor Omnibus Company merited a lengthy denunciation. Over the next few months the London Electrobus Company, the Motor Car Emporium, Securities Exchange and the National Motor Mail Coach also came under the magazine's critical spotlight.[32] It was all part of a pattern. Beall was putting the squeeze on Lehwess.

In July *Motor Finance* was one of the few publications to write a critical piece about the commercial launch of the electrobus. It repeated at length the criticism in Stanley Spooner's *Automotor Journal* and then added some. Arguing that the company would be running at 'a dangerously low margin of profit' the article urges 'investors to remain unimpressed by the laudatory accounts by non-technical reporters now appearing in the press, concerning the alleged advantages of electrically propelled buses'.[33]

In October 1907 Lehwess did a deal with Beall to halt the deluge of criticism. It was a meeting of well-matched minds. Beall agreed to stop the attacks on Lehwess's companies; Lehwess agreed to take out some expensive adverts in *Motor Finance*. Lehwess agreed to let Beall have a slice of the electrobus swindle and in return Beall would help Lehwess (and Longman) offload their shares in the London Electrobus Company. The first sign of this new alliance came in mid-October when the Electric Van Wagon and Omnibus Company placed a full-page advert on the back cover of *Motor Finance* extolling the virtues of battery-powered electric vehicles.[34]

The next month the magazine published its scoop – a three-page account of the London Electrobus Company's annual general meeting. The meeting was told that most of the shares were now held by 'friends of the directors, who did believe in the potentialities of the electrobus, and these gentlemen, who had the pluck to go forward and show what grit they had would undoubtedly reap their reward'. The chairman of the London Electrobus Company told the meeting that the company wanted to raise £70000 to put 100 electrobuses on the streets.[35]

Two days after the annual meeting Beall registered a new company, the Motor Share and Investment Trust. The 'plucky gentlemen' were Lehwess and Longman. Between them they owned around 80 per cent of the electrobus shares. But far from reaping the rewards from all their pluck and grit Lehwess, Longman and now Beall became partners in a conspiracy to unload these unwanted shares on to an unsuspecting public through the Motor Share and Investment Trust.

There was now an abrupt change in the tone of *Motor Finance*'s reporting. In place of its critical coverage of the electrobus, it now lavished unstinting praise while denigrating the motor bus. Motor buses were 'in disgrace in the City of London' because of their 'terrible effluvia and injurious vapour'. The electrobus, 'owing to its smooth and noiseless running, freedom from breakdowns and slow depreciation, can be run profitably and bring a handsome return to all interested in its success,' claimed the magazine. It was, the magazine predicted, 'sure to be a dividend earner' and cannot fail 'to be the motor omnibus of the future'.[36]

On the back of the company's highly successful November meeting, and on the same day that the latest puff in *Motor Finance* appeared, the London Electrobus Company made another attempt to raise more capital to buy more buses. This wasn't a public share issue like the one in April 1906. Instead the company wrote to both its current shareholders and those who had taken the company's offer of a refund asking them to consider buying more shares and offering them the opportunity of buying a single deferred share for every ten ordinary shares they bought. On paper this was an attractive deal – if the London Electrobus Company ever made a profit.[37]

Most of the shares in the electrobus company – the ones it had originally offered the public back in 1906 – were ordinary shares. But there was also a small number of shares, originally earmarked for Lehwess and his acolytes, called deferred shares. These were potentially very valuable. Effectively the promoters were making an each-way bet when they set up the company. In the event that the company failed they stood to make extortionate profits from the bogus patent and other advance fees. But if the electrobus was a runaway success the promoters planned to take an equally extortionate slice of the profits.

If the company made profits it would pay shareholders a dividend. The ordinary shareholders would receive the first 10 per cent of any dividends. But any profits above this threshold would be divided equally between the ordinary and the deferred shares. As there were very few deferred shares in circulation if ordinary shareholders received several pennies in dividends the holders of deferred shares could look forward to dividends measured in shillings.

In its circular to shareholders the company explained that it wanted to increase its capital to £100000. The last six months' results showed that investors could confidently expect a return of 17½ per cent, it said. 'It is impossible not to admire the beautifully smooth and noiseless running of their omnibuses,' reflected the city editor of the *Daily Mail*. But, he warned, estimates such as these are more easily made than fulfilled. If the markets believed that the electrobus shares were going to earn 17½ per cent, then the price of London Electrobus Company shares would be considerably higher than it was.[38]

The sight of the electrobus quietly gliding along the streets of the capital was certainly seductive. More than 150 of the existing shareholders were tempted to increase their stakes in the company. Even some of those who had gone to court to get their money back after the original fiasco now decided that the company wasn't such a bad job after all and again placed their money and their trust in the London Electrobus Company. This limited share offer raised just over £7000, underscoring the confidence that ordinary investors had in the electrobus's prospects.

The company's plan was to make a fresh share offer to the public in the New Year. The first rumours of this share offer began to circulate in December. But at the same time Lehwess and Longman also wanted to sell the 40 000 shares that they still held, mostly in the names of companies such as Securities Exchange and the Asiatic Bank. This posed a dilemma: heavy selling would inevitably depress the share price, which had to be maintained if they were to attract fresh investors in a new public share offer. The strategy they adopted was to sell a trickle of shares on the back of the publicity for the fresh public share offer.

A few weeks into the New Year the Motor Share and Investment Trust began sending out circulars to people on Beall's extensive suckers' list – people who were known to be susceptible to get-rich-quick schemes. The circular gave them the opportunity to buy electrobus shares for 16s 6d (82.5p), promising a profit of 3s 6d (17.5p) by June. The *Daily Mail*'s level-headed city editor was not impressed. 'We think it would be unwise to accept the offer,' the paper advised. The last time electrobus shares had changed hands they fetched just 15 shillings.[39]

Chapter 12

The Other Brighton Run

Shortly before 8 am on Easter Sunday 1908 a small expectant throng gathered in front of the Hotel Cecil in the Strand. Parked outside the hotel was a brand new electrobus, straight out of the workshops of the Electric Vehicle Company – the new and less cumbersome name for the Electric Van Wagon and Omnibus Company.

It was a time for celebration. The Electric Vehicle Company had just sold its first electrobus outside London, the first of an order for 14 electrobuses. The press duly admired the gleaming new vehicle. After breakfast a group of specially invited guests and journalists were going to deliver the electrobus to its new owner – a Brighton bus company – by driving south to Brighton and then having lunch beside the sea at the Hotel Metropole.[1]

The Brighton run had totemic status in motoring circles ever since the original emancipation run in 1896. The distance from London to Brighton by road is a little over 52 miles and with several steep hills on the way it was a convincing test of any vehicle. The electrobus had been dogged by persistent claims that its limited range made it impractical as an alternative to the petrol bus. Running to Brighton on a single charge would dispel any doubts about its battery power.

The publicity stunt was the brainchild of Captain John Taylor, whose firm Steele Lockhart had just been hired by the London Electrobus Company to manage its public relations in the run-up to the fresh share offer. The Brighton run was the curtain raiser for the flotation. Taylor certainly presented an impressive public face. Here was an outwardly upstanding pillar of society, a retired army captain and a magistrate.

However, Taylor had a chequered past. As a young man he'd had an unhappy relationship with cards and the turf, leaving in his wake a series of unpaid gambling debts. He then sought his fortune on the Stock Exchange, serving a financial apprenticeship with Hooley, and becoming closely associated with Bottomley. By the early 20th century Taylor was promoting mining companies in the Gold Coast (now Ghana). In one case his persuasive public relations talents pushed up the price of a company's shares from £1 to £4 on the Paris Bourse, despite the absence of a valid mining concession.[2] If anyone could turn the electrobus into a gold mine it was Captain Taylor.

Packed with representatives of the press, the electrobus left the Hotel Cecil promptly at 8 am, followed by a small squadron of polluting petrol-powered vehicles. All went well until Redhill, some 20 miles south of London, when the rear axle began to overheat. The company engineers added an extra link to the driving chain to reduce the load on the axle. This failed to do the trick. Ten miles further on the passengers were alarmed to see flames licking around the rear axle. The bus came to an abrupt halt. Rather than miss their lunch at the Metropole most of the passengers transferred to the accompanying vehicles, while the engineers cooled the axle.

The lunch, hosted by the Electric Vehicle Company, had much of the flavour of a modern car launch. There was a strong contingent of newspapermen from London and one local reporter was moved to comment in some awe on the numerous lovely ladies

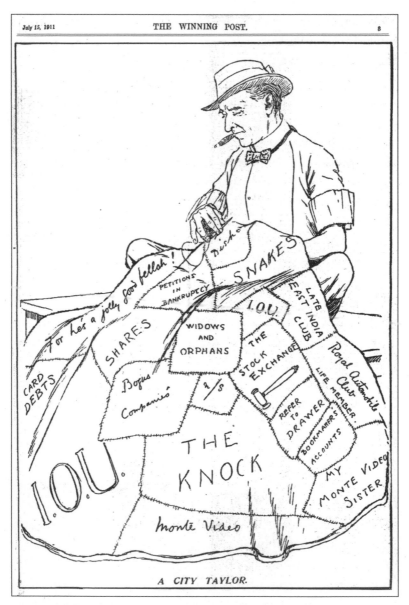

A CITY TAYLOR.

Figure 9 The electrobus publicist: Captain John Taylor, weaving a patchwork quilt of bogus companies, bankruptcies and bad debts. As caricatured by the *Winning Post* in 1911.

attending the lunch. Over the port and brandies Captain Taylor explained away the hiccough en route. It was a teething problem that could have happened to any new vehicle that hadn't been run-in and it had nothing to do with the bus's electrical equipment. He toasted the press and concluded his speech with the Edwardian catch phrase of the day: the electrobus, he declared, had 'come to stay'. An American newspaperman who replied to the toast for the press laboured the point, saying that the electrobus is 'going to get right there'.[3]

The much-delayed electrobus didn't get right there – or at least not on schedule. It arrived after lunch, swooping downhill into Brighton to the sound of a posthorn. The razzmatazz continued with the bus making an afternoon tour of the town centre. Captain Taylor stressed to reporters that not only had the bus travelled to Brighton on a single charge but it still had enough juice left in the batteries to run for another 20 miles or so. The trip proved, said Captain Taylor, that its batteries did not significantly limit the range of the electrobus.

Most reporters were impressed by the bus and bought into Captain Taylor's spin. The *Standard* reported that 'with the exception of a slight mishap to one of the driving wheels the vehicle ran through to Brighton and was received at the seaside resort with great enthusiasm'. The reporter from the *Times* was a little more cautious. 'The trial cannot, however, be regarded as conclusive in view of the delays en route.'[4]

It took a rather more hard-bitten hack from the trade press to uncover the subterfuge. 'We are at a loss to understand the bluster and fuss about running of accumulator-propelled omnibuses between London and Brighton,' wrote the reporter from *Commercial Motor*. Normally the electrobus carried a battery containing either 42 or 44 cells slung beneath it, which gave it a range of around 36 to 40 miles. So how did it make the 52-mile run to Brighton? It was time for a bit of investigative journalism.

Turning up the seats on the lower deck the reporter found 32 extra cells concealed beneath them and a further 12 cells hidden at the rear of the vehicle. Effectively the electrobus was carrying two batteries – with a combined weight of 3.5 tons. The extra weight meant the bus was overloaded and that almost certainly explained the hot axle.[5]

The Brighton run was the culmination of a three-month PR campaign, designed to capitalise on the good publicity generated by the previous November's annual general meeting and paving the way for a fresh public share offer in the spring of 1908. The campaign had begun shortly after the meeting with a conducted tour of the electrobus garage in Horseferry Road, showing reporters in the trade press how the batteries were exchanged, how they were charged and answering detailed questions about the operation. Everyone who visited the garage, including experts from the trade press, was impressed by how slick the operation was and how well-engineered the buses were.[6]

Until now the electrical trade press had maintained a sympathetic but slightly sceptical attitude to the electrobus. Electric trams and the manufacturers of tramway equipment provided one of the major sources of advertising revenue for the electrical press, so they supported the tram over the rival motor bus. But they didn't quite know what to make of the electrobus: was it a detestable rival to the tram or an ally in the struggle with the motor bus? After the garage visit, it was clear the electrical papers had been won over.[7]

So too was the motoring press, which until that point had been overtly hostile – because if electric vehicles succeeded they could damage the prospects of the motor vehicle, which in turn could affect their advertising revenue. *Commercial Motor* praised the well-arranged garage. Even confirmed petrol-heads such as Stanley Spooner, editor of the *Automotor Journal*, who had led the campaign against the electrobus, were coming round. Two years ago, commented the journal, 'it was perfectly clear that nothing but a scandalous waste of public money could result from so reckless a piece of bad company promoting'. But after being given unrestricted access to the company's operations, both in the garage and on the road, the journal was 'forced to the conclusion that the undertaking is now quite a legitimate – and even promising – field for the private financier who seeks a speculative opening rather than a safe investment for the capital at his command'.[8]

Predictably, *Motor Finance* was a stalwart cheerleader for the electrobus. The electrobus was 'the acme of perfection', it said in January 1908. In February it claimed that the electrobus was the only solution to the current discontent about noisy motor traffic. In March it observed that the public could see for themselves 'that although derelict petrol buses may be seen along any of the principal routes, the electrobuses are always to be seen threading their way through the traffic with clockwork regularity'.[9]

Beall excelled himself in April – the week before the new public share issue. Arguing that electrobuses cost half as much to run as motor buses, he concluded: 'Can there be any doubt that the electrobus will be the greatest dividend earner that ever ran on wheels in the streets of London…? We have no hesitation whatever in advising our readers to subscribe for the shares now being issued.'[10]

It had been a well-judged public relations campaign. Any criticism in the trade press had been stifled. Even the *Automotor Journal* had been neutralised.[11] The national press habitually kept a close eye on the trade press – it was often a useful source of stories – so the absence of any substantial technical criticism meant that the national press was likely to welcome the new share issue.

The new prospectus was published on 27 April 1908, almost exactly two years after the original flotation. It was the company's third attempt to raise capital and it invited the public to buy the rest of the unsold shares, all 240 000 of them. The prospectus was accompanied by a new brochure, doubtless the fruit of Captain

Taylor's public relations expertise, which extolled the virtues of the electrobus with almost religious fervour.

'When New Thoughts, New Ideas and New Methods are put before us, we are apt in our Conservatism to regard them lightly,' ran the introduction. 'Nimbler brains than ours grasp their Possibilities, their Beauty, their Utility…and afterwards in Leisure and Repose enjoy the Fruits of their Perspicacity.

'The paths of the Progress of all Great Things are paved with the regrets of countless multitudes who saw, but learned too late.'[12] Hallelujah!

A report by Sir Douglas Fox and Partners added immensely to the credibility of the prospectus. This is what would attract serious investors. Fox was a distinguished civil engineer who had designed many of the railways in southern Africa, including the bridge over the Victoria Falls, as well as working on London's new tube railways. His company, the pre-eminent consulting engineers of the day, had been retained by the London Electrobus Company.

Fox made extensive tests of an electrobus and concluded that it would be cheaper to run than a motor bus and that wear and tear would be lower. 'We can see no analogy between the numerous and complicated working parts of the petrol omnibus, operating under adverse conditions and subject to frequent ill-usage and the comparatively few substantial and simple parts of the electrobus equipment.'[13]

The company also revamped its board. Two new directors joined for the share issue. They were Jacob Atherton, who had a long track record in the electricity industry and was seemingly a good catch for the company, and Sir Henry Dering, who became the new chairman. In practice Atherton was less of an asset than it might seem. He took almost no interest in the batteries – the most critical part of the bus's equipment.

Dering was also judged a valuable addition in some quarters. 'The company has a good business board with Sir Henry E Dering

JP, DL, as chairman,' claimed the *Daily Express*. The *Daily Express* was too easily impressed. Dering was the archetypal guinea-pig director. He had only recently inherited his baronetcy and was in the process of garnering as many directorships (and their lucrative fees) as possible – without being particularly concerned about how dodgy a company was.[14] His eyes were firmly fixed on the job's remuneration. Allowing his title to adorn the electrobus prospectus earned Dering a yearly income of £400.[15]

The prospectus met none of the criticism that had accompanied the share issue two years before. The general tone of comment was one of cautious optimism. 'The vehicle appears to be a superior article to its competitors, but more experience must be obtained before it is proved that it is also superior in profit-earning capacity,' said the *Economist*.[16]

The *Daily Mail*, in a piece probably penned by its city editor Charles Duguid, the foremost financial journalist of his day, adopted a similar tone. 'The prospectus…contains many good points and all of us hope that the electrobus company will succeed. Especially encouraging is the report of such an eminent firm as Sir Douglas Fox and Partners.' However, he wrote, it was disappointing that having run electrobuses for nine months the prospectus still only contained estimates of costs, rather than actual figures.[17]

A more analytical view of the company was to be found in the trade press. *Commercial Motor* tempered its praise with a shrewd caveat: 'Subject to proper management this company's prospects are amongst the brightest of the day.'[18] *Electrical Review* also drew a clear distinction between the electrobus and the company behind it. The public much prefers the electrobus to the 'stench, noise and other nuisance' of the petrol vehicle, it reported. But it accused the company of holding out extravagant hopes without convincing data to back them up. 'We may like the electrobus and we wish it success but to approve of its prospectus we find…absolutely impossible.'[19]

On 25 April, the Saturday before the share issue opened, there was a sophisticated attempt to rig the market in electrobus shares. Rigging the market in shares was an illegal but common practice. The price for ordinary shares had been languishing around 15 shillings for several months, partly because Beall had been slowly selling off the shares owned by Lehwess and Longman. This made it extremely difficult for the London Electrobus Company to persuade the public that buying shares at their full price of 20 shillings was a good investment.

The deferred shares were once again used as bait to snare new investors and persuade existing ones to up their stakes. On 16 April – two weeks before the new public share offer – the company gave just over 1500 deferred shares to a select group of investors. These favoured shareholders, like the Asiatic Bank, were all fronts for Lehwess.[20] This manoeuvre gave Lehwess a huge majority of deferred shares: only 400 were held by ordinary investors. Immediately after distributing this largesse the company divided each of the £1 deferred shares into four 5-shilling shares.

The terms of the share issue were that investors who bought 20 ordinary shares in the London Electrobus Company were also entitled to buy one of the 5-shilling deferred shares. It was impractical to rig the market in ordinary shares: any attempt to push the share price up above the £1 mark by buying heavily risked producing an embarrassingly expensive number of takers. But it was possible to rig the market in deferred shares because there were so few in circulation. Lehwess and his accomplices owned the vast majority of them. They had cornered the market.

Late in the day on Friday 24 April and on into Saturday morning a few traders on the Stock Exchange started acting on instructions from Beall and Lehwess to buy electrobus deferred shares. They found very few sellers – Lehwess was not selling – and the result was that the price of these shares skyrocketed.[21]

When the Stock Exchange closed on Friday deferred shares with a face value of 5 shillings were changing hands at 10s 6d (52.5p) and on Saturday morning the deferred shares shot up still further, reaching 18s 9d (94p) by close. The *Daily Mail* rightly smelled a rat. 'Such an advance on a Saturday morning is rather too prodigious to carry conviction as to the probability of its being maintained.'[22]

The share issue was not a resounding success. This was not entirely surprising. While the sharp rise in the value of deferred shares dragged up the price of ordinary shares to their face value of £1 for a short time, the price soon started to fall back. For most of the week electrobus ordinary shares could be bought on the Stock Exchange for a less than the company's share offer. Why buy from the company at £1 if you could buy the same share for 2 or 3 shillings less from a stockbroker?[23]

No serious investor would. But more than 300 new people did invest in the new shares. They were almost all unworldly small investors, the usual collection of tailors, nurses, schoolmasters, a footman, several spinsters and widows. The share issue raised more than £20 000, most of which was money from genuinely new people.[24] On paper at least this new money should have enabled the company to buy nearly 30 additional electrobuses.

Chapter 13

The French Sailors

At 10 am on 27 May 1908 nine electrobuses lined up in the forecourt of London's Charing Cross railway station. The electrobuses were there by order of the Admiralty, which had hired them for the day. Their mission was to pick up and help entertain 260 French sailors who had travelled up to London from Dover by train.

The electrobus jaunt was part of the celebrations surrounding the great Franco-British exhibition at White City in West London. The exhibition was designed to cement the Entente Cordiale, which the two countries had signed four years earlier. The French president Armand Fallières travelled to London to join King Edward VII and Queen Alexandra in making an official visit to the exhibition. The bluejackets, as the sailors were nicknamed, were the crews of the French cruiser *Léon Gambetta* and two destroyers, which accompanied the French president on his voyage across the English Channel.[1]

The commission was a publicity coup for the London Electrobus Company, which decorated its buses in the French colours of red, white and blue for the occasion. It was a perfect spring day and the sailors crowded on to the waiting electrobuses, jostling to get a coveted seat on the top deck. Once installed, they set off on a scenic tour of London on their way to the exhibition, waving their hats to the people lining the streets who had stopped to watch the spectacle.

For the first time the king had given special permission for buses to use the roads in the royal parks, so one of the first stops on the sightseeing tour was Buckingham Palace. It was a PR gift: a line of electrobuses with the French sailors crowded on top cheering the king. Naturally, the London Electrobus Company had a photographer on hand to record the scene.

The visit was a convivial occasion. The French president and the king attended a reception at St James's Palace, before a lengthy lunch and even lengthier speeches at the Guildhall. Arguably the bluejackets had the better time. They visited the exhibition then adjourned for lunch which the Admiralty laid on at a West End hotel. The menu included fish and chips – with the refinement of a parsley sauce to suit Gallic palates – as well as several fine wines and, for the more adventurous, British beer. After lunch the sailors boarded the electrobuses and went to the Palace Theatre, where the matinee included ventriloquist Arthur Prince and his dummy 'Sailor Jim'. Entertainment finally over, the sailors climbed back

Figure 10 A publicity coup: a line of electrobuses outside Buckingham Palace on 27 May 1908, with French sailors crowding on to the top deck of the buses to cheer the king.

aboard the buses and were returned to Charing Cross in time to catch the 7 pm train to Dover.

One of the chief aims of the exhibition was to showcase the latest technology and promote trade between the two nations, their empires and the rest of the world. The French sailors were agog to see detailed scale models of dreadnoughts, the new British battleships, and stopped to examine them in minute detail. There were dozens of motor buses that the Admiralty could have hired to ferry the bluejackets around London but the electrobus's advanced technology fitted perfectly with the image the British government wanted to project: the subliminal message was cutting-edge technology coupled with Anglo-French trade.

The electrobus was not an exclusively British product: there were several French connections. The first electrobus had a French motor. French money had paid the rates on part of the electrobus garage for a critical period. Furthermore, there was a realistic prospect that the French would adopt this pioneering technology.[2] The previous year Parisian councillors on a fact-finding visit to see how London was coping with the motor bus problem visited the electrobus garage. Like everyone else who saw the garage the councillors were very impressed by the technology. Following that visit the Compagnie Générale des Omnibus de Paris sent two engineers to make a detailed inspection of the electrobus operations. Part of the reason for the Parisian company's interest was that its concession was soon coming up for renewal. The choice of a silent and fume-free technology could help to influence the decision to renew its concession.[3]

In an effort to capitalise on this wave of positive publicity Lehwess launched an extensive marketing campaign to sell electrobuses around the country. Whatever else he was, Lehwess was an energetic salesman.[4] Brighton had been the first town outside London to buy the electrobus and now he hoped other towns would follow suit. In the summer of 1908 Lehwess embarked on a nationwide roadshow, taking a demonstration electrobus around the country and putting it through its paces in towns that were likely prospects.[5]

The roadshow started at Cheltenham. The burghers of this genteel spa town had a well-advertised aversion to the motor bus and local dignitaries were given a series of rides around the town centre. The electrobus was warmly welcomed, both by local councillors, who were in a position to license an electrobus service, and by the local press which ran a series of enthusiastic articles about the electrobus.[6] The roadshow then travelled on to Oxford, Loughborough and York offering free rides to local dignitaries before returning to London towards the end of July.

'The electrobus which visited Oxford on Friday made a favourable impression on a great many of the city councillors and others who rode in it...there was a welcome absence of the noise and odour associated with the motor bus,' wrote one reporter. It wouldn't replace the electric tram, but 'should do splendid work in supplementing tram services'.[7]

Lehwess carefully tailored his sales pitch to each town. In Oxford the electrobus would provide a feeder service for trams, carrying passengers to the nearest tram stop. In Cheltenham the electrobus would remove the need for the noisome motor bus and could be run on a route where there weren't any tramlines. In York, where the corporation was considering replacing the town's horse trams with electric trams, the electrobus would remove the need for trams altogether.

Perhaps the local papers in York weren't as fulsome in their coverage as the Electric Vehicle Company had hoped. Lehwess quickly made up for the deficiency. One seemingly public spirited individual thought the event should be noticed and wrote to the local papers. 'Just recently I have seen going about the narrow streets of our old city an electrobus, which seems eminently adapted to the needs of a city like this. And a proper service of these would be much better adapted and more appropriate than any system of electric trams.' If the letter read like the Electric Vehicle Company's public relations pitch that is because it was. Identical letters appeared in two of York's papers from an address that was a lodging house used by short-stay commercial travellers.[8]

Throughout 1908 Lehwess tried to interest towns in the electrobus, asking more than a dozen town councils for licences to run the buses.[9] Sometimes the approach was made by the Electric Vehicle Company, sometimes by the International Motor Traffic Syndicate and sometimes the London Electrobus Company. The names were virtually interchangeable and it often seemed to depend on no more than which sheet of headed notepaper came to hand.

Eastbourne was one of the best provincial prospects. This upmarket seaside resort on the south coast of England was vehemently opposed to electric trams. It considered them too working class and councillors feared they might deter the better class of visitor. The council had set up the world's first municipal motor bus company in 1903 to help fight off the prospect of the dreaded tram.

The motor buses may have fended off the tram but they generated a flood of vociferous complaints. Property owners and ratepayers told councillors that the continued running of 'the evil-smelling and noisy petrol buses...was proving seriously detrimental to private property and was threatening the reputation of the town'.[10]

The electrobus seemed the ideal solution, satisfying both the anti-tram faction and the noise protesters. Representatives from the council and the bus company twice travelled to London to inspect the electrobuses. 'I have inspected these 'buses on service and find they work very smoothly indeed, the accumulators which I inspected at the depot giving very little trouble,' said the bus company's general manager.[11]

The sticking point for the council was the cost. The corporation had spent a lot of money setting up its motor bus service and there was a general feeling that the investment hadn't been wholly successful given the scale of complaints about noise. Having had its fingers burned once the corporation wasn't keen to repeat the experience.

Already the council faced the prospect of scrapping its first four buses, or converting them into dustcarts, as one councillor suggested. The Electric Vehicle Company told the council it could supply an electrobus for the same price as a petrol bus. The sticking point was the cost of all the extras: modifying the garage to recharge batteries and the cost of the batteries themselves, which weren't included in the price of the bus. Once all these extras were included the corporation reckoned it could buy six new petrol buses for the price of four electrobuses.[12] For almost a year the corporation dithered before eventually deciding to stick with petrol power. Several other provincial English towns were also seriously interested in electric buses.[13] Among them was Torquay, the Queen of Watering Places on the English Riviera as the town billed itself. Torquay was on the point of scrapping its steam buses. The London Electrobus Company wrote to the council in August asking for a licence to run electrobuses along the promenade. The council agreed and gave the company the welcome news in October.[14] And then, apart from a letter from the company in November saying that arrangements were in hand, everything went mysteriously quiet. The council never heard from the company again and never saw an electrobus gliding along the town's gracious promenade.[15]

It was an extraordinary marketing campaign. The Electric Vehicle Company could not supply electrobuses fast enough to keep up with the orders it already had from London and Brighton. Ever the salesman, Lehwess was repeating the same legerdemain that he had performed at the Motor Car Emporium. He was selling buses that he didn't have – and had no prospect of having

– two or three times over. The campaign bordered on the delusional with the consummate con man showing every sign of believing his own sales patter.

One of the signs that the original 1906 flotation wasn't quite right had been the plan to supply hundreds of electrobuses from a former stables in West London. The premises were not large enough to hold more than a few buses. The Electric Vehicle Company now had its works in a backyard behind a Victorian villa in the South London suburb of West Norwood. The yard was much the same size as the stables in Holland Park and had previously been occupied by a specialist hand-built car maker, who had moved out of London because the premises were too small.[16]

Nevertheless, the electrobus made steady progress in the capital throughout 1908. It was the first bus to have lighting on the top deck and at night the brightly illuminated bus stood out from the dark mass of other traffic.[17] The April share offer had produced a new influx of money and the number of electrobuses was now increasing. The company began a second bus route, which ran along the Edgware Road – where the silent passage of an electrobus went unnoticed by diners quietly enjoying their meals in the Oxford Restaurant – and on into London's north-western suburbs.[18] The electrobuses were demonstrably popular with the travelling public. According to surveys conducted by Douglas Fox's consulting engineers you were less likely to find an empty seat on an electrobus than on an electric tramcar.[19]

There was a huge fund of sympathy for the electrobus in almost all quarters. When Paul Taylor, a magistrate at Marylebone police court, tried an electrobus driver for speeding he gave the bus an unsolicited testimonial, which the company duly wove into its publicity material. 'I think that the electrobuses ought to be supported and I hope they will be a success and that electricity will eventually abolish petroleum from the streets.' His sympathy only went so far, however: he fined the driver 10 shillings.[20]

In November the company unveiled an electrobus with a covered top. The Metropolitan Police had previously only allowed tramcars to have a covered upper deck because of concerns that a top-heavy bus might topple over. A demonstration for reporters showed the operation's continuing flair for publicity. The test run started at the Hotel Cecil in the Strand and went on to St Paul's Cathedral before returning the newshounds to the hotel for a slap-up lunch. The London Electrobus Company commissioned an engineering report from the magazine *Commercial Motor* which argued convincingly that with a heavy lead battery slung under the bus the centre of gravity was extremely low, making it far less likely to topple over than a petrol bus. The Metropolitan Police still refused to license a bus with a covered top.[21]

The railway companies were also surprisingly supportive of the electrobus. They normally regarded motor vehicles as competition and were not disposed to do them any favours. Motor buses were

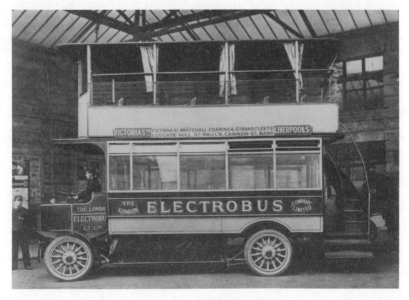

Figure 11 An electrobus with an experimental covered top. A news agency photo taken at Victoria Station probably in November 1908.

banned from the forecourt of London's Victoria Station, because the noise and fumes offended passengers using the station. In November the companies made an exception to their rule and allowed electrobuses to use the station forecourt.[22]

The rumble of discontent about motor vehicle noise continued throughout the year. At the end of February a number of influential people had written to the home secretary complaining about the 'injurious and distracting noise caused by motor omnibuses'. The letter, which had been orchestrated by the Betterment of London Association, was signed by no fewer than four earls and a duke plus sundry other titled gentry.[23]

The letter argued that the electrobus should be the benchmark for any regulation. 'It appears that the only line of motor omnibuses not complained of is that of the London Electrobus Company. As the entire service of this company runs quietly and smoothly it would seem that some standard of permissible noise might be set up and that any vehicle exceeding – or not conforming to – that standard should not be allowed in the streets of the metropolis.'[24] The London Electrobus Company naturally agreed. Its chairman Sir Henry Dering proclaimed that there was a panacea for the present outcry against petrol buses. And that was the electrobus.[25]

The public outrage about noise was manifestly genuine despite the involvement of Bowden Green and his Betterment of London Association. The protests continued, culminating in an extremely well-attended meeting at Mansion House in June 1908, chaired by the lord mayor and attended by many highly influential people in the Square Mile. This was a critically important meeting, which had the potential to change the way traffic was regulated.

The purpose of the meeting was 'to consider the question of preventing or abating noisy and dangerous motor traffic in the City of London'.[26] A handful of petrol bus supporters also attended the meeting. The operators and manufacturers of petrol buses felt – with some justification – that they were fighting for the survival of their industry.

At the end the meeting approved a watered-down resolution to appease them. It called on the government to clamp down on excessive noise, noxious fumes and speed but it now acknowledged 'the benefits that have accrued from the introduction of motor-power'.[27] The amendment would turn out to be an important concession.

The meeting agreed to send a high-powered deputation to the home secretary, headed by the lord mayor and including some of the most senior figures in the City. This was a protest that Herbert Gladstone had to take seriously.

In the run up to the deputation Lewis McIver, an influential Liberal MP who chaired a parliamentary committee investigating traffic over London's bridges, wrote to the *Times* saying that the present state of motor traffic in London was intolerable. 'Our present grievances are noise, smoke, smell, undue speed, and for the traveller, undue vibration. The electric carriage is guiltless of all these offences.'

McIver went on to suggest a radical departure in government policy – what amounted to positive discrimination in favour of the electrobus. 'Why…instead of confining themselves to the negative check of taking over-noisy and over-smelly vehicles off the street, should not the authorities have power to favour and encourage the virtuous electric cab and electrobus? A very slight preference would do it. Or must we continue to have free trade in smell, noise and occasional murder?'[28]

McIver was probably alluding to the well-publicised death the previous month of a three-year-old girl, who was crushed by the wheels of a motor bus in the East End of London. The accident triggered a four-hour riot during which the angry crowd attacked every passing bus. Extra police had to be drafted in to rescue the bus crews.[29] However, his point was seriously undermined by the untimely demise of Ernest Cooper, a clerk in the Foreign Office. On the day McIver's letter was published, Cooper was crossing Whitehall in the middle of the evening rush hour when he was run over and killed by an electrobus.[30]

Confronted by the lord mayor's deputation, Gladstone blamed other bodies, such as the London County Council, for failing to tackle motor bus noise and fumes. He seized on the concession at the Mansion House meeting about the benefits of motor vehicles and emphasised he did not want to do anything that might damage the growing motor industry.[31] Gladstone was reluctant to consider new legislation and held out the prospect of the problem solving itself, with petrol buses 'being supplanted by an electric omnibus with equal carrying power which would run at reduced speed'.[32]

Elsewhere the electrobus continued to attract plaudits. In September the bus was showcased at the annual meeting of the British Association for the Advancement of Science, one of the most prestigious events in the scientific calendar and a forum where scientists from many different disciplines could exchange ideas and review progress. That year's meeting was held in Dublin and opened by the BA's president Francis Darwin, the son of Charles Darwin. Among the diverse range of topics was the Meteorological Office's progress in forecasting wind speeds from measurements of barometric pressure, how folding layers of rocks formed the Alps and efforts to reduce mortality from bovine tuberculosis by pasteurising milk.

On the final day of the meeting Sir Douglas Fox, the electrobus company's consulting engineer, gave a paper on 'Railless Electric Traction' – electric buses which did not run on rails. He spoke about two alternatives, trolleybuses, which drew their electric current from a pair of overhead wires and which were being experimented with in mainland Europe, and electrobuses, which took their power from batteries.

Illustrating his talk with lantern slides – the Edwardian equivalent of a Powerpoint presentation – Fox told his audience that the key question was whether electric trams or motor buses would be the future of urban transport, whether the commuters of the future travelled on rails or not. The tramcar was superior to the motor bus in both comfort and capacity, but he doubted whether Britain's municipal tramways were making a profit. 'The electrobus,' said Fox, 'was probably a more formidable rival than the petrol omnibus, not only to the horse omnibus but also to the tramway.'

Fox left his audience in little doubt that the electrobus had a bright future. When the electrobus was first introduced many experts doubted whether the technology was up to the job. His figures dispelled all doubt. A fully laden electrobus, weighing 7.5 tons, could run 40 miles on a single charge and cope with steep hills without causing any damage to the batteries. Its electricity consumption was about the same as a tramcar and the wear and tear of the electrobus was far less than that of a motor bus because it had fewer moving parts.

'The many attractive features of the electric omnibus as compared with the petrol omnibus must dispose everyone interested in urban transportation to wish for it all the support, moral and financial, necessary for its development and perfection,' said Fox.[33]

To round off the year the electrobus won a theatrical accolade. At the end of 1908 the impresario Herbert Beerbohm Tree was mounting his Christmas show *Pinkie and the Fairies* at His Majesty's Theatre in London's Drury Lane. This was a decidedly upmarket panto. The star of the show was Ellen Terry and among the cast were two budding starlets who went on to become well-known actors in their own right. Tree's own daughter, Viola, played the Sleeping Beauty, and Miss Stella Patrick Campbell – the daughter of Mrs Patrick Campbell – was also cast as a fairy.

Under the terms of the council's special licence that allowed young girls to perform on the West End stage, Tree had to arrange for them and their mothers to be taken home after the evening performance. He chose to convey them in style, by hiring a private electrobus. The brilliantly illuminated bus not only saw the girls safely home but was also an effective advert for Tree's Christmas show – and the electrobus.[34]

Chapter 14

A Black Hole

By most yardsticks 1908 was a year of solid advances for the London Electrobus Company. It had pulled off a series of publicity coups both big and small, from the Brighton run to a prominent role in the festivities surrounding the Franco-British exhibition. Political pressure was now mounting on the government to clamp down on the noxious nuisance of the motor vehicle – which could only improve the electrobus's prospects still further. To dispassionate observers the electrobus was the most promising technology on the streets of London, although there were reservations aplenty about the conduct of the company.[1]

Despite its evident progress, the company's annual general meeting was delayed and the accounts were late, which is not normally the sign of a company enjoying healthy finances. In stark contrast to the previous year's meeting the annual general meeting of 1908 was a hole-in-the-corner affair. It was held three days after Christmas, a time, as one commentator put it, much 'favoured by companies of the baser sort' to discourage attendance by shareholders and journalists.[2]

The meeting was again held in Lehwess's favourite venue, the Hotel Cecil. There was a certain historical resonance behind his liking for the Hotel Cecil. The man who financed this opulent 1000-room hotel on the south side of the Strand was the notorious

Victorian fraudster Jabez Balfour. Shortly before the hotel opened in 1896 Balfour, as the author Benny Green put it, 'found himself short of £8 million or so and was invited to spend the next 14 years in a cell trying to remember where he had put it'.[3]

So why was the London Electrobus Company, previously so keen to trumpet its successes, suddenly so publicity shy? The answer was simple. There was a black hole in the company's finances that defied explanation and could only partially be concealed in the accounts.

Right from the beginning the electrobus company's figures never quite made sense. The amount of money it raised, or claimed it had raised, was never matched by the number of buses on the streets. The original share offer had raised £46 000, the company told its shareholders at their first meeting in August 1906. The company said it had ordered 30 electrobuses, ten of which would soon be delivered. When the electrobus service eventually started a year later it had only six electrobuses, although the company maintained there would soon be 50. By the time of the AGM in November 1907 it still had only seven buses. The company then promised to put a hundred buses on the road, provided it could raise more money to buy them. By the summer of 1908, there were still only a dozen buses on the streets.

The lack of electrobuses piqued the curiosity of *Commercial Motor* during the summer of 1908, possibly as the result of a tip-off. 'It is an eminently unsatisfactory feature that only 12 vehicles are in service, at a time when the company has got through approximately £50 000.' The reporter then rather spoilt this devastating insight by claiming that at £700 a time the electrobus was costing the company twice as much as it should. The magazine was forced to retract this claim by Lehwess's legal team. It had mistakenly thought that £700 was the cost of an electrobus chassis and not the cost of a complete bus.[4]

The subsequent apology has a libel lawyer's fingerprints all over it and shouldn't necessarily be taken at face value. 'We have recently had the opportunity of looking into the terms upon which the Electric Vehicle Company of West Norwood… [supplies] accumulator-driven omnibuses…largely through the instrumentality of Dr E E Lehwess, to the London Electrobus Company. We find that, after the expenses of assembly and erection are taken into account the directors of the latter company are not paying an unreasonable price for the complete vehicles.'[5]

Despite its grovelling apology, the magazine was on the right track. At the time a complete motor bus – including a chassis and a body – which was considerably more complex to make, cost in the region of £550 to £750.[6] Furthermore, at these prices the motor bus was ready to run: you just needed to fill it up with petrol and the first passengers would soon be tendering their fares. Even at £700 the electrobus wasn't ready for the road. It needed batteries, which had to be bought or leased. They could cost half as much again as a bus. The magazine did the sums. The Electric Vehicle Company was certainly making an enormous profit on its electrobuses. A few months later the magazine reverted to its original view that the price being charged by the Electric Vehicle Company for the electrobus bus was 'distinctly high'.[7]

However, the magazine's fundamental point was even better. By the end of 1908 when the company had raised £75 000 it still only had 20 buses. The London Electrobus Company had swallowed huge amounts of money but had little to show for it. Where had all the money gone?

The contrast between the electrobus company and two other companies then trying to get a toehold in the lucrative London bus market is revealing. Both companies had a capital of around £20 000 – less than a third of the electrobus company's bankroll. The London Central Omnibus Company, which ran conventional petrol buses, put its first buses on the road in October 1907. Nine months later it had 16 of them. The Metropolitan Steam Omnibus Company began with seven buses in November 1907; six months later it had 20 steamers on the road.[8] If these concerns could do it why couldn't the London Electrobus Company? It is true that the very first electrobuses needed some presumably costly modifications to the transmission but this doesn't even begin to explain the huge discrepancy.[9] Why was the electrobus company such a bottomless pit?

In November 1908, just before the delayed annual general meeting, the London Electrobus Company produced a fresh bombshell: it was mortgaging the company's assets. The company wrote to its shareholders saying it needed even more capital to expand its fleet of buses. This was its fourth attempt to raise money from the public. Instead of trying to foist more shares on investors it was inviting the public to buy £50 000 of debenture bonds, which it said would enable it to put 100 electrobuses on the road.[10]

Debentures can be a legitimate financial instrument, but they were never going to be popular with existing shareholders. On paper debentures could be extremely attractive for investors who wanted a secure income. Anyone subscribing to the electrobus debentures, which were sold in £1 units, could expect to receive 6 per cent interest a year. Furthermore, the bonds were secured on the company's assets.

But debentures were not a good deal for existing shareholders. The debenture interest took priority. It had to be paid before the company could pay any dividends to shareholders. Issuing debentures meant the prospect of shareholders receiving a dividend receded sharply. It would take a remarkable recovery in the company's financial fortunes before it paid any dividends.

For the shareholders this was a double whammy, because debentures were a mortgage. And like any mortgage, if the company failed to keep up the interest payments its property could be repossessed. With no realistic prospect of any dividends and an increased risk of losing everything the electrobus share price was bound to go into free-fall.

The press was surprisingly sympathetic to the debenture issue. 'It would certainly be a loss to London and a severe setback to our great progress in vehicular traffic if the Electrobus Company were allowed to expire for the lack of more capital, which the directors assert is all that it needs,' was the verdict of the *Daily Mail*.[11] Equally upbeat was *Commercial Motor*, once one of the company's sternest critics, although its view may have been coloured by the fact that the London Electrobus Company had recently commissioned it to produce an engineering report on the stability of an electrobus with a covered top. The magazine generously conceded that 'widespread anticipations of disaster' that it had forecast had 'proved entirely wrong and baseless'.[12] Increasing the size of the electrobus fleet was the surest way to increase profitability.

This was a fair point. The shortage of electrobuses was a particular financial headache for the company, in a way that would not be nearly so serious for a company running petrol buses. Then – as now – small fleets of electric vehicles can often be uneconomic

Figure 12 In with the new, out with the old: traffic outside the Bank of England in a photograph probably taken in 1908, with motor buses and an electrobus vying with horse power for supremacy on the streets of London.

to run because of the overheads. The 20 electrobuses rattled around in the capacious garage in Victoria and much of the expensive electrical equipment, such as the battery chargers, stood idle.

As the shareholders sat in the Hotel Cecil waiting for the AGM to start the tardy accounts did not make happy reading. The company had notched up significant losses in its first year of operation. But the results for the latest quarter – July to October – were rather better and lent some credibility to the claim that more buses would make the company profitable. In this quarter the company had made a modest operating profit – even if it was less than £10. The directors could say that they were beginning to turn round the loss-making company.

As chairman, Sir Henry Dering gamely claimed that the electrobus was now a proven commercial success and that the issue of debentures would provide more buses and result in a steady stream of dividends for shareholders. 'Experience has proved to your directors the profitable earning power of the electrobus and, with the necessary working capital to augment the fleet of buses there is no reason why in the near future the shares should not be on the dividend list.'[13] This rosy assessment may have given rise to cautious optimism among electrobus shareholders. If it did it was unwarranted.

The year's well-publicised successes had obscured some more worrying changes in the company. In a boardroom reshuffle in the spring, Ernest Rowbottom, the man who had worked so hard to make the electrobuses a practical proposition, resigned. The lack of electrobuses prompted a second resignation: John Musgrave, a director of Wilkinson Sword Company, walked out in September. His resignation forced Lehwess to take a formal position with the company. He briefly became a director to help make up numbers on the board – although he resigned shortly before the AGM.[14]

More mysteriously, the company's independent auditors disappeared. Ever since the Companies Act of 1900 limited companies had to have their accounts audited. The purpose of this legislation was to safeguard the interests of shareholders and to prevent fraud by managers and directors.[15] By law auditors were appointed by shareholders – and not the directors. The electrobus auditors had been duly reappointed by the shareholders in 1907. But sometime after the share offer of April 1908 they resigned or were forced out by Lehwess, who was by far and away the largest single shareholder. Just why they left was never explained to the ordinary shareholders.

Consequently the electrobus company needed a new auditor and Captain John Taylor knew just the man for the job – Thomas Jehu Garlick. Garlick was much more than a run-of-the-mill accountant. He had helped Captain Taylor to set up Steele Lockhart, the PR wizards retained by the electrobus company, and audited its accounts. Garlick was a City wheeler-dealer and much in demand by the financial world's shadier characters.

Garlick was closely associated with a number of ventures with both Taylor and Frank Shackleton, the younger brother of Ernest Shackleton, the heroic Antarctic explorer. Frank Shackleton, who was a director of Steele Lockhart, was one of the rogues of the Edwardian age and is generally believed to have stolen the Irish Crown Jewels. This trio were behind the recent flotation on the London Stock Exchange of Maxim's Ltd, the English company that now owned the legendary Parisian restaurant and which was chaired by another familiar name, Sir Henry Dering.[16]

Dering and Garlick were plainly on good terms. Garlick even stood in for Dering at the press lunch following the experimental run of an electrobus with a roof.[17] None of the journalists at the Hotel Cecil that day seemed to question why the company's independent auditor was in the apparently compromising position of deputising for the chairman.

At the same time that Garlick was auditing the electrobus accounts – and those of Maxim's – he and Shackleton were also making frequent trips to Tavistock in Devon. The focus of their attention was an elderly spinster, who they were pressurising into buying worthless shares in a company promoted by Steele Lockhart that allegedly had interests in Argentina. Their high-pressure sales technique worked and before long they had emptied the spinster's bank account and reduced her to penury. For both men, this was a scam too far. It would take a few years for the law to catch up with them, but both would later be jailed for this fraud.[18]

Even Garlick's undoubted auditing skills couldn't completely conceal the black hole in the electrobus accounts. The company's 20 buses cost £700 each, or £14000 in total. Yet the electrobus company had paid the Electric Vehicle Company more than £31000 for buses. So what had happened to the other £17000? The only explanation in the accounts is that these were payments in advance for new buses. In effect, the electrobus company had paid for two dozen ghost buses.

There is a coded hint in the footnotes to the accounts that these figures might not be wholly accurate, probably added so Garlick could evade any legal blowback. He says 'the expenditure upon the assets is stated at the amount allocated thereto by the company's officials'. In other words, he hadn't checked the figures.

On top of this the company had huge promotional expenses, which had ballooned by 60 per cent over the previous year and were now only a few pounds short of £20000. Most of this increase was down to substantial payments the electrobus company had made to Steele Lockhart – a company in which Garlick, Shackleton and Taylor shared a common interest.[19]

All this may have passed the shareholders by in the Hotel Cecil. The AGM had been scheduled for 12.30 pm, coinciding with what for at least some shareholders was the most important business of the day – lunch. Some shareholders may have been reluctant to drag out the meeting with probing questions about the accounts and risk any delay to their lunch.

One man, however, had read the accounts closely and was alarmed at the rate the company was haemorrhaging money. He was Jacob Atherton, one of the electrobus company's directors. Atherton hadn't always taken a close interest in the company's affairs but shortly after the AGM – it would be nice to think this was over the lunch the directors enjoyed in the Hotel Cecil's restaurant immediately after the meeting – he had a heated row with Lehwess over the company's lavish spending and resigned.[20]

But there could have been another explanation for the financial black hole. The electrobus shareholders were constantly being spun the line that only a lack of capital was holding back the company and it is true that when the electrobus company raised money from shareholders, in April 1906, November 1907 and April 1908, the influx of cash was used to buy more buses. But each time the company raised fresh capital it spent only a fraction of it on buses.

Lehwess was undoubtedly siphoning cash out of the electrobus company. But was some part of the black hole because the largest single shareholder had not paid in full – and in cash – for his shares?

This kind of deceit was not uncommon. In the shadowy world of Edwardian finance people acquired large blocks shares without ever paying for them in full – or providing any services in return for shares. Earlier in 1908 another company promoted by Shackleton and Taylor handed over £15 000 of shares to its chairman. He was never required to pay for them. And who was this lucky chairman? It was Thomas Jehu Garlick.[21]

Chapter 15

The Sell-Off

In June 1908 the Archdeacon of Mashonaland received a letter out of the blue offering him some free electrobus shares. The Motor Share and Investment Trust was offering one free deferred share for every ten ordinary shares that the archdeacon bought. This buy-ten-get-one-free offer was particularly attractive and the letter laid it on thick. 'The collective return on each 100 ordinary and 10 deferred [shares] should amount to about £26 per annum on the outlay of each £100,' claimed the trust.[1]

The Motor Share and Investment Trust had extended the same generous offer to everyone on its suckers' list. The compilers of these lists, known at the time as widows' lists, collected the names of well-heeled single women, widows and professional folk like clergy who lived in the country, ingenuous people with spare cash who were likely to be taken in by share scams. According to Edward Beall, who as a regular user of these lists was in a good position to know, one of those being hawked around the City of London at the time had the names of 108 000 'women, capitalists and shareholders'.[2]

The trust's letter was accompanied by a four-page glossy advertising supplement from *Motor Finance* detailing the offer of 'a limited number' of shares in the London Electrobus Company. The shares were 'a progressive and remunerative investment'.

The magazine itself had a lengthy supporting article, which proclaimed the electrobus the victor in the 'battle of the buses'.[3] The supplement featured several of the electrobus company's publicity photos including one of a line of electrobuses outside Buckingham Palace full of the French sailors cheering the king, a picture taken just the week before.

No sooner had the French sailors returned home than the push to sell electrobus shares moved into overdrive, as the trust pushed out a series of circulars trying to offload shares held by the swindlers. The trust emphasised that the offer of a free deferred share was very valuable, because the 5-shilling shares had been traded on the Stock Exchange for close to £1. 'As the number of shares is limited, applications will be considered in strict order of priority,' it claimed.

The shiny supplement in *Motor Finance* had all the appearances of being an official share offer: it certainly fooled some journalists who initially thought it was a repeat of the April share offer.[4] But this was not an official share issue. It was not designed to raise money for the electrobus company. It was simply a way of offloading the swindlers' shares.

Between them, the electrobus swindlers still owned a large number of electrobus shares and now they wanted rid of them as fast as possible. The share offer of April 1908 had forced them to soft-pedal any sales to avoid depressing the share prices. Now there was no longer any need for restraint. In the two months following the April share issue more than a third of the electrobus company's shares changed hands. The Asiatic Bank handed over nearly 20 000 shares to the Motor Share and Investment Trust while Taylor sold all his holdings, which were mostly held in the names of Steele Lockhart, his wife and a couple of clerks in Taylor's office. The investment trust – and the editor of *Motor Finance* – sold off these shares in small parcels directly to the public.[5]

Some of the readers who received letters from the investment trust sought counsel from the newspapers, many of which ran a financial advice column, a sort of agony aunt for small investors. The advice offered to one reader was very much to the point. 'As a speculation electrobus shares are fairly attractive. I gather from your letter that the Motor Share and Investment Trust are offering 10 500 at £1 a share. You can buy as many as you want on the market at 12s 6d, or perhaps a trifle cheaper.'[6]

The Archdeacon of Mashonaland – today part of Zimbabwe – and his brother, who was a rector in Norfolk, were blissfully unaware of all this ungodly business lurking in the background. They both had a touching faith in the written word and believed that the free shares were an unmissable offer. The two clerics sent off their cheques for £40.

The contrast between the behaviour of the small shareholders and the characters behind the swindle could not have been greater. The small shareholders were a loyal lot, who continued to have faith in the future of the electrobus. Only a few of them ever sold their shares. Almost all the shares that ever came up for sale were being sold by Lehwess and his accomplices. One circular from a firm of 'stockbrokers' claimed that a distressed client urgently needed to sell some electrobus shares to meet a pressing liability and this client was prepared to part with shares worth a pound for only 15 shillings.[7] After a lull over the summer the sell-off picked up again in the autumn.

By the end of the year only Lehwess still had a significant stake.[8] Longman had sold his shares through the Motor Share and Investment Trust. However, Longman did not enjoy the close working relationship that Lehwess had forged with Beall. Although Beall had sold Longman's shares he seems to have forgotten to pay him.

In October 1908 Longman's company Securities Exchange sued the Motor Share and Investment Trust, Edward Boyle (who was Beall) and Lehwess, demanding accounts for the electrobus shares that they had sold. The court papers show that the Motor

Share and Investment Trust was the conduit for share sales by the electrobus swindlers and that Beall and Lehwess were part of a conspiracy to offload electrobus shares on an unsuspecting public.[9] Longman won his case when it eventually came to court four months later. Beall failed to pay and so Longman bankrupted the Motor Share and Investment Trust, which was forced into liquidation.

By the autumn of 1908 electrobus shares were in the doldrums; the price was depressed both by Lehwess selling off his holdings and by a fares war. In the face of plummeting profits caused by the conversion from horse to petrol London's three largest bus companies had formed an alliance. The combine, as it was called, controlled about 85 per cent of London's buses. Among its first moves was to increase bus fares to improve takings and replenish the companies' depleted coffers. 'We got tired of losing money,' the London General told the press.[10] The electrobus company held its fares at the old level – a 1d fare for short journeys in central London – which boosted the number of passengers but not the profits. A fares war with a large company would undoubtedly have worried the combine. However, the fleet of electrobuses was far too small for this fares war to be more than an irritant.

The fares war ended in December when the combine reduced its fares. The electrobus company was quick to claim the credit. 'By adhering to the old penny fares we claim to have broken the combine, which raised the prices in the middle of December,' said Arthur Riding, who was now the electrobus company secretary.[11]

The share sell-off continued in the New Year. In January 1909 a select group of investors received a letter offering them cheap electrobus shares. A firm of stockbrokers had a limited number – only 800 – to sell at the unprecedentedly low price of 13s 9d. The stockbrokers behind this circular were a previously unknown firm called Albert E Griesbach and Company, an outfit operating from a poky office in Covent Garden, which wasn't even listed in the telephone directory. The stockbrokers were simply another front for Beall. Griesbach was one of Beall's clerks and the Covent Garden office was rented by Beall.[12]

Over the next few months Griesbach pumped out circular after circular emphasising how remarkably profitable electrobus shares would be. One of these came into the possession of the *Financial Times*. 'Considering that the current market quotation for the shares is about 2s 9d a deal at the figure mentioned by Albert E Griesbach and Company would be remarkably profitable – for Albert E Griesbach and Company,' sniffed the paper.[13]

But the gem among these circulars, the product of a truly inventive mind, was sent to shareholders in the Army and Navy Stores, a well-known London department store close to Victoria Station. It made another unmissable offer and one the Army and Navy Stores shareholders shouldn't overlook – a limited number of £1 electrobus shares – once again there were only 800 of them – and once again the unusually low price was 13s 9d.

'These electric omnibuses,' said Griesbach, 'have been running past the stores in accordance with an arrangement with the [stores] and have been well patronised and much appreciated by [shoppers] and shareholders.' The special relationship between the Army and Navy Stores and the electrobus was an 'amusingly fantastic' claim, said the city editor of *Truth*. The route of the electrobuses did indeed take them past the Army and Navy Stores on Victoria Street. But there wasn't any arrangement with the store. Lots of companies ran their buses along Victoria Street.

An offer that was too good to miss? Not so, said *Truth*. 'The generosity of the offer will be appreciated when I mention that on the Stock Exchange you can buy these shares at about 1s 6d.'[14]

By spring the spate of circulars had dried up. In practice the shares had become unsaleable. For Lehwess the game was up.

He had sold around 7000 through these circulars in the first six months of 1909 but it was becoming increasingly difficult to sell electrobus shares at almost any price.[15] On top of that a legal action was looming which threatened to throw an unwelcome spotlight on his activities.

Chapter 16

A Veil of Secrecy

In June 1909 a High Court action comprehensively shredded the veil of secrecy that surrounded the London Electrobus Company. There might have been suspicions – and occasionally accusations – that Lehwess was one of the chief wheeler-dealers behind the company, but irrefutable evidence was difficult to find.

This changed when American battery tycoon Charles Gould sued Lehwess. The subsequent court case shone a powerful spotlight on the murky goings-on behind the London Electrobus Company. The case proved that the Asiatic Bank and Trading Corporation and the International Motor Traffic Syndicate were no more than fronts for Lehwess and it unmasked him as the controlling godfather behind the London Electrobus Company.

The trigger for Gould's court action was an attempt to close down his British company, the Gould Storage Battery Company Limited. The company sported impressive notepaper emphasising its international connections. It had offices in Regent Street, the centre of London's West End, and it was the European representative of the Gould Storage Battery Corporation of New York, which had a capital of $5 million and offices in Boston, Chicago, San Francisco and Toronto, Canada, with a factory in New York State.

Gould held a majority of shares in the British company. However, he was based in New York, and so unable to play any timely part in the company's business. Day-to-day control was in the hands of its chairman, Captain Locock, and the main British shareholder, the Asiatic Bank.

In late September 1908 the British Gould company held an extraordinary general meeting, at which shareholders were told that the company couldn't continue in business because of its debts. They were asked to approve putting the company into voluntary liquidation.

It was patently a trumped-up liquidation, designed to give the company a discreet burial away from prying eyes. Only two shareholders attended the meeting, Locock and a representative from the Asiatic Bank – Edward Ernest Lehwess. The company's assets were the 15 sets of batteries that Gould had shipped to England, which were leased to the London Electrobus Company. Its liabilities amounted to £175 – not the sort of debt mountain that would force a company with such impressive international backing into liquidation.[1]

Locock, who had been appointed liquidator at this strange shareholders' meeting, duly called a meeting of creditors, which by law had to be advertised in the press.[2] During this process the news reached Charles Gould in New York, who now realised he had been suckered. Up to this point Gould had been labouring under the illusion that his British company was cash-rich, with thousands of pounds in the bank. So where had all the money gone? Gould, who held the majority of shares, objected to the liquidation and halted it.

Not a man to be bilked, Gould then sued Lehwess for £3200 – the cost of the batteries – claiming that he had been defrauded. Lehwess was starting to become a familiar figure in the law courts. The Gould case opened in May 1909, a month after the Motor Car Emporium had attracted such unflattering publicity in the case of the false prospectus issued by the Edinburgh bus company.

The international dimension of the case meant it attracted widespread coverage in the Fleet Street papers, unlike the

Edinburgh case which had been of more interest to the provincial press. Much of the hearing was spent unravelling the byzantine links between Lehwess and the London Electrobus Company.

Lehwess's cross examination by Gould's lawyers was particularly damaging, because it betrayed the extent to which Lehwess dominated the electrobus company and how he used his front companies to deceive Gould – and by extension the general public – about his involvement.[3]

Not only was the Asiatic Bank one of the main shareholders in the Gould Storage Battery Company Limited, it was also a significant shareholder in the London Electrobus Company. There was, said Gould's lawyers, something of an element of Asiatic mystery about the corporation. It had signed a contract saying it would use its best efforts to persuade other companies to use the Gould batteries and in return for these valuable services had been given a stake in the British Gould company. In cross examination Lehwess was asked about his links with the corporation. The lawyers probed: Lehwess dissembled.

– 'Are you a director of the Asiatic Banking and Trading Corporation?'

– 'No I am not.'

– 'Are you a secretary or any other official?'

– 'I had better tell you what it is,' he eventually conceded. 'It is a promoting syndicate which we registered ten years ago when we were looking at some concessions in Russia and Asia.'

Bit by bit the story dribbled out. The corporation was a Channel Islands company. Despite having a nominal capital of £1 million, its paid-up capital amounted to just £7. Lehwess was one of the seven founding shareholders. By the time the case came to court it had been wound up. Lehwess had to concede that any dividend on the electrobus shares held by the Asiatic Bank would be paid to him and that he had concealed from Gould that the corporation was just Lehwess under another name. The judge could scarcely believe his ears.

– 'You were the Asiatic Banking and Trading Corporation?' he asked incredulously.

– 'As I explained to your lordship, I was.'

– 'I warn you, this is serious. You did not write to Mr Gould to tell him you were the Asiatic Banking Corporation?'

– 'I did not tell him anything at all about it.'[4]

Lehwess was a little more forthcoming about the International Motor Traffic Syndicate. Asked about the syndicate, he said:

– 'That is my trading name, I own it. I have done business for years under that name and have an account under that name.'

He then claimed that it was not a limited company. This was false, although it was true that the company had failed to fulfil its legal obligation to file its annual return for 1908.[5] Had he really forgotten the celebrations at the Oxford Restaurant that followed the company's registration?

The cross examination was spread over two days with the judge becoming increasingly irritated by Lehwess's evasive answers. At one point he was asked if he was chairman of the Electric Vehicle Company.

– 'I believe that I am chairman or managing director or something of that sort still.'

Lehwess was similarly vague about the extent to which he controlled the London Electrobus Company and was forced to admit that he had deceived Gould about his role.

– 'Did you tell Gould that you had half of the shares and that you could control the company?' asked the judge.

– 'I can't say my Lord. I rather think not.'

Lehwess argued that the Gould batteries were not up to the job and that the electrobuses were now using batteries made by the German Tudor company. The Tudor batteries were undoubtedly better suited to the job, according to reports in the trade press, and the Gould batteries were not lasting well.[6] But that didn't really change the fundamental point: Lehwess had conned Gould into shipping the batteries to Britain, used them to start the electrobus service and was now refusing to pay for them.

The result of the court case – a victory for Gould who was awarded £2500 – was rather less important than the damage it did to the electrobus company. The directors were revealed as little more than Lehwess's compliant tools.

Two weeks after the case ended Lehwess suddenly recovered from the temporary amnesia he suffered under cross examination and brought the International Motor Traffic Syndicate's file at Companies House up to date. It turned out that Lehwess was a director and that he and his mother Jenny held the bulk of the shares.[7]

Lehwess took the case to appeal to try to overturn the verdict. The appeal court was unhappy about the way the damages had been calculated and sent the case for retrial, which ended in a compromise. The full terms of the compromise were never disclosed, but Gould withdrew his accusations of fraud in return for what must have been a significant pay-out.[8]

During these protracted legal proceedings – and probably prompted by them – Companies House asked the British Gould Storage Battery Company if it was still in business. Locock's reply was a nice piece of deceit. 'The only business that it ever carried on was the leasing to the London Electrobus Company of certain batteries. These batteries are now valueless for working purposes their only value consisting of the lead in which they are constructed.' He went on to explain that the electrobus company had the batteries and that the Gould company was broke, claiming: 'The shareholders attend no meetings and seem to evince no interest in the company whatsoever.'[9]

Lehwess was clearly the dominant figure in this shady web of companies. In a later legal case his private secretary, Elsie Ractliffe, described the way he ran one of them. The Electric Vehicle Company, she said, was a one-man company controlled from beginning to end by Lehwess. The directors and other officials were completely under his influence and gave him carte blanche to do whatever he wanted. There can be little doubt that he ran his other companies on the same lines. Ractliffe was close to being the most sympathetic witness possible for Lehwess. She was a trusted servant of his family for several decades to the point where she was the executrix of Jenny Lehwess's will.[10]

After the Gould case the next item on the agenda for the London Electrobus Company was paying the interest on the debentures it had issued at the end of the previous year. The electrobus debenture issue had not been a resounding success. On paper the sale of debentures had swelled the company's coffers by nearly £12000. Where did the money go? No one knows. There were never any accounts. The first interest payment was due in June 1909. The electrobus company defaulted on the payments.

Just over half of the debentures were held by Lehwess, although there must be some doubt whether he ever paid for them.[11] Now that the electrobus company was behind with its payments the holders of these debentures could foreclose on the mortgage at any time they chose. All it would take was a majority vote. Lehwess had tightened his grip on the electrobus assets.

Chapter 17

The Greek Adventurer

The long-suffering shareholders in the London Electrobus Company must have choked on their toast and marmalade when they opened their morning post on Wednesday 14 July 1909. For among the envelopes on the breakfast table was a lengthy letter from one D J de Lyann, the editor of a magazine called the *Cosmopolitan Financier*. De Lyann had a scheme for reconstructing the London Electrobus Company. He was writing to ask for the shareholders' support and – predictably – their money.

De Lyann said he had been asked to intervene by several subscribers of the magazine who were 'large shareholders' in the electrobus company. The company was in temporary financial difficulties, he said. But once these difficulties had been surmounted electrobuses were clearly the future of public transport and 'your enterprise possesses exceptional opportunities of practically monopolising the passenger traffic in the metropolis'.[1]

Only 14 electrobuses were currently on the road, he said, because the company lacked the money to repair them. His solution was to set up a new company, the Reorganisation and Control Syndicate, which under his benevolent supervision would take control of the electrobus company's assets and provide an immediate injection of cash. The company was paying an exorbitant price for its electrobuses, claimed de Lyann, who further claimed to have an option for cancelling the contract with its suppliers – the Electric Vehicle Company.

After the company had been reorganised it would be able to raise further funds, increase its fleet to 50 buses and pay a dividend of 28 per cent on ordinary shares. All he wanted from electrobus shareholders to reach this nirvana was for them to invest £1 in his syndicate for every £5 of electrobus shares they held.

The shareholders had to make up their minds quickly, however. De Lyann told them that his options for carrying out the scheme expired at the end of the following week and without a reconstruction their shares would be worthless. He boasted that the scheme had the backing of the newest director of the electrobus company Lieutenant-Colonel Charles Mordaunt Fitzgerald. In a follow-up letter to wavering shareholders de Lyann laid it on thick. 'I am by no means satisfied that all have grasped the gravity of the situation, or indeed appreciate the efforts that are now being made by Lieutenant-Colonel Fitzgerald and myself on their behalf.'

Truth was scathing about the scheme. 'In the long run people who have refused to have anything whatever to do with this Reorganisation and Control Syndicate will, I think, have cause to congratulate themselves upon having thoroughly grasped the situation,' said the magazine.[2]

The figures in the circular were pure fantasy, especially the jaw-dropping claim of a 28 per cent dividend. Who, shareholders might have wondered, was de Lyann? Who were the big shareholders backing this astounding scheme? And why such urgency? The short answer was that de Lyann was the journalistic *nom de plume* of Demetrius John Delyannis, another con artist working the fringes of the Edwardian financial world. He was already well known to *Truth*. His entry in the *Truth Cautionary List*, the magazine's annual guide to the blackmailers, swindlers and other ne'er do wells of the era, describes him as a 'Greek adventurer [who] has bamboozled the public by means of various financial schemes'.[3]

Figure 13 The Greek adventurer: Demetrius J Delyannis as portrayed in the *Cosmopolitan Financier*, the reptile journal he owned and edited.

The electrobus shareholders could not know it but Delyannis had teamed up with Lehwess – the unnamed large shareholder backing this fantastic scheme – to devise a new way of fleecing investors. This unlovely pair calculated that the electrobus shareholders were worth yet another shakedown. Lieutenant-Colonel Fitzgerald, the electrobus director endorsing the scheme, was very much Delyannis's man. He was chairman of Cosmopolitan Publications, the publishers of the *Cosmopolitan Financier*.

The urgency of the mooted reconstruction became apparent a few days later. It had nothing to do with Delyannis's options and everything to do with a forthcoming legal action. A London battery company was trying to bankrupt the London Electrobus Company. The firm had around £1000 of batteries on hire to the electrobus company and it hadn't been paid. Given all the recent publicity about Lehwess cheating Gould out of his accumulators the firm was understandably keen to recover its batteries and ensure that it was paid.[4]

To add to the electrobus shareholders' woes the landlord of the electrobus garage was on the point of sending in the bailiffs to seize the electrobuses because of rent arrears. However, this was a phoney demand. For Lehwess owned the lease on the electrobus garage through one of his fronts, Improved Electric Traction. The rent demand was simply a manoeuvre designed to pre-empt the legal action and establish Lehwess as a creditor of the electrobus company in the event that the battery firm forced the electrobus company into liquidation.[5]

So who was the Greek adventurer now taking centre stage in the electrobus saga? Demetrius J Delyannis was a nephew of Theodoros Delyannis, the recently assassinated prime minister of Greece, and a cousin of the Greek ambassador to France. In photographs he strikes a self-important pose, a man with a splendid handlebar moustache who is developing middle-age spread and doing his best to hold it in for the photographer. Delyannis and his younger brother, a deputy in the Greek parliament, had come to London after the death of their uncle. But that was about as deep as the veneer of respectability went.[6]

Demetrius Delyannis had been forced to flee Greece for Paris to escape his creditors. After he had left Greece he was declared bankrupt and faced the threat of imprisonment if he returned to the country.[7]

Soon after he arrived in London Delyannis set up a company to acquire a waterworks back home in Greece. The venture was still-born and in September 1907 he renamed the company the Atlas Banking Corporation and began publishing his own reptile journal, the *Cosmopolitan Financier*.[8]

One distinctive feature of the magazine – one that was highly unusual in a magazine ostensibly specialising in high finance – was a column written by an enigmatic Greek astrologer called Madame Catinomany. Readers were asked to think of a particular eventuality, such as electrobus shares paying a 28 per cent dividend, and while continuing to hold this thought in their mind they should shuffle a pack of cards and turn up three of them. It wasn't clear from all this hokum if the pack should include the joker. All they then had to do was to send details of the cards they had turned up to Madame Catinomany's office in Regent Street – together with six penny stamps.[9]

Hundreds of ladies and gentlemen were 'spellbound and amazed' by the great astrologer's predictions, according to her adverts. 'My great success in the trials made by the editor of the *Cosmopolitan Financier* with his readers throughout the United Kingdom have secured me an extensive circle of clients, admirers and supporters.'[10] This particular advert was accompanied by an unintentionally hilarious photo of village girls and water carriers 'queuing up to have their fortune told' by Madame Catinomany in some bucolic Greek grove. The rather more down-to-earth interpretation of the photo is that they were queuing to draw

Figure 14 At home with Madame Catinomany: from the *Wheel of Fortune*, April 1908, a short-lived reptile journal published by Demetrius J Delyannis.

water from the village well. At least one employee of the *Cosmopolitan Financier* doubted that Madame Catinomany existed. Fortune telling was more than an idiosyncratic sideline. It was a useful source of names of credulous people for anyone compiling a suckers' list.

The fortunes of the Atlas Bank and the magazine were closely bound together. 'You will never see a paid tip or puff as editorial or otherwise in the *Cosmopolitan Financier*,' proclaimed Delyannis high-mindedly.[11] Yet the *Cosmopolitan Financier* plugged the Atlas Bank from its very first issue. In December 1908 the magazine featured a lengthy article on the 'fundamental principles of investment' by Bertram R King, 'the able managing director of the Atlas Banking Corporation and for many years connected with the London Stock Exchange'.[12]

King was Delyannis's right-hand man but he did not have long experience with any recognised financial firm. His connections with the Stock Exchange amounted to a couple of bucket shops – a spell managing a provincial branch of the London and Paris Exchange and another as a director of the Anglo-Continental Investment Syndicate. Both went bust in 1909, the Anglo-Continental with debts of £1350 and assets of 8s 9d.[13]

The Atlas Bank was no more above board than other bucket shops. Much of its 'business' was simple stock swindles. There were dozens, if not hundreds, of them. People bought shares, paid for them and never heard from the bank again, let alone receiving their share certificates.

Truth was a tenacious critic of Delyannis and warned its readers of 'the undesirability of dealings with the *Cosmopolitan Financier*, or Cosmopolitan Publications, or the Atlas Banking Corporation'.[14] Delyannis started libel proceedings in an attempt to gag his most dogged adversary. The tactic partly worked. *Truth* was forced to soft-pedal its criticism to avoid aggravating any libel. Delyannis eventually dropped the action, but it gave him enough breathing space to develop his latest scam – the Reorganisation and Control Syndicate.[15]

Events moved swiftly after de Lyann's initial letter to electrobus shareholders. The next week the syndicate was registered at Companies House. Delyannis, the saviour of the electrobus, was a director. There was obvious collusion between Delyannis and Lehwess. The day after the syndicate was registered Lehwess – who controlled the majority of the debentures in the electrobus company – called in the receivers. It was a fact that Delyannis was able to announce before the event.[16] Perhaps he had been consulting Madame Catinomany.

The new arrangements were byzantine. The electrobus company told its shareholders that the receivers would protect the company's property: 'the directors think you need have no alarm,' they wrote. The company would be run in consultation with a committee, 'under the chairmanship of Mr de Lyann, who is undertaking arrangements for financing the company. A scheme will shortly be forthcoming to reorganise our finances.'[17]

On the streets of London the electrobuses continued to glide quietly along their routes. But there were fewer of them. At the peak in the autumn of 1908 the company had up to 20 buses running on two routes, with the first bus taking to the streets at 6 am and the last returning to the garage at midnight.[18] By the summer of 1909 the service was increasingly patchy. The electrobuses were still just as comfortable, noiseless and fume-free, but would-be passengers had to wait longer and longer for a bus to arrive.

The flow of optimistic publicity in the press also dried up.[19] The *Cosmopolitan Financier* was now virtually alone in continuing to puff the electrobus in a series of articles that lasted for the rest of the year.[20] Anyone who had seen electrobuses 'will be readily convinced of their startling superiority over the steam or petrol vehicle,' claimed the magazine. The only bus that could make a profit, it declared, was the electrobus. Only a lack of investment was holding back the ultimate triumph of the electrobus.[21]

'Travel in Luxury,' proclaimed adverts in the *Cosmopolitan Financier*. 'If you hate smoke and fumes and the rattle and hustle of the petrol motor 'bus RIDE IN AN ELECTROBUS.' The company, claimed the ads, is 'now under new and efficient control'.[22] The electrobus chairman, Sir Henry Dering, urged his shareholders to back the syndicate.[23] It was the fifth attempt to relieve electrobus shareholders of their nest-eggs. More than £6000 flowed into the syndicate in the second half of 1909, with about two thirds of the money coming from people with a stake in the London Electrobus Company. The rest were either shareholders in Cosmopolitan Publications, people who had been taken in by the publicity in the *Cosmopolitan Financier* or were on Delyannis's sucker lists.[24]

'Regular readers of the *Cosmopolitan Financier* and more particularly those who have joined me in the Reorganisation and Control Syndicate know of the great interest I have at all times manifested in...electrically propelled omnibuses,' Delyannis wrote. 'I am a great believer in this mode of propulsion. I had great faith in the London Electrobus Co. when it was floated, and was bitterly disappointed when it got into financial difficulties... But in spite of all its troubles and trials...I never lost faith in its eventual triumph.'[25]

Delyannis was never a man to put his money where his mouth was. Despite his great faith in electric buses his name does not appear in the London Electrobus Company's share registers and his investment in the Reorganisation and Control Syndicate amounted to one share, costing £1.[26] The only real evidence of any previous sympathy for the electrobus was a critique in the *Cosmopolitan Financier* of the 'abominable nuisance' of the motor bus. The article, published under the headline 'Noise Fiend of the Metropolis', was a diatribe about the racket made by motor buses – and barrel organs. It was written by Thomas Bowden Green.[27]

It would not take the gifts of Madame Catinomany to foresee the crash of Delyannis's empire. There was a harbinger of things to come in August 1909 when Bertram King, Delyannis's factotum and 'able managing director' of the Atlas Bank, was successfully sued for £50 that he had borrowed and forgotten to repay. In court, King's reputation for financial probity was forensically shredded. He was forced to concede that his cheques often bounced and claimed that he no idea how many outstanding court judgments there were against him.[28]

By the end of the month the bank was in deep trouble and its creditors were circling. One of them sent in the bailiffs. The Atlas Banking Corporation shared its offices in the City with its new bedfellow the Reorganisation and Control Syndicate. Delyannis, the bank's 'presiding genius', as *Truth* dubbed him, was ready and waiting. The bailiffs were turned away empty-handed. The office furniture and everything of any value in the office either belonged to him or the Reorganisation and Control Syndicate. The Atlas Bank had sold the furniture to the syndicate to pay the rent, Delyannis claimed, brandishing a receipt under the sheriff's nose. The ink on it was barely dry.[29]

In October the creditors forced the bank into compulsory liquidation. The bank had debts of £10 000 and assets of £3 in cash. The bank had advertised that it paid 7 per cent interest on deposits. One widow who took up the offer received her first payment on schedule, and then the interest stopped. The bank gave cheap loans to people who deposited valuables, such as stocks and shares, in its strong room. The bank promptly sold the valuables or pledged them elsewhere. 'A lot of money appeared to have found its way into the concern,' said the official receiver, who investigated the bankruptcy, 'but the books…were so badly kept that it was impossible to trace where it had gone.'[30]

None of this chicanery was calculated to help save the electrobus company. If the company was to be put on a proper footing it needed to increase the size of its fleet and run more buses. Instead, by the end of the year, the number of electrobuses on the road had dwindled to five – barely disturbing the eerie calm of the capacious garage.[31] The flow of cash into the syndicate's coffers had failed to result in any new electrobuses from the overpriced Electric Vehicle Company or anyone else, and the electrobus company hadn't even kept its existing buses roadworthy.[32]

Delyannis and Lehwess decided it was time to pull the plug on the London electrobuses. In late November they made a covert offer to sell them to the local bus company in Brighton.[33] The Brighton company was sworn to secrecy.

While they waited for the Brighton company to make up its mind Lehwess sold all the company's assets to the Reorganisation and Control Syndicate for a knock-down price. The fleet of electrobuses, which had cost the electrobus shareholders £14000, was sold to the syndicate for £1000 in cash – plus a nominal £2000 in the syndicate's shares.

On 3 January 1910 the Reorganisation and Control Syndicate formally took over the electrobus concern. Shortly afterwards the rump of the London Electrobus Company went into voluntary liquidation. The liquidator was Thomas Jehu Garlick. He continued to be the liquidator for the next 13 years – including the period when he was doing nine months' hard labour in Wormwood Scrubs following his conviction for defrauding the Devon spinster he and Frank Shackleton had ruined.[34]

Chapter 18

The Whistleblower

The morning of Monday 3 January 1910 was dull, but quite mild for the time of year. The loyal commuters waiting on the pavement for their electrobus were by now used to watching a few noisy jolting petrol buses pass before they eventually saw the bright lights of their smooth and comfortable ride approaching. That morning the wait was unusually long. One by one the passengers drifted away and caught one of the despised alternatives. And if the wait seemed to last for ever that is because it did. The electrobuses were firmly locked up in their Horseferry Road garage. There were no electrobuses that day, or the next. They would never run in London again.[1]

The last London electrobus disappeared into the garage in the midwinter gloom at the start of January. On 3 January the Reorganisation and Control Syndicate took over the electrobus company and all its assets. The next issue of the *Cosmopolitan Financier* sported a glossy supplement extolling the virtues of the electrobus garage, which the syndicate had just acquired.[2]

Nearly 300 people had invested in the Reorganisation and Control Syndicate believing its pledges to bring the electrobuses under new and efficient management. Naturally enough they were looking forward to seeing their brightly lit electrobuses gliding along the capital's streets. Certainly the syndicate had ambitious plans, if you believed Delyannis.

The syndicate would raise £100 000 through a fresh share offer Delyannis had promised the previous November when he told shareholders of his plans for the future. It would set up a new operating company to run the buses. The money would be enough to buy a hundred new electrobuses enabling the new operation to pay shareholders a phenomenal 100 per cent dividend. Furthermore, Delyannis had plans for new pullman electrobuses, 'luxurious and tastefully equipped electric cars upholstered in morocco [leather]'. The public would willingly pay an extra penny to travel in such style and comfort, he said.[3]

In the middle of January the London Electrobus Company held its final shareholders' meeting, called to rubber-stamp its voluntary liquidation. The meeting was remarkably well attended. Around 50 shareholders squeezed into the Atlas Bank's old boardroom, which now belonged to the Reorganisation and Control Syndicate.

In normal circumstances only a handful of mourners would have bothered to attend the company's final meeting. But these were not normal circumstances. For several months reports had been circulating of dissension on the electrobus board.[4] The precise nature of the dispute was obscure, but it now became evident that one of the directors, William Roberts, was the source of the dissent.

Roberts had been on the board right from the beginning. He had also been a director of other equally shady companies, including the Edinburgh bus company, when he had loyally defended its decision to buy buses from Lehwess. Roberts was no longer part of the charmed inner circle. The week before the shareholders' meeting he wrote to them warning that they were being ripped off.[5] The Reorganisation Syndicate, he wrote, had bought the company's assets for a tenth what they were worth.

Roberts did not attend the electrobus company meeting, which was chaired by Dering. Dering tried to placate the shareholders, but the bottom line was they had no say in this sale. The company's assets were owned by the debenture holders. However, Dering told them, the Reorganisation and Control Syndicate planned to set up another company to run the buses and all the electrobus company shareholders who invested in the syndicate would profit from this reconstruction. He urged the shareholders to back the scheme.[6] The other electrobus director at the meeting, Lieutenant-Colonel Fitzgerald, also endorsed the plan. The shareholders voted to wind up the electrobus company. They had no other option.

The game plan was fairly transparent. There was a well of public support for the electrobus – and investors had a track record of backing the electrobus with hard cash. Delyannis and Lehwess were hoping to run the swindle all over again through an entirely new company untainted by the bad odour surrounding the London Electrobus Company.[7]

Roberts and other small debenture holders tried to block the sale. But it was a lost cause. Lehwess held the majority of electrobus debentures and could out-vote all the rest. Roberts went to court in January, claiming the electrobuses were being sold too cheaply, but after a couple of months he dropped the case.[8] The action cost the syndicate 'a few hundred pounds in legal fees', complained Delyannis in March. This was the last time the *Cosmopolitan Financier* mentioned the electrobus.[9]

The Reorganisation Syndicate had bought the electrobus company as a going concern. But despite all the pre-launch hoo-ha it never ran a single electrobus.[10] Nor did any successor company. The contrast between the grandiose plans for developing the electrobus service and the complete absence of electrobuses on the road was all a bit mysterious, thought one journalist. 'It is difficult to discover exactly what is happening, but if reports in circulation are accurate, the whole of the Electrobus Company's business, lock, stock and barrel, is now in the hands of Dr Lewis.'[11] The rumour mill was spot-on: between them Delyannis and Lehwess had a stranglehold on the company's assets.

By now though the tide of events was running strongly against Delyannis. Two days before the electrobus company's final meeting the official receiver held a public inquiry into the bankruptcy of the Atlas Bank. Delyannis tried to distance himself from the bank by claiming that he had resigned a long time before. The official receiver wasn't fooled: he knew that Delyannis controlled the bank up to the day it went bust. The next day's newspapers were full of how the bank had swindled its customers and some reporters made the connection between Delyannis, the Atlas Bank and the Reorganisation Syndicate.[12]

After the failure of the Atlas Bank other branches of the Delyannis empire began to fall like dominoes. Cosmopolitan Publications went bust and the *Cosmopolitan Financier* was taken over by new owners. Delyannis prepared the ground for a last-gasp attempt to revive the electrobus swindle but nothing came of it and his interest switched to rubber and oil shares.[13]

The turning point in Delyannis's career as a con man came with the publication of a deliciously scurrilous pamphlet naming and shaming him. The pamphlet was written by a whistleblower who could tell the inside story about the collusion between Delyannis and Lehwess, because he had worked on the *Cosmopolitan Financier*. The author of this pamphlet was to be Delyannis's undoing.

There couldn't be a much greater contrast between the pamphlet's author William Saxby, a sometime sub-editor on the *Cosmopolitan Financier*, and Delyannis. Saxby was employed casually at 3 guineas a week, while Delyannis earned £1000 a year from his job as editor – quite apart from the profits of his scams. Saxby lived modestly in Wandsworth. Delyannis could afford to live at fashionable addresses in Kensington and Park Lane.

Saxby was a habitual drunk and commonly to be found at the bar of various watering holes around Fleet Street. Delyannis, on the other hand, was teetotal and was so offended when he once saw

Saxby staggering out of a public house he stopped employing him for a while. Delyannis insisted that Saxby signed the temperance pledge before he would take him on again.

There was another key difference between the two men. Unlike Delyannis, Saxby had a stubbornly honest streak. Saxby had a conscience about puffing the shares of worthless companies, making false attacks on companies and being compelled by Delyannis to pen the distorted and misleading articles that were published in the *Cosmopolitian Financier.*

In the late afternoon of 26 February 1910 Saxby took a hansom cab to Threadneedle Street, the centre of the City of London, to distribute his pamphlets. He gave them to a number of newsboys selling the evening papers and told them they could sell the pamphlets for a penny each – and keep the money. The City was soon awash with copies of 'The Story of Demetrius John Delyannis, alias D J de Lyann, alias the *Cosmopolitan Financier*, the vulture of the West' in which Saxby denounced Delyannis as a rogue, swindler and bucket shop-keeper.[14]

'The manner in which one weekly financial paper, published in the City of London, is conducted constitutes without doubt a grave public scandal,' Saxby wrote. The management of the *Cosmopolitan Financier* was 'incompetent and dishonest'. 'Bankrupt alike in purse and reputation [the magazine] is compelled from week to week to attack or refrain from attacking, as best suit its purpose', certain financial figures. The magazine gained spurious credibility by attacking bucket-shop keepers, claimed Saxby, while Delyannis himself ran 'a glorified bucket shop' – the Atlas Bank.

Thanks to his bankruptcy in Greece, Delyannis was a man 'who cannot go back to the land of his birth to the home where his family are honoured and where the many great and at the same time noble acts of his forebears are held in kindly and loving remembrance,' explained Saxby. 'He put himself without the pale; he remains outside today.'

The pamphlet went on to point out that fortune tellers could be prosecuted under the Vagrancy Act and that the great Madame Catinomany was Delyannis in disguise. The astrologer's adverts in the *Cosmopolitan Financier* gave an address in Regent Street. This was a small back room on the third floor, which Delyannis rented for 10 shillings a week. Madame Catinomany had never been seen in Regent Street or indeed anywhere else, and Delyannis dictated her predictions to a typist.

Delyannis was provoked into launching a prosecution for criminal libel, which was exactly what Saxby and his backers had intended. If Delyannis failed to prosecute he would be irredeemably branded a cheat and a rogue. Saxby was sent for trial at the Old Bailey. The case caused a mild sensation. But for Saxby, this was a game with high stakes. If he lost, he risked a prison sentence – and Delyannis had secured the services of Richard Travers Humphreys, one of the most eminent barristers of the day.

The case started in June. The main focus was the swindles Delyannis had perpetrated. A series of defence witnesses testified to the Atlas Bank frauds, explaining that they never received the shares they'd paid for or that valuables they had deposited at the bank had vanished. However, the case also shone a searchlight on the close links between Delyannis and Lehwess at this period. Saxby said that his editorial work for the *Cosmopolitan Financier* was carried out in interconnecting offices in the City of London that were shared by the Atlas Bank and the Reorganisation and Control Syndicate. The sole reason for setting up the Reorganisation Syndicate, he said, was to acquire Lehwess's worthless electrobus debentures.

Saxby revealed that he had written the report of the syndicate's AGM in November 1909. The meeting had been ignored by the mainstream press. But it was covered in some detail by the *Cosmopolitan Financier*, which proclaimed the 'splendid results of three months' work' and said that there had been a substantial increase in takings and a great reduction in costs.

Saxby swore that the report he had originally written had been accurate, but Delyannis had later falsified it. The article published in the *Cosmopolitan Financier* 'is not a fair report of the proceedings at all,' said Saxby. 'The continued loss of the running of the buses of the electrobus company was not allowed to be shown. They wanted to obtain more shareholders and the object was to make it appear that things were quite good.'[15]

Delyannis had also tried to airbrush out the links between Lehwess, the London Electrobus Company and the Reorganisation and Control Syndicate. 'Whereas in the discussion I put in the names of the real speakers he altered them,' said Saxby. In the printed report Delyannis had changed Lehwess to Lewis and John Neely, the company solicitor of the old electrobus company, became Mr Kelly.[16]

The association between Delyannis and Lehwess went far wider than the electrobus. A month after the Reorganisation Syndicate meeting Saxby penned an account of a Cosmopolitan Publications meeting. According to the report that appeared in the *Cosmopolitan Financier* the meeting at the Waldorf Hotel was well attended. In fact there were just ten people there and only one was a shareholder. The rest of the people, who included Lehwess and Neely, were cronies of Delyannis.

The *Cosmopolitan Financier* devoted two pages to the report. It was all fiction, said Saxby. Delyannis and Lehwess dictated the outline of the story to him, telling him what to write. According to the article a Mr Laxon played a prominent part in the meeting. It was an outrageous fabrication, said Saxby. No one called Laxon was there. The name had been borrowed from the sports pages. Bill Laxon had no connection with Delyannis; he was the professional billiards champion of Johannesburg and at the time he was in South Africa.

The jury was unimpressed by the prosecution. They exonerated Saxby and added a damaging rider to their verdict: 'We find that...

the pamphlet was substantially correct and that a public service has been rendered by its publication.'

'The failure of his proceedings against [Saxby]…leave no doubt as to the real character of the man,' wrote *Truth*, which was naturally delighted. 'The evidence that has been given during the liquidation of the Atlas Bank, and in the course of the long trial at the Old Bailey shows that since he has been in this country he has been simply living on his wits by a course of unscrupulous roguery. He has displayed great cunning in keeping himself outside the reach of the criminal law, but whether he has entirely succeeded in doing so is a point which might well be tested in the public interest.'[17]

Although the libel case exposed the behind-the-scenes skulduggery of Delyannis and Lehwess the fate of the electrobuses hadn't become any clearer. When the electrobus company issued debentures in 1909 it appointed two trustees to ensure that there was no hanky-panky. In practice this provided no real protection, because Lehwess held more than half the debentures. But the trustees still felt some moral responsibility towards the minor debenture holders.

One of the trustees was Roger Yelverton, a barrister and former chief justice of the Bahamas. In an open letter to the press he said that the point of setting up the syndicate was to reconstruct the company and put the electrobuses 'back on the streets'. But the buses were nowhere to be seen – at least not in London.

'I have twice…written to the secretary of the syndicate to inquire what success had attended its efforts in the above direction,' wrote Yelverton, 'but possibly by inadvertence, I cannot obtain any reply to my inquiry.'[18]

Chapter 19

A Franchise in Fraud

On Thursday 19 January 1911 Henry Semple, a surgeon living in
Devon, was flabbergasted to receive a demand for money from
the Reorganisation and Control Syndicate. The letter was headed
'private and confidential' and it was signed by the syndicate's
secretary, Edward 'Ted' Riches – an associate of Delyannis. Semple,
who had bought 50 shares in the syndicate, read the letter with
mounting dismay and disbelief. According to the letter an annual
general meeting had been held on New Year's Eve, an otherwise
unreported event. The meeting was told of a looming legal action,
in which the syndicate was trying to recover 'buses, parts etc., to
the value of £3400 '.

The letter went on to say that the company was having difficulty
in pursuing the action because it did not have enough money. Riches
asked shareholders to 'lend' the company one shilling for every
share they held. 'It is essential and expected that all shareholders
addressed will promptly respond, otherwise this action may be
dismissed and the company deprived of this substantial asset. In
view of this pressing emergency I shall be pleased to have your
remittance for the amount as at the foot.' Semple's letter asked him
to send a cheque for £2 10s.[1]

It was all quite puzzling for the benighted shareholders. This
was a company that had raised a substantial sum of money just

over a year ago. It hadn't run any buses. Yet it was suddenly short of money.

The shareholders could also be forgiven for wondering who exactly the syndicate was planning to sue because the letter didn't specify the target of the legal action. The answer to this last question emerged over the following weeks. It was the International Motor Traffic Syndicate – in other words Dr Edward Ernest Lehwess.[2] What was going on?

The origins of this legal action went back to the beginning of 1910 when the Reorganisation and Control Syndicate took over the electrobus business. On 11 January 1910 there was a clandestine meeting at the electrobus garage in Victoria. Four people were there: Delyannis and Riches represented the Reorganisation Syndicate, Roger Yelverton, the barrister who had a watching brief for the electrobus debenture holders, and Lehwess. During the meeting Delyannis secretly agreed to sell Lehwess eight electrobuses for £100 each. 'It was a regular juggle in my opinion,' said Yelverton.[3]

This underhand deal was temporarily put on ice when Roberts, the dissenting electrobus company director, tried to halt the sale in the High Court. But in April, after that threat had evaporated, Lehwess went to the garage. The buses had been run into the ground and many needed repairs to make them roadworthy. Lehwess selected the best eight vehicles and had them taken away. The International Motor Traffic Syndicate bought the buses for £800 and sold them on to the Electric Vehicle Company for an undisclosed sum. The Electric Vehicle Company then sold them on to the Brighton, Hove and Preston United bus company, the same company Lehwess had secretly offered the buses to five months earlier. According to the chairman of the Brighton bus company – one source in this story who is undoubtedly trustworthy – Brighton paid £3411 for eight second-hand electrobuses – a mark-up of 325 per cent.[4] Naturally Brighton also needed batteries to power all these buses. So Lehwess removed 19 sets of batteries from the electrobus garage and sold them to Brighton for £100 apiece.[5]

Not long after this Lehwess finished plundering the electrobus assets. Lehwess, in the name of Improved Electric Traction, held the lease on the garage. The seemingly cash-rich Reorganisation Syndicate was suddenly unable to pay the rent. So Lehwess got a warrant to seize the syndicate's assets. The bailiffs removed the remaining electrobuses to satisfy a rent demand of just £292.[6] Delyannis was clearly complicit in this pillage because the syndicate was not short of money and was happily settling other bills around the same time.

It was an extraordinary denouement to the electrobus swindle. Over the past five years somewhere in the region of £70 000 to £95 000 had been subscribed to provide London with an electric bus service. All of it had been skimmed off by the fraudsters who had flocked to join the swindle. All that remained were eight second-hand buses running in Brighton.

By the spring of 1910 Delyannis's main interests increasingly lay elsewhere. The boom in motor shares had run its course. Rubber and oil were the new flavour of the month. Demand for these commodities was burgeoning. The rapidly growing number of motor vehicles needed fuelling and councils were increasingly spraying roads with tar to keep down dust. The combination of rough roads and heavy new motor vehicles created a huge demand for tyres. The expanding electrical industry also needed rubber for insulation. So the smart money switched from investing in motor vehicles to rubber and oil. And where the reputable financiers went the rogues were not far behind.

Delyannis set about rebuilding his empire. In place of the *Cosmopolitan Financier* was his new sham magazine, *Rubber Investor*. His flagship interest was Rubber and Oil Consolidated Investments, a collective investment company that was similar, in theory at least, to a unit trust. The company invested in rubber shares and small investors could buy small stakes in Consolidated Investments. 'Buy a few shares in the Rubber and Oil Consolidated Investments and blame me if you should not double your money within this year,' proclaimed Delyannis.

Consolidated Investments moved into the Atlas Bank's old offices, alongside the Reorganisation Syndicate. It was a convenient arrangement for all concerned. Ted Riches, for example, was secretary of both Consolidated Investments and the Reorganisation Syndicate, while the chairman of Consolidated Investments was Sir Henry Dering, the last electrobus chairman.[7]

Given the stench of bad publicity generated by his failed libel case, it was now Delyannis's turn to keep a low profile. He was not a director of Consolidated Investments nor did his name appear anywhere in the *Rubber Investor*. Ever suspicious, the city editor of *Truth*, who only a couple of weeks before had administered a 'parting kick' to Delyannis after the collapse of his libel case, sent a reporter to track down the people behind this dubious new magazine. The magazine's office was occupied not by a team of reporters, but by a solitary typist, who had until recently worked for Cosmopolitan Publications. She helpfully redirected the reporter to the editor, who was to be found at the offices recently occupied by the Atlas Bank. 'The cat, so carefully concealed, then emerged from the bag – a remarkably fine old tom in the person of the aforesaid Demetrius John Delyannis,' wrote the reporter.[8]

By the middle of 1910 Delyannis had begun to plan his exit. Always a shrewd operator, he could read the writing on the wall, even without the aid of his astrological alter ego. He began the process of transferring his franchise in fraud to a Swiss swindler called Joseph Chansay. Zurich-born Chansay was one of the most prolific fraudsters of the era. His name was a gift to headline writers: 'A Chansay Promotion', 'A Chansay Company's Affairs' and then 'Another Chansay Promotion'.[9]

Like Delyannis, Chansay had his own sham financial magazine and his own much-criticised bucket shop.[10] In the summer of 1910 Consolidated Investments moved from Delyannis's offices to a suite that Chansay rented in a handsome new office building in the heart of London's financial district.[11] A few weeks later the Reorganisation Syndicate made the same move. In parallel to these physical moves a complex series of share deals saw Chansay take control of all Delyannis's companies.

Delyannis and Lehwess undoubtedly had an agreement on sharing the spoils. However, Chansay was not party to this understanding and in late June he launched a series of legal actions against Lehwess's front companies. His first ploy was to try to stop the sale of the buses to Brighton. It was too late – the buses had already gone south to the seaside.[12]

The case of the missing electrobuses didn't come to court until the following February. The Reorganisation Syndicate, now controlled by Chansay, sued both Lehwess, in the guise of the International Motor Traffic Syndicate, and the Brighton bus company. The Brighton company was effectively – and unfairly – being accused of receiving stolen goods, and had probably been included in the action because it was more likely pay up in the event of a win than Lehwess.

Eight of the syndicate's electrobuses were now running in Brighton, while the rest had been broken up for spares after being seized by Lehwess's bailiffs. The reason for the court action, said the Reorganisation Syndicate's lawyer, was to decide 'which of two injured parties was to suffer and the hero of the piece, or the villain, whichever way they looked on it was Mr. Lehwess, a doctor of science'.[13]

The judge, who was decidedly unimpressed with the stories told by either side, dismissed the claim. A couple of weeks later the two syndicates were back in court before the same judge. Lehwess had perjured himself. He had originally told the court that the electrobus batteries were on hire and the Brighton company was taking over the hire arrangement. But the batteries weren't on hire at all: the electrobus company had bought them, which Lehwess knew when he gave evidence. It also seemed to have slipped his mind that the Brighton company had paid him £1900 for the batteries.[14]

In July 1911 the Reorganisation Syndicate was back in court again. On the strength of the *Cosmopolitan Financier*'s glowing – but falsified – report about the 'splendid results' from running the electrobuses and its plan to put 50 electrobuses on the streets of London, Stephen Jones, a City solicitor, had invested in the syndicate.[15] He was dismayed to discover that the syndicate had failed to run a single bus. He was supported by Yelverton, who added the intriguing information that in the autumn of 1909 two or three other respectable suitors had expressed serious interest in taking over the electrobus service and running the buses.

Delyannis didn't turn up in court. With the authorities starting to take an increasingly close interest in his affairs he skipped the country in the spring of 1911. He never returned.[16] Jones won his case for misrepresentation, with costs. But it was a pyrrhic victory. 'Whether the victory would be worth anything or not I do not know,' was the judge's wry comment.[17]

The Greek adventurer was still listed as a director of the Reorganisation Syndicate but he no longer controlled it. Towards the end of June 1911 Helier Alexandre Vincent, a 40-year-old clerk from Jersey – and one of Chansay's trusted sidekicks – turned up with a debenture bond issued by the syndicate. Six months earlier the Reorganisation Syndicate had mortgaged its assets in return for £500 – issuing a debenture bond that paid 6 per cent interest. The bond had been made out to 'bearer'. Now that the syndicate had defaulted – it didn't even make the first payment – Vincent had the final say in what happened to it.[18]

Debentures were the Edwardian swindler's get-out-of-jail free card and the debenture dodge was a Chansay hallmark.

It was a way of looting the assets of a dying company while cheating creditors and shareholders of their rightful due.[19] Debentures can be a legitimate way of raising corporate finance, just as taking out a mortgage is a perfectly respectable way of buying a house. But in the hands of a swindler like Chansay a debenture was just a means of spiriting assets out of the reach of shareholders. Indeed there was no sign that the syndicate ever received £500 for the debenture – from Vincent or anyone else.

There was little chance of the debenture dodge ever being exposed. It was, said *Truth*, after one rare successful prosecution, 'a species of company swindle which has too often been practised with impunity'. A solicitor told *Truth* that he had 'come across lots of cases in which there was no moral doubt that this fraud had been perpetrated…but the legal proof required for a successful prosecution is not always obtainable'.[20]

Vincent lost no time in consolidating his hold over the syndicate. On 15 August he appointed a receiver: an accountant called Julius Wilson Hetherington Byrne. Byrne was the discerning fraudster's receiver of choice. As long ago as 1899 the *Financial Times* ran an exposé of his activities under the headline 'How Mr Byrne Uses Up Bad Eggs'. The article, which featured a sarcastic recipe for omelette à la financière – take seven bad eggs and skim off the profits – suggested that Byrne would cook books to order.[21]

At the time Byrne was peddling a scheme for amalgamating seven gold mines. None of the individual mines had ever struck gold but Byrne was confident that when they were brought together the magic of amalgamation would make them highly profitable. 'Mr Julius W H Byrne,' said the *Financial Times*, 'possesses a remarkably discriminative memory. It is quite unable to retain any unfavourable point in regard to any property he is liquidating, but it registers most vividly anything that will look well in a prospectus.'

Many of Byrne's clients were doubtless paragons of respectability. Others were more interesting. He was the obvious choice for Delyannis in April 1910 when he needed a liquidator for Cosmopolitan Publications.[22] Now he was Chansay's choice for interring the Reorganisation Syndicate.

Towards the end of 1911 half a dozen shareholders in the Reorganisation Syndicate combined forces and took legal action to force an inquiry into the goings-on at the syndicate. The group included the Devon surgeon Henry Semple and City solicitor Stephen Jones, and there is strong circumstantial evidence that Colonel Alfred Mayhew's cleanup the City campaign was actively supporting the shareholders. The head of the group was Michie Fraser, a retired civil servant in the diplomatic corps.[23]

Fraser told the court that the syndicate had been set up to take over the electrobuses as a going concern. Lehwess had comprehensively looted the company's assets. The result was that the syndicate had 'never carried on the business or indeed any business at all since January 1910'. According to the syndicate's latest accounts – dating from January 1911 – it had raised £6500 in cash, mostly from small investors. So it was a bit of a puzzle that a cash-rich company like this should want to take out a mortgage for £500.

'The company has assets more than sufficient to pay all moneys due under the said debenture and sufficient to pay the unsecured creditors a part of their debt,' thundered Fraser. He wanted 'an enquiry as to the circumstances in which the company was promoted and has carried on its business – so far as it had carried on business – and the said debenture was created by the company'.

The shareholders won their case and forced the syndicate into compulsory liquidation. Byrne was kicked out of his job as liquidator, and replaced by the Board of Trade's official receiver. So it was Henry Winearls from the official receiver's office who at the end of March 1912 convened a meeting of creditors and shareholders at his offices in Carey Street to explain to them where their money had gone. The story that emerged was a sorry one. The syndicate had been founded by Delyannis, said Winearls, but he had been 'unfortunately unable to trace the whereabouts of Delyannis, who, according to the other directors and the secretary, controlled the affairs of the company'.[24]

This wasn't quite true. Chansay had been in sole control of the syndicate since the middle of 1910. In a tight corner like this the scoundrels running the syndicate needed a scapegoat if they were to escape censure or even prosecution. Delyannis was the obvious fall guy. He was, after all, one of the architects of the whole swindle and – equally importantly – he wasn't around to deny his role. Winearls said he had found nearly half the cash raised by the company, but this was likely to be swallowed up by various creditors. So the shareholders got nothing more than the moral satisfaction of revealing the murky goings on behind the syndicate.[25]

Many of the key figures in the later stages of the electrobus swindle, such as Sir Henry Dering, were also prominent in Rubber and Oil Consolidated Investments. Under Chansay's malign influence this company went on to become one of the more infamous swindles of the early part of the 20th century. Its fortunes were closely tied up with the financial linchpin of Chansay's empire, the Anglo-European Bank. The swindles operated by the bank would culminate in both Chansay and Vincent being charged with fraud.

Almost all of the directors of companies in the Chansay empire were either guinea pigs, like Dering, or one of his clerks, like Vincent. Either way they exercised no control over their companies. One of Dering's fellow directors of a rubber and tea company was endearingly candid about his role after the company went bust. He told the official receiver he knew nothing about rubber or tea and his only financial interest in the company was the fees that it paid him.[26]

Consolidated Investments claimed its funds would be 'carefully invested in shares of various first class rubber plantation companies and oil companies'.[27] Instead the investors' money was poured into a variety of Chansay's rotten companies.[28] The story of one of these companies would have sounded uncannily familiar to the poor shareholders in the Reorganisation Syndicate. The Aywara Rubber and Cotton company was set up to exploit plantations in the Gold Coast. The chairman was Dering. The company failed to produce any rubber or cotton. A debenture holder then appeared from nowhere and took control of the company, putting in a liquidator. The debenture holder was Vincent; the liquidator was Byrne.[29]

In 1913 Chansay put Consolidated Investments into voluntary liquidation. Predictably, Byrne was the liquidator. This turn of events prompted a shareholders' revolt and the official receiver had to intervene. Winearls was again the man given the job of investigating. He uncovered a story riddled with deceit. The company's only real asset, some rubber shares worth nearly £5000, were put on deposit with the Anglo-European Bank, which sold them as soon as it got its hands on them.[30]

Not long afterwards the bank also went bust. The official receiver again investigated. Some of the books had gone missing. Those that the receiver found told an outrageous tale. 'The bank sold the securities without the knowledge of the owners and… presented fictitious accounts,' reported the receiver. The bank's accounts, which were audited by Byrne, 'were a device for concealing these facts'.[31]

The receiver's investigation was hampered by the absence of key figures at the bank. Chansay had gone abroad 'temporarily' and Vincent had been unable to resist the attractions of a protracted foreign holiday. 'Chansay did his swindling very successfully, and he had the prudence to go abroad while he was still at liberty to do so,' was the verdict of *Truth*, which called for Chansay to be extradited from the continent and put on trial at the Old Bailey.[32]

On 28 January 1914, warrants were issued for the arrest of Chansay and Vincent on charges of fraud and false accounting. In April Vincent, who had been in Paris for over a year, returned to England and gave himself up. Chansay was arrested in Genoa, while the British authorities tried to extradite him.[33] But under Italian law extradition had to take place within two months and justice ran out of time. It was impossible to prosecute Vincent without Chansay and the case against Vincent collapsed.[34]

Chapter 20

The Battle of The Buses

In stark contrast to the great fanfare of publicity that greeted Brighton's first electrobus in April 1908, the arrival of the latest batch of electrobuses two years later was furtive. The second-hand London electrobuses that Lehwess had sold to Brighton in April 1910 were virtually smuggled into the town. The local newspapers seemed oblivious to the event. There was only an oblique reference in the trade press to an increase in the number of electric vehicles in Brighton.[1]

The twin seaside towns of Brighton and Hove were the only place outside London to have electrobuses. The buses took their place alongside the electric trams that Brighton Corporation had run since 1901. The trams were fume-free and nowhere near as noisy as petrol buses. But Hove was vehemently opposed to allowing Brighton's trams on its genteel streets.[2] The two town councils were at loggerheads. Brighton wanted to run its trams in Hove, while Hove was implacable in its opposition. The most absurd manifestation of this stand-off was a short section of tramline which extended a few dozen yards from a junction in the north of Brighton, pointing like a dagger towards the heart of Hove before ending abruptly at the borough boundary.[3]

Hove shared its anti-tram attitude with the upmarket seaside resort of Eastbourne and well-heeled parts of central London, such as Chelsea, Kensington and Westminster. The residents of these wealthy parts of London mounted a long-running and largely successful campaign to keep trams out of central London, partly because the tramlines interfered with the use of their carriages and partly because trams had a lower class image because of their cheap fares. As Lady Chichester's lawyer said when opposing one tramway, it would be 'intolerable to have the tagrag and bobtail disgorged before her ladyship's lodge'.[4]

Ironically, the areas that were steadfastly opposed to trams were among the most vociferous when it came to complaining about motor buses. *Truth* didn't mince its words: 'The pig-headed shopkeepers and residents of the West End of London have stolidly set their faces against tramways…They have thereby brought on themselves an infinitely worse evil.'[5]

The noisy and smelly motor buses were detested just as much beside the sea as they were in London. The two councils had to deal with a continual stream of complaints from residents in both Brighton and especially Hove about the damage they were doing to the seaside resort. The coastal councils may have found it difficult to cooperate over transport but their ratepayers were united in their opposition to motor buses.

In November 1907 Hove Borough Council received a petition signed by 545 people with a long list of complaints about motor buses. Noise and smell came top of the list. 'They are not only detrimental to the welfare and prosperity of this beautiful town, but are also calculated to drive away many of the residents and visitors.' In a move that was clearly coordinated, Brighton received a similar petition complaining about the motor bus's 'dangerous speed, enormous weight, unbearable noise, unpleasant smells'.[6]

Shortly after these petitions one of Lehwess's front companies offered to replace the motor buses with electrobuses.[7] To placate the ratepayers – and forestall the possibility of another bus company gaining a toehold in Brighton – the local bus company arranged to buy some electrobuses from the Electric Vehicle Company. The first was delivered in April, followed by three more, although the company took more than a year to deliver them.

The two councils were very happy with the results. One of the few points they could both agree on was that electric buses, which ran on the main bus route linking the twin towns, were far superior to motor buses. The Brighton, Hove and Preston United Omnibus Company – known as the United – was cautiously pleased: 'The running of the electrobuses has proved so far satisfactory but it remains to see whether they are a financial success,' said the United's secretary.[8] True to form the Electric Vehicle Company had been slow to deliver and the United sought out different suppliers of quiet buses, buying some hybrid petrol-electric buses as well to compensate for the shortfall of electrobuses.[9]

Once the electrobuses had stopped running in London, Brighton had the world's largest fleet of battery-powered buses, a record unmatched until the early 1990s, when the Tennessee city of Chattanooga built up a fleet of twelve electric buses. In many ways the trial of electrobuses in Brighton and Hove was more significant than the one in London because it lasted so much longer – giving plenty of time to assess the pros and cons of electric buses free from the malign influence of the London swindlers.[10]

The arrival of the electrobuses did nothing to quell the discontent of those within earshot of the main bus route. If anything, the silence of the electrobuses only highlighted the racket made by motor buses. Canon John Flynn, whose church was on the bus route, complained about the din during divine service and asked Hove to ban motor buses on Sundays. The council sympathised with the clergyman and asked the bus company if it was possible to have an all-electric service on Sundays. The bus company said it wasn't, although it would try to run more electric buses.[11]

What held it back was largely the difficulty in recharging batteries. In London the electrobus company had a slick system for replacing exhausted batteries. Brighton's bus garage was geared up to the demands of petrol buses: filling fuel tanks, carrying out engine repairs and machining parts. It was not designed to provide a quick turnaround for electrobuses. So cumbersome were the arrangements that the United could run only three electric buses at any one time.

To solve this problem the company leased some land from Brighton Corporation and in October 1908 began to build a charging station to make better use of its electrobuses and expand its fleet. When the charging station opened the following June it was able to charge 16 sets of batteries simultaneously. This was the only purpose-built charging station for electric buses ever built in Britain. The building still survives.[12]

The design of the new charging station was a compromise as it housed both hybrids and electrobuses. The type of hybrid the United had bought was essentially a petrol vehicle, running a generator that supplied current to electric motors that drove the rear axle. Because the hybrid bus generated its own electricity its batteries did not normally need to be charged from the mains. The electrobuses, however, had to swap their batteries at least twice a day and the flat batteries then needed recharging. The swap took ten minutes using the company's home-made trolleys – two or three times longer than it did in London.[13]

None of this did anything to silence the growing grumbles about noisy motor buses. Councillors on the towns' powerful watch committees – council committees that controlled the police and which had the power to grant or rescind bus licences – were getting restless. Hove kept asking the United why it wasn't running more electrobuses. The council ratcheted up the pressure on the company by cutting the duration of petrol bus licences from one year to four months – while renewing electrobus licences for a full year.

Chapter 20

In October 1909 the ratepayers of Hove presented another petition about the evils of the petrol bus, this time signed by more than 600 people. Such was the public outcry that the United replaced motor buses in the west of the borough with horse buses.[14] A month later 500 Brighton ratepayers followed suit with their own petition, listing the usual complaints about noise, vibration, noxious smell, the effect on their health, how the motor buses were destroying the rateable value of properties and how the wheels of speeding buses sprayed both passers-by and shop windows with mud, a euphemism for a mixture of liquid and solid horse excrement.

The ratepayers who signed the petition were some of the most influential citizens in the town. And in case councillors failed to grasp the point the covering letter pointed out that almost all the ratepayers on the main bus route had signed it and that between them they paid more than £36 000 a year to the council in rates.[15]

As a result of this pressure Brighton's town clerk wrote to the United in December 1909 demanding to know when it was going to increase the number of electric buses. The bus company pointed out that it had already spent £12 000 building the charging station, leasing the land from the council and buying electric buses and that electric buses were 'much more expensive to run than petrol buses'. The United asked for and was given assurances that if it bought the eight second-hand London electrobuses Lehwess had recently offered the company it would not be wasting its money and the council would not grant licences to any rival firm running petrol buses.

Complaints about motor buses rumbled on. The United's standard response was to try to shift the blame. It argued that the principal cause of bus noise was the poor state of repair of the roads – which was the council's responsibility. 'My directors also venture to draw your committee's attention to the road in front of

194

Hove Town Hall, which is very worn,' was one tongue-in-cheek response.[16]

There can be no doubt that electrobuses banished the problem of noise and fumes wherever they ran. 'The silence of these buses was much appreciated by the public,' said the United's company secretary.[17]

Continuing complaints prompted Hove to ask the chief constable to investigate to provide an independent view of the problem. His report points the finger firmly at the petrol bus. At the time of his investigation the United was running more than twice as many petrol buses as electrobuses. Over a period of three years the police recorded more than 150 complaints about petrol buses, but only a dozen about the electrobuses.[18]

At its peak in 1911 the Brighton bus company had a fleet of 17 electric and hybrid buses, in addition to 25 petrol buses. Almost all of the electric buses operated on the main bus route linking Brighton and Hove, which ran past Canon Flynn's church.[19] For a time the electrobuses vied for supremacy with the petrol-powered buses, but they struggled on gradients, especially the stiff 1 in 11 incline up to Brighton's clock tower.

The United scrapped its hybrid buses before the start of the First World War, but kept the popular electrobuses, including the second-hand ones it had bought from London. After the outbreak of war petrol was in short supply and the government's war department requisitioned the company's horses, so the electrobuses kept on running – amply justifying claims that the small number of moving parts meant they would be less prone to break down and would last longer than petrol vehicles.

Towards the end of 1916 the Brighton bus company was taken over by Thomas Tilling, a large and long-established transport operator that ran buses and other commercial vehicles in towns all over the country.[20] Tilling continued to run electrobuses but with little enthusiasm.

As a result of the takeover, details of the electrobus operating costs emerged in the trade press, possibly with the aim of softening up local councillors prior to scrapping the electrobuses. The cost of operating electric buses had always been controversial. The electrobus company had insisted that the electrobus was cheaper to operate than a petrol bus. The United stressed how expensive they were.[21]

In theory, because the same company ran both types of bus over the same route, comparisons should have been easy. But while the take-home message was clear – the running costs of the elderly electrobus were higher than a modern petrol bus – the figures were curiously incomplete. There were detailed costs for the consumption of electric current and battery maintenance, which reflected badly on the electrobus, but the figures for keeping the buses roadworthy, which may have been significantly lower for the electrobus, were not available. Instead there were some anecdotes about how the strain of climbing the single hill on the route caused the motors to overheat and the insulation to fall off the electrical wiring in flakes.[22]

Part of the reason for the higher running costs was that despite the councils' enthusiasm for the electrobus the United was paying over the odds for its current, even though it used off-peak electricity to charge its batteries. Brighton Corporation supplied the company from its own power station and was more concerned with boosting the power station's profits than giving the electrobus a helping hand. In 1911 the corporation's electricity works boasted an increase in sales of almost 14 per cent – a large part of which was the result of 'the extra electrobuses, which the company had added to its fleet'. The corporation charged the bus company nearly twice as much for electricity as the electrobus company had paid in London and almost 50 per cent more than it was charging the corporation's own trams.[23]

What is indisputable is that the electrobuses were durable. Few, if any, contemporary petrol buses lasted anything like as long.

In the capital, the London General reckoned that the new standard buses introduced in 1910 would last five years and clock up 150 000 miles over their lifetime. Each of Brighton's electrobuses ran more than 200 000 miles in a ten-year life.[24]

The electrobuses continued to run in Brighton and Hove until April 1917. The technology that had taken the twin towns by storm in a blaze of publicity ten years earlier simply fizzled out. Thomas Tilling asked Brighton to license its electrobuses for a further three months, adding the caveat that the buses would not be used 'unless a further shortage of petrol should compel the company to do this'. The councillors remained keen to keep their electrobuses. Brighton wrote to Tilling wanting to know what steps the company was taking to put the electric buses back on the road.[25]

Two weeks later Tilling replied: the electrobuses were unsafe because 'it is impossible to obtain spare parts,' they wrote. No one had made any spare parts for at least six years. The stock of spares from the electrobuses that had been broken up in 1910 had been exhausted, so any new parts would have to be made from scratch. And that required skilled labour. The combination of a dearth of spares and wartime labour shortages meant the electrobus had reached the end of the road.[26]

The last time an electrobus made headlines was in January 1917. Alice Scutt, a domestic servant, was crossing the road in Hove. It was her evening off and she was going out. One of Lehwess's second-hand buses was approaching at about 4 miles per hour.

The driver sounded the gong because of some nearby road works. But Scutt did not see or hear the approaching bus. Nor did the driver see the 39-year-old Scutt in the gloom. The bus passed the road works. 'I felt a severe jolt,' said the driver. 'I pulled up at once, I went to the rear of the bus and found the body of a woman doubled up between the nearside back wheel and the mudguard of the bus. The hind wheel appeared to have passed over her head.' Alice Scutt was dead.[27]

Chapter 21

Boom, Bounce and Bust

In early 1910 a charwoman walked into a firm of stockbrokers. She hadn't come to black the grates or polish the brass, she was there on business. She had 10 shillings in her purse and she told the astonished clerks that she wanted to put it all into rubber shares. Another woman wrote to a firm of brokers enclosing 7½d and asking them to 'buy her a good rubber share which would rise'. It was the height of the rubber boom. On the Stock Exchange the frenzied trading in rubber shares reached such a peak that one trader fainted. His plight was discovered only at the close of business when the shouting throng dispersed and the unsupported trader slumped to the floor. These were just some of the stories doing the rounds during the rubber boom.[1]

For most people in the City the boom was highly profitable, although it did have its downside. The more sporting souls in the Square Mile were dismayed to discover a staggering increase of 6 shillings in the price of a dozen golf balls – the result of the soaring price of rubber.[2]

The rubber bubble took off in a big way in the first months of 1910. Britain's demand for rubber – much of it for tyres – was growing. The country was importing more than three times as much rubber as it had been twenty years earlier. In 1907 the price of rubber was just over 5 shillings a pound. Two years later it was

9 shillings and the bandwagon gathered pace in the spring of 1910 until the price reached a peak of almost 13 shillings at the end of April.[3]

The bounce in the price of rubber was felt almost everywhere. In the first two months of 1910 more than 50 new rubber companies were registered, trying to tempt the public into buying more than £5 million of shares. Most of these new companies priced their shares in units of just 2 shillings, instead of a pound, to make it easier to trade small amounts of shares and to attract a new class of investor – making the shares accessible to the nation's charwomen.[4] Everyone it seemed was going rubber crazy. The *Financial News* capitalised on the mood by launching a column called 'Voice of the Rubber Public'. Even *Truth* began publishing regular analyses of rubber shares in its financial columns alongside more familiar features like 'Round the Bucket Shops'.[5]

With their eyes fixed firmly on the main chance Beall and Lehwess, like Delyannis, moved away from the motor trade and into promoting rubber and oil companies. Beall and Lehwess continued the close collusion they had established in the electrobus swindle and now turned their skills to milking the rubber boom. They were intimately involved with two new companies. In mid-February they set up a shell company called the Lee Syndicate. Towards the end of the month the Lee Syndicate in turn promoted a new rubber company, Victoria (Malaya) Rubber Estates, which was perfectly poised to profit from the boom.

Although details differ there are clear parallels between the new promotion and that of the electrobus company. Both gulled investors with a misleading prospectus, which concealed the secret profit that the promoters intended to pocket. In the case of the electrobus flotation the device for raking off this secret profit was a pointless patent; in the case of the Victoria company it was an unacknowledged commission.

The Lee Syndicate was a paper company, with a paid-up capital of £22. In early 1910 it acquired almost 8000 acres of land in Malaya and then sold it on to Victoria (Malaya) Rubber Estates. With the rubber boom in full swing the Victoria company then issued its prospectus, aiming to raise £80000 from the public. In the event it raised just over half its target.[6]

Neither Beall nor Lehwess featured on the returns of either firm at Companies House. Their notoriety was such that neither man was keen to broadcast his connection with the companies.[7] The Victoria Rubber prospectus painted a rosy picture of a healthy estate, with trees just waiting to ooze latex. But when the company sent out a representative to inspect its assets he found the plantation overgrown and neglected.[8]

In the normal course of events the directors of the Victoria company would be the promoters' nominees who could usually be relied on to be compliant. But Beall and Lehwess had a singular stroke of misfortune – which turned out to be a lucky break for the shareholders. Just weeks after the share offer the chairman died. The relatively successful share offer had loosened the ties between the promoters and their offspring and the Victoria company was cut adrift to prosper as it might. Two new independent directors joined a revamped board. The result of these boardroom upheavals was to weaken the promoters' grip on the board and prompt an outbreak of independence.[9]

The new directors took a fresh look at the company's promotion and were dismayed to discover that the Lee Syndicate had made a secret profit of £12000 in addition to the fees it charged for promoting the Victoria company and underwriting the share issue. The Lee Syndicate claimed it had paid £48000 for the property. However, the Victoria company discovered that the owner in Malaya had received only £36000. Where had the rest of the money gone?[10] In 1911 the shareholders made a clean sweep of the boardroom removing all the original directors and electing new ones to replace them.[11]

The new board examined all the correspondence with the Lee Syndicate and came to a harsh conclusion. The real object of setting up this company, the directors deduced, was to cover up the operations of Lehwess and his associates and to conceal the profits which they hoped to make.[12]

With the threat of a damaging legal action looming Beall and Lehwess plotted to regain control of the Victoria company. In place of the defunct *Motor Finance* Beall now had a new sham financial magazine, *Rubber and Oil*, which he planned to use to undermine the Victoria company's new management.[13]

Beall had always steadfastly denied that he had anything to do with *Rubber and Oil*. In its very first issue of 1911 the magazine wished its readers a happy New Year and then carried a point-blank denial that Beall was in any way connected with it. 'There is no foundation for the rumour that…Edward Beal [and a number of other people] are contributing to *Rubber and Oil*. The suggestion that these distinguished persons have any connection with the paper is baseless.'[14] Maybe spelling his own name wrongly was a double bluff – intended to throw readers off the scent – but the denial was a lie.

In October Beall launched an attack on the Victoria company's board for contemplating legal action. He warned shareholders that the directors were diverting money that should be used for planting rubber trees into a lengthy legal action. 'Litigation is more valuable to the solicitors than to the shareholders,' he said.[15]

On 28 November, one of Beall's stooges – a man called Edward Alleyn – was handed a small bundle of shares in the Victoria company by the Lee Syndicate. Three days later Alleyn wrote to shareholders alleging gross mismanagement by the board. He asked the shareholders to back his call for an extraordinary meeting which would set up a committee – headed by Alleyn – to investigate the company. The circular was followed by a flurry of letters to the financial press. The directors defended themselves while an anonymous writer calling himself 'investigator' – who was probably Beall – attacked the board.[16]

The agitation for a meeting was backed by a firm of accountants: Herbert Gowar wrote to shareholders asking them to fill in forms demanding an extraordinary meeting. It was not completely coincidental that Gowar was currently winding up one of Lehwess's electrobus companies – Improved Electric Traction.

Improved Electric Traction had been set up with 'a considerable bank balance of its own', according to its secretary. The company enjoyed rental income from the electrobus garage and would have undoubtedly added to its bank balance when it seized the remaining electrobuses, which were broken up to sell as spares to Brighton. Gowar was singularly unsuccessful in uncovering the whereabouts of the company's considerable assets, either in the bank or elsewhere. The bank balance, he said, was £3 10s, and he couldn't find anything else. The cost of liquidating the company meant that he was already out of pocket, he whined in one letter to Companies House, following up this sob story with the claim that the shareholders have all apparently disappeared, a story that would have sounded all too familiar to the clerks at Companies House.[17]

The agitation was effectively a takeover bid. If Alleyn's committee gained control of the Victoria company it intended to drop the court action. The Victoria directors, however, responded vigorously, writing to shareholders urging them to keep faith with the board.

Early on Christmas Eve 1911 Lehwess travelled from London to Beall's country house at Sunningdale to plot the agitators' response. Adopting a new tactic, they turned their attention to the proxy votes of shareholders who would be unable to attend the meeting. Later that day many shareholders received an unseasonal card in the post: it was from the agitators, posted in Sunningdale, and it asked them not to give their votes to the directors. Two days after Christmas the morning post contained yet another circular from Gowar, asking shareholders to give their proxy votes to the agitators.[18]

After this preliminary bombardment the decisive battle took place at a well-attended and refreshingly rowdy meeting of shareholders on 3 January 1912. The Victoria directors had done their homework well. The chairman launched a withering broadside publicly exposing the two conspirators.

'I think it can be irrefutably proved that behind the Lee Syndicate, who were the nominal promoters of the company, there were two gentlemen – Dr Lehwess and Mr Edward Beall – the latter having been formerly a solicitor,' said Sydenham Blandy, the Victoria company's new chairman. Lehwess, he went on, claimed to be a director of the Lee Syndicate – although this fact was not registered at Companies House – and Lehwess had promised to pay for the Victoria shares still held by the Lee Syndicate. These shares hadn't been paid for so Lehwess owed the company 'a large sum of money', said Blandy. He went on to say that Beall was to share in the promoters' secret profit.

'Furthermore,' said Blandy, 'we have information that satisfies us that Mr Edward Beall, under the name of Albrecht and Co, of 2 Thames Chambers, Adelphi, gave the first instructions for the preparation of the prospectus of this company. In this way I say that Dr Lehwess and Mr Edward Beall can be shown to have been concerned in the promotion of this company.' These gentlemen, declared Blandy, are 'the real agitators against the company' and behind the plan to hand over control of the company to a committee.[19]

These public revelations about Lehwess and Beall were fatally damaging to their attempt to wrest back control of the company. Blandy disclosed that Beall was a former solicitor. Some of those present may have remembered why he had been struck off – he had been imprisoned for fraud. When Blandy alluded to Beall's past, with all the restraint that was due in a public place, the news of his fraud conviction spread quickly in the febrile atmosphere of the meeting. The mere mention of Beall's name – and his name cropped up several times – led to audible cries of dismay.

The conclusion was inevitable. The plan to set up a committee was defeated by a large majority. What's more, the meeting passed an overwhelming vote of confidence in the directors. Beall and Lehwess retired to lick their wounds. Their reaction came in the bizarre form of an intemperate 'letter' in the correspondence column of *Rubber and Oil* and a couple of bitchy diary items. The lengthy letter accused Blandy of 'pure and undiluted calumny' and lying 'the blackest of lies'. Readers might have puzzled over exactly who were the victims of this calumny – for neither Beall nor Lehwess were mentioned in the letter, which was signed Albrecht and Co.[20]

Who was Albrecht and Co? Anyone familiar with Beall's career would have recognised it as one of his fronts. For once there was a real person behind the name. He was Rudolf Albrecht. Albrecht was married to Kate Merchant, who in turn was the daughter of James Merchant – Beall's right-hand man.

The now unstoppable Victoria court action created an acute problem for Lehwess because he was also facing a difficult court case over another one of his rubber promotions. The Malaya case was due to be heard first – and Lehwess was concerned that it would give unwelcome prominence to his dealings with the convicted fraudster Beall, which could prove extremely damaging in the other court case.[21]

Lehwess's other promotion was South Sumatra Rubber Estates.[22] Its prospectus, also launched at the peak of the rubber boom in April 1910, claimed that there were upwards of 30 000 rubber trees on the plantation owned by South Sumatra Rubber Estates. Investors rushed to back this fine prospect and the share issue was oversubscribed. But the company failed to produce a single pound of rubber let alone any profits, income or dividends. By 1911 shareholders wanted to know why.[23]

The answer wasn't hard to find: the 16 000-acre 'plantation' the company had bought was 'impenetrable jungle'. The disgruntled shareholders forced an investigation. The investigators found that the reports from two independent experts who vouched for the accuracy of the prospectus had been written on the same typewriter and had 'the appearance of being typed at the same time by the same person'.[24] They also found irregularities in the books and over-generous payments, including expenses, to various figures including Lehwess. The shareholders went to court saying they had been sold a false prospectus.

As his troubles mounted Lehwess decided it would be good to get away for a while. In January 1912 he sailed to America. In March he was enjoying some female company at the plush Hotel Shelburne in Atlantic City – she signed the register 'Mrs Lehwess' – and celebrating the early spring weather with the fashionable throng on the boardwalk.[25]

The Victoria company, not surprisingly, was eager to quiz Lehwess about his activities in court; not surprisingly, Lehwess was less keen. So while he was stepping out on the boardwalk his lawyers were at the High Court in London explaining that he had been taken ill in America and brandishing a doctor's certificate declaring Lehwess unable to undertake the rigours of an ocean voyage. The court postponed the hearing.

In April the Victoria company discovered that Lehwess was after all sailing back to Europe, although not to face the music in court. His lawyers explained that he was travelling to the French Riviera 'under doctors' orders'. It was an unlikely story and the Victoria company's lawyer suggested in an aside laden with innuendo that 'there might be reasons why he was anxious not to appear'.[26]

In truth there were several reasons why it was convenient for Lehwess to be abroad. The official receiver was about to publish his report on the Reorganisation and Control Syndicate, which could make uncomfortable reading. But the main reason was the

Chapter 21

impending South Sumatra action in which Lehwess was being sued for expenses he had taken out of the company. In May the lawyers were back in court. Lehwess was now in Menton, on the Riviera, suffering from 'nervous prostration'.

This time the Victoria company's lawyer was blunt about the motive for these manoeuvres. There was another court case pending, he said, and 'Dr Lehwess was very anxious that the present action wasn't tried before the other'. For someone so sick, Lehwess 'seemed to be able to travel a good deal,' observed the judge.[27]

The courts finally caught up with Lehwess in June, with the two cases being heard at the same time. On one notable day Lehwess had to leave off justifying his expenses claims from the South Sumatra company and rush to the court next door to answer questions about his links with Beall in the Victoria company.[28]

The Victoria company's court hearing confirmed the findings of Blandy's earlier investigation, showing how closely Beall and Lehwess had been working together – although the answer had to be dragged out of Lehwess's solicitor bit by reluctant bit. The solicitor, John Neely, was forced to concede that most of the missing money went to a man called Robert Asch. Who was Asch? He was a relative of Lehwess. Another £2000, said Neely, went to a man called Boyd.

– 'What is Boyd's real name?'
– 'Mr Edward Beall, I think.'
– 'You have heard of Mr Edward Beall, an ex-solicitor?'
– 'Yes.'
– 'And he has been in prison?'
– 'I don't know.'
– 'Do you know Asch?'
– 'I have met him.'
– 'Is Asch some relative of Dr Lehwess?'
– 'He is a connection. I don't think he is a blood relative.'
– 'Is Asch the gentleman who got a commission…for £12 000?'

– 'I suppose so.'

– 'Did you ask what Asch had done for the £12 000?'

– 'Certainly not.'[29]

When it came to his turn to be cross examined Lehwess did his best to conceal his links with Beall and the secret commission. But the attempt fell apart under questioning.

– 'Have you heard of Albrecht and Co?'

– 'Yes,' said Lehwess.

– 'They, Boyd and Beall are one and the same?'

– 'Yes.'

– 'What are Albrecht and Co?'

– 'They had a paper called *Rubber and Oil*.'

At this point the judge intervened. He wanted to know if the articles published by *Rubber and Oil* were related to Beall's share of the commission.

– 'Did it [*Rubber and Oil*] mention the company?'

– 'Yes.'

– 'Favourably or unfavourably?'

– 'Favourably.'

– 'I suppose it had nothing to do with the commission, had it?'

Lehwess conceded that Beall was going to share the secret commission with Asch.

Lehwess lost the court case – and still failed to pay so the Victoria company bankrupted the Lee Syndicate. In the end the Victoria company recouped the secret commission and compromised with Lehwess over the unpaid shares, accepting half the sum he owed.[30]

The Victoria company emerged from the grasp of Beall and Lehwess in a far better state than the electrobus company. The plantation finally started to produce rubber and in 1916 the company even started to pay dividends. The plantation went on producing rubber until the 1990s when the trees were cut down and palm oil replaced rubber.[31]

Chapter 22

The Master Blackmailer

Towards the end of 1913 Thomas Webb, the editor of the *Critic*, set a trap. It was designed to snare the most notorious gang of blackmailers of the day. When the trap was finally sprung it would result in long prison sentences for three of the gang's leading members, including the brains behind it – Edward Beall.[1]

Beall used his reptile journals to put the squeeze on dubious financiers. It was this slightly unorthodox means of introduction that led to his close working relationship with Lehwess and gained him a slice of the electrobus swindle. Magazines like *Motor Finance* and his latest venture *Rubber and Oil* liberally dispensed praise or brickbats about companies – not according to any intrinsic merit of the companies' operations but according to the money Beall thought he could make out of them. The technique had changed little since the days when Beall was blackmailing Hooley.

One of Beall's lieutenants would visit a company and explain that *Rubber and Oil* was about to publish a damaging attack on the company, which would drive down the share price and damage investors' confidence. The only way to stop the attack was to pay hush money. Alternatively, *Rubber and Oil* might print an effusive article about the company's amazing prospects. They could have 2000 copies of the magazine to distribute how they pleased. It was a snip at £500 – or sixty times the cost at the magazine's usual price.[2]

One of Beall's victims was a financier with rubber interests in Panama. Blackmail negotiations like these were highly sensitive and normally conducted through intermediaries so that both sides could, if necessary, deny having taken part in any discussions. In May 1913 the financier contacted Webb at the *Critic* to ask if he could help stop the attacks in *Rubber and Oil*.[3] Webb had toned down the *Critic* after the edgy editorship of the previous owner – Henry Hess – who had himself been jailed for fraud. Under Webb's editorship the magazine became less virulent in its attacks on bucket shops and the City's other detritus – and a much duller read.[4]

Webb was far more than a simple journalist; he was also a financial fixer and publicist. For the right price he could arrange for favourable articles about companies to appear in the financial press, lauding the achievements of anyone who was prepared to pay the piper. After being contacted by this financier the worldly wise Webb picked up the telephone and rang *Rubber and Oil*, speaking to a man who called himself Walter Miles. In return for £80 in gold Miles agreed to stop the attacks, expressing the wish that 'it would lead to further business'. After this deal Miles would ring Webb from time to time to ask 'if there was any more business on'.[5]

In November Miles turned up uninvited at the *Critic*'s offices and asked if Webb could arrange some 'business' with a man called Richard Barnett. Barnett had extensive interests in oil, from Romania to Trinidad and Venezuela. His Venezuelan oil company had just been comprehensively rubbished in *Rubber and Oil*. The company had spent more than £60000 drilling for oil and had struck only water. It was, crowed *Rubber and Oil*, 'a formidable sum for striking pure water at 333 feet'.[6]

Miles asked Webb if he knew Barnett. *Rubber and Oil*'s Christmas supplement was to contain a special feature on another of Barnett's companies, Roumanian Consolidated Oilfields. 'A similar attack on the Roumanian Consolidated would easily knock

5 shillings off the price of the shares,' said Miles. 'My people,' he added disingenuously, 'have no desire to continue the attack on Mr Barnett and wish to avoid further unpleasantness.'[7]

For once Beall had picked the wrong target. The watery results of his Venezuelan drilling may have been galling for the shareholders, but Barnett, who had trained as a barrister, was an honest man and not susceptible to blackmail. When Webb warned him about Beall's plan, Barnett turned to his solicitors, who got in touch with Scotland Yard. Between them they set up an elaborate sting to nail the elusive Edward Beall.

From this point on Webb ceased to be a neutral go-between and his every move was choreographed by the police at Scotland Yard, who relayed their instructions to him through Barnett's solicitors. Miles phoned Webb to arrange a meeting. Webb said he was very busy and asked if the meeting could be held at the *Critic*'s office. Miles agreed and said one of his colleagues called James Hayes would come to meet him. The reason for Webb's insistence on the venue had nothing to do with pressing deadlines or his other editorial labours. It was so that Barnett's solicitors had time to stage-manage a trap.

On 25 November James Hayes left his office in the Strand and took a cab to Webb's office in the City of London. It was the first time the two men had met. Miles had been a young man in his mid-twenties. He lacked gravitas and was not quite the sort of person Webb expected to carry out serious negotiations with. Hayes, in his mid-60s and sporting a splendid handlebar moustache, was much more the type. He was an accountant and clearly had a good head for figures. Ostensibly the purpose of the meeting was for the two men to do a deal on behalf of their principals, Barnett and Beall, and halt the damaging attacks.

Webb was the epitome of hospitality. Hayes sat down while Webb poured them drinks. Webb sent out the typist leaving the two men alone to have a full and frank discussion with no danger of being overheard.[8]

The two men were not quite alone, however. Sending out the typist was merely a ruse to put Hayes at his ease. An internal door leading to another room was slightly ajar. And sitting hidden behind the door scarcely daring to breathe was a private enquiry agent, Philip Willis, a retired sergeant in the Metropolitan Police, who was taking notes of what was said. Willis was there to provide the vital corroboration – evidence of blackmail that would stand up in court.

Webb's opening gambit was to offer £500, an amount he thought the Romanian group would pay. Hayes said they wanted £2000 in a mixture of cash and shares. Following the script dictated by Scotland Yard, Webb said he would convey the demand to Barnett. The real aim of these manoeuvres, however, was not to negotiate a suitable sum for the hush money but to flush out Beall.

Webb questioned whether Hayes had enough clout with Beall to ensure the attacks stopped.

'Beall has nothing to do with it,' said Hayes.

Webb knew better. 'You go and tell that in the country places, but do not tell it to a man who has been in the City 18 years,' he retorted.[9]

Hayes then claimed that he did not have influence with Beall but Miles did.

The next morning Webb took a telephone call from *Rubber and Oil.* The man at the end of the phone said his name was Carter and asked whether they could meet that afternoon in the Cabin Tea Rooms in the Strand. Webb recognised the voice as belonging to Miles.

When Webb turned up for the meeting he was met by Hayes, who explained that he had come in Carter's place. At the next table, also taking afternoon tea, was another ex-policeman, ex-superintendent Leach. Leach's presence was no coincidence; he was there to eavesdrop on the conversation. Webb said that Barnett was not prepared to hand over any shares but was willing to pay

£1000 in cash. Webb pressed Hayes to tell him exactly who it was that he was dealing with.

'There must be some responsible editor of *Rubber and Oil* and it is imperative that I should know who it is,' said Webb.

'Well, you can have it pat. Beall is the editor of *Rubber and Oil*, but I am second-in-command and Carter and Miles come after me,' said Hayes.

'That is not what you told me yesterday,' said Webb. 'If you occupy this position how long have you been on *Rubber and Oil*?'

Hayes said he had been on the magazine since it began and before that he had been on *Motor Finance*.[10]

The problem for Scotland Yard was how to ensure that Beall was snared as well as the more minor players in the blackmail. The police were well aware that Beall was the mastermind behind dozens of similar attempts at blackmail but they always lacked enough hard evidence to secure a conviction. Beall distanced himself from anything that could be construed as blackmail and left the dirty work to others. Payments were made in gold because it was untraceable.[11]

Following the meeting Webb went to see Beall himself at the offices of Albrecht and Co, just off the Strand. As far as Beall was concerned these delicate negotiations were about to reach a very successful conclusion.

'As regards the sum of £1000,' said Webb, 'I don't think there will be any difficulty about the money being forthcoming; but it is important, if the money is paid, I should have the assurance from you that there will be no renewals of the attacks.'

Beall's reply was a masterpiece of deceit. 'Mr Webb, I assure you my great characteristic has always been loyalty, and I give you my word that after this arrangement there will be no attacks.'[12]

Beall had a secret phone number, which was not listed in the telephone directory and which was only given to blackmail victims towards the end of negotiations, so that they could arrange payment. He gave the number to Webb.

The next day Webb rang Beall on the secret number and this time Barnett's solicitors and ex-police sergeant Willis listened in on an extension.

'Referring to our conversation yesterday, I think I shall be able to get it for you this morning. How shall I bring it?' asked Webb.

'All gold,' said Beall. 'I am afraid that it will be heavy, but I think it will be best.' Webb kept the appointment. But instead of bringing a heavy bag of gold he brought two police officers, who arrested Beall.[13]

A week later Edward Beall, aged 63, and 67-year-old James Merchant – Hayes's real name – were hauled up before the magistrates at Bow Street charged with demanding money with menaces. The police also issued a summons for the arrest of Walter Miles. The public prosecutor was notoriously reluctant to take on difficult financial cases so Barnett mounted a private prosecution. He hired the redoubtable Richard Muir as prosecutor.

Muir later wrote that this gang of blackmailers had for a long time terrorised dozens of public companies into paying hush money. 'The principal malefactor in this wholesale campaign of blackmail studiously kept himself in the background, although his identity was well known to the police,' Muir recalled. 'Dozens of dubious concerns paid huge money, until eventually the blackmailers made the mistake of trying to extort a large sum from a company that had nothing to fear.'[14]

Four days after the proceedings began Thomas Walter Carter, aged 26, gave himself up and admitted that he had used the name Walter Miles when he had visited Webb. A month later two other members of the gang were arraigned, including Kendall Robinson, a financial journalist who had been city editor of the *Globe*, a London evening newspaper, but who because of a drink problem had been reduced to working for the likes of Chansay and Beall.[15]

The difficulty in blackmail prosecutions is persuading the victims to appear in court, because they have something to hide.

Figure 15 The master blackmailer: Edward Beall snapped smoking his
trademark cigarette on his way to the Old Bailey in 1914.
From the *Financial News*.

In the years before the First World War London's financial centre
was a small place. Most financiers, legitimate and otherwise,
had offices in the Square Mile, or just outside. In this close-knit
community rumours spread with frightening speed and most of
Beall's targets decided it was cheaper to pay hush money than risk
the rumour mill.

Barnett and his solicitors had persuaded five of the victims of
1913 to give evidence. They all told remarkably similar stories. One
victim was George Broadbridge, who had interests in a number
of companies as well as renting offices to Captain Taylor. Taylor,
dubbed an 'evil genius' by *Rubber and Oil*, had been at odds with
Beall ever since the last days of the electrobus company and his
companies were frequently the subject of Beall's attacks.

Broadbridge was dismayed to receive a request for a list of shareholders of one of his companies from someone who was operating out of one of Beall's addresses. For those in the know it was the classic sign of an impending attack. *Rubber and Oil* began its attack and Beall distributed the magazine to all Broadbridge's shareholders, blockading his offices with people carrying *Rubber and Oil* sandwich boards, adorned with slogans such as 'Broadbridge's Bantlings', casting doubt on the legitimacy of Broadbridge's operations.[16] The point of the sandwich boards, said Muir, was to annoy the directors of the companies, frighten shareholders into selling their shares and so depress the share price.

Another victim was Edward Boxall of the Premier Oil and Pipe Line Company, who had been approached by a man calling himself Miles. Boxall had initially paid £900 in hush money. The attacks in *Rubber and Oil* ceased – only to be taken up by some ferociously damaging circulars sent to shareholders by a J Wilson of the Oil Bureau and Share Exchange. Boxall went to see Beall and asked him who Wilson was. Beall said he would make enquiries. Beall came back and said that for a further £400 the bureau's circulars would cease. Boxall paid up.[17] What Beall did not tell him was that Wilson was an alias used by Carter and that the Oil Bureau and Share Exchange operated out of an office rented by Merchant.

Muir built up his case against Beall with typical thoroughness. Although all the charges related to events in 1913 the police, who had kept Beall under surveillance since he came out of prison in 1902, knew that the blackmailing business went back many years. Beall had set up a web of deceit to thwart any attempt to prove he was the man behind the blackmail. He maintained at least three separate offices, all within easy walking distance of each other, with different operations based in each office. On top of that the main characters all used a bewildering array of false names.

Chapter 22

The task of unravelling the tangle of false names was made easier because one of Beall's associates turned King's evidence. Beall had changed his name by deed poll to Boyle when he came out of prison. But he was also known as Boyd. Merchant was normally known as Hayes – although he sometimes used the name Wilson. Teresa Grimshaw, a typist who worked closely with the two men for several years on both *Motor Finance* and *Rubber and Oil*, knew Beall as Clement and Merchant as Hayes. Carter was often known as Miles, or Mills, and he told the court that when he was first hired to work for these characters, Merchant was calling himself Whitaker.[18]

The magazine *Rubber and Oil* was owned by a private company called Rubber and Oil. There was also a linked company called the Rubber and Oil Trust & Investment Corporation, which had a sideline in share dealing for the magazine's readers. The directors of the investment corporation were Rudolf Albrecht and 'Robert Whitaker', according to the return at Companies House filed by 'Walter Miles'. Anyone who had looked into the Motor Share and Investment Trust and its efforts to offload electrobus shares might have found these names oddly familiar. The directors of the trust were Walter Miles and Robert Whitaker.[19]

The existence of Walter Miles became a running legal gag during the trial – both before the Bow Street magistrates and when the case was heard at the Old Bailey. At one stage Beall even hired a lawyer to represent the absent Miles in court, who just before Christmas 1913 gave a bravura performance – cross examining one victim about the difference between Carter and Miles even though Carter had already admitted to using the name Miles.

Beall continued to insist that the mythical Miles had a separate existence, in defiance of overwhelming evidence. But Beall was no match for Muir's forensic skills.

Beall told Muir that he and Merchant owned the company Rubber and Oil.

– 'Who were the directors?'

– 'No directors.'

– 'There were no meetings?'

– 'No.'

– 'Any minute book?'

– 'No.'

– 'A sham company?'

– 'I don't say so.'

– 'Will you be surprised to hear that Mr Walter Miles was a director?'

– 'He was.'

– 'You said there were no directors?'

– 'I think he was a director.'

– 'Did he ever direct?'

– 'I think he attended some meetings.'

– 'You said there were no meetings?'

– 'I was not present at any meeting.'

– 'What did he do?'

– 'I don't think he did anything.'

– 'Had he any control over the money, or anything?'

– 'No.'

– 'Did he get any fees?'

– 'I believe he did.'[20]

As the inquisition went on so Beall dug himself deeper into the hole. Miles, he claimed, was a friend of Merchant's. He was an artist. Muir was keen to know where 'Miles' was now, especially as the police had been searching for him for more than two months. Beall continued with evasions, saying that a few months earlier he had met with an accident. He further embroidered the story with the claim that Miles had been run over by a motor car in the Strand and was paralysed down one side.[21]

With the trial going badly Carter tried to do a deal with the prosecution. He told the lawyers: 'if the prosecution will let me down lightly I will say anything you like'. When Muir asked him about this in court Carter burst into tears.

Eventually, the jury retired. They took just 15 minutes to find Beall, Merchant, Carter and Robinson all guilty. 'I am not at all convinced that I am sentencing all the blackmailers in London by a long way,' said the judge, Charles Darling, when handing down the sentences. 'The people who set the traps and gave evidence did a great public service.'[22]

Robinson, who was in poor health, was fined £50. Merchant was jailed for 18 months, a light sentence because of his age, and Carter, who the judge said was 'the servant of brigands', got nine months. Beall was given five years.[23]

'It is no exaggeration to say that the news of the conviction of Edward Beall, the notorious blackmailer, ex-solicitor and ex-convict, was received in many a City office with a sigh of intense relief,' was the verdict of Webb, writing in the *Critic*.[24]

Beall's sentence was not too severe, commented the *Financial Times*. 'It will at all events remove from the City for a long time one of the most dangerous swindlers that it contained – dangerous not only on account of his misapplied ability, but because he seems to have constituted a centre of corruption for others.'[25]

Both Beall and Merchant appealed against their convictions and their sentences. Beall pleaded for a reduction in the length of his sentence on the grounds of ill health, because of 'chronic insomnia'. Both appeals were unsuccessful.[26]

Chapter 23

The Trendsetter

'London,' wrote H G Wells, is 'a great place. Immense. The richest town in the world, the biggest port, the greatest manufacturing town, the Imperial city, the centre of civilisation, the heart of the world.'[1]

During Queen Victoria's reign London had become the world's largest city. Cities around the world looked to London to see how it coped with its growing pains. They copied and emulated its successes – and sometimes avoided its mistakes. London's leading position in the global economy was firmly established by the Great Exhibition of 1851, the first of its kind, and the city's reputation as a trendsetter continued until the First World War.

London had the first gas street lighting. London had the first pneumatic tube for sending urgent messages to and from the Stock Exchange. Its pioneering sewage system rid the capital of waterborne diseases. London had the world's first underground railway. And the underground launched the public use of escalators when one was installed at Earls Court in 1911. Travellers were so wary of this revolutionary moving staircase that the underground hired a man with a wooden leg to ride the escalator to prove to the able-bodied that it was safe.

London also led the world in introducing motor buses. The replacement of the horse was far from a straightforward commercial decision: horse buses were cheaper to run than early motor buses. Companies bought motor buses to keep abreast of the new technology. The London motor bus boom of 1905–07 was not mirrored in other cities, which adopted a more cautious approach. By 1909 London had around 1000 motor buses – far more than any of the world's other great cities. Paris had about 150 motor buses while Berlin had around 100.[2] In New York, the Fifth Avenue Coach Company, the city's pre-eminent bus operator, had only 80 motor buses as late as 1911.[3]

The future of transport had reached a tipping point. The rival technologies of electricity, steam and petrol were vying to replace the faithful horse and only a slight nudge would tip the balance one way or another. The internal combustion engine would emerge the victor in this epic struggle and become the technology of choice for cars, buses and goods vehicles. But there was nothing inevitable about this victory and a small nudge at a critical moment could have produced a dramatically different outcome, certainly as far as commercial vehicles were concerned.

The most reliable early figures for the number of vehicles adopting the new means of locomotion come from the United States. Electricity and steam were the early front runners. In 1900 there were nearly 34000 cars with steam and electricity each fuelling nearly twice as many cars as the petrol-powered parvenus.[4] Electricity and steam were both partly proven technologies. Steam had powered the railways for 70 years while electric motors had recently become common on tramways. One of the less probable outcomes in 1900 was that a motor that depended on harnessing the power of a series of controlled explosions would win this technological struggle. 'It is only a question of a few years,' wrote one commentator, 'for the petrol and steam cars to be placed in museums and shown as monstrosities of the past.'[5]

However, it soon became apparent that the odds were stacked against the electric car. The most practical role for an electric car was as a local runabout. Their owners could go for a drive during the day and leave the battery to be charged overnight. But the petrol car tapped into a deep vein of individualism. Many early motorists had previously been cyclists and the bicycle had whetted the appetite for touring in both America and Europe. Bike rides in the country were a popular social activity in the late 19th century.[6] Exploring the wide open spaces by car was an obvious extension of cycle touring for early motorists. But for drivers of electric cars touring was an impossible dream, because of the lack of supporting infrastructure.

The basic infrastructure for motoring in a petrol-powered car was established very early on and this was true on both sides of the Atlantic. An American motorist who toured Britain by car in 1907 remarked that motor-supply depots were as numerous as inns along the main road from London to Coventry. 'Supplies of all kinds are to be had every mile or two. The careless motorist would not have far to walk should he neglect to keep up his supply of petrol.' Finding places to charge batteries was far more problematic.[7]

In the United States too, the obstacles faced by electric cars were formidable, as one American observer noted. 'The lack of proper charging facilities outside of the larger cities and towns is discouraging to those who are fond of touring. Gasoline is available everywhere and the supply can be promptly replenished, while charging a battery is always a slow job.'[8]

Electric car manufacturers fought back with adverts for one model making the extremely optimistic claim that it was 'good for 100 miles on one charge', but their efforts were fatally undermined by a lack of suitable infrastructure and a lack of standardisation.[9] There were public recharging points, but motorists venturing further afield would find the voltage incompatible or that their plug wouldn't fit. On top of that vast swathes of America didn't have electricity, even in urban areas.[10] It was a similar story in Europe where electricity was often only supplied in towns.[11]

The emphasis on long-distance motoring was really a side issue. Most journeys were local and could easily be made in an electric car. But Detroit, the town that became a metaphor for the motor industry, was already adept at selling motorists what they didn't really need. The idea of a touring car was a seductive ploy that helped to shift cars off the showroom forecourts. As one trade magazine based in Chicago put it: 'The things a gas car can do, but seldom does, are the things a brand new driver thinks he wants to do and the things an electric will not do.'[12] The car makers sold a vision rather than a vehicle. 'A manufacturer,' wrote the American journalist John Keats decades later, 'would commit economic hara-kiri if he were to sell us a car on truthful grounds.'[13]

For motor cars the decisive nudge came from Henry Ford's introduction of the Model T in 1908. The Model T was the world's first mass-produced car: Ford had taken up and improved production techniques that had been pioneered on electric cars. Its starting price in 1908 was $850 and as more people bought the car so the economies of scale kicked in and the price plummeted. By the mid-1920s it sold for $290.[14]

Clara Ford may famously have preferred electric cars because husband Henry's were too noisy, but the cost of a Detroit Electric which Clara bought in 1914 was around $2000. Of course, this was a top-of-the-range model and there were much cheaper ones, but nothing to match the price of the Model T. The average car buyer looked at the price tag and ignored the noise. By the 1920s the electric car was headed towards extinction: almost all cars on sale in America and Europe had petrol engines.[15]

The eventual triumph of petrol as the fuel of choice for commercial vehicles followed a rather different trajectory. The fortunes of the delivery vehicle were closely tied up with those of the bus. 'Steam, petrol or electricity?' asked the adverts. Despite the tainted source – this was an advert placed by the Electric Van Wagon and Omnibus Company – it was a fair enough question at the time.[16] Delivery vans had much in common with buses. The chassis for buses and goods vehicles were practically identical; it didn't matter if the vehicle was carrying sacks of coal, barrels of beer or people.[17]

Frank Searle, who as chief engineer of London's leading bus company was better placed than almost anyone to pick the winning technology, expected it to be steam.[18] His reasoning was impeccable, even if it turned out to be wrong. Steam vehicles were quieter than petrol, they didn't need troublesome gearboxes and they didn't have the range restrictions of battery power. The ideal motor bus needed to be clean, reliable and noiseless. 'The petrol bus does not fulfil these conditions. My firm belief is that we shall have to revert to the steam engine,' he wrote in June 1908.

Perhaps Searle's verdict was partly conditioned by the parlous state of his bus company, the London General, which that year lost the phenomenal sum of £140 000 as it struggled with the changeover from horses to unreliable motors. It was an exaggeration to say – as people did – that petrol buses broke down every five minutes. But not much of one.[19] It looked as though the company was heading for a breakdown like its buses. This was an opportunity that the electrobus could have capitalised on. But its potential was sapped by the swindlers milking the company's coffers.

There was certainly no shortage of interest in electric buses. Two London bus operators were sufficiently impressed by the electrobus to conduct their own experiments with electric buses.[20] When Paris drew up the terms of its new omnibus contract in 1910 it deliberately worded the contract to leave open the prospect of electric buses in the future.[21] The British government's Board of Trade, which had set up a special group to monitor London's traffic problems, was cautiously optimistic about the prospects for electric buses. 'If they can be worked at a profit they ought to succeed…Electricity has great advantages over all other kinds of power for public vehicles and if it could be adopted generally the well-founded objections to mechanical vehicles would disappear.'[22]

Commercial vehicles were the most promising market for battery power. Lead-acid batteries might be brutish and crushingly heavy, but they were surprisingly delicate. They couldn't be left uncharged for long, they couldn't be charged too fast or over-charged. Private motorists often failed to meet these demanding requirements and as a result their batteries died on them early.

Garages that ran commercial vehicles – either buses or lorries – had staff who knew how to care for batteries, as *Scientific American* pointed out. 'Electric trucks are best adapted for use in large fleets by department stores and others…because they require charging facilities and should be under the supervision of a battery expert.'[23]

Electric lorries and delivery vans became popular on both sides of the Atlantic.[24] They had largely predetermined routes and limited local mileage, which meant predictable demands on their batteries which could be recharged at a central garage. Upmarket stores were particularly keen on using electric vans for deliveries because they didn't want to disturb and annoy their wealthy customers. Gimbels and Tiffany in New York had fleets of electric vans. Harrods, the fashionable London shop, used only electric vans for deliveries until the end of 1918. The posh people's store continued to run electric vans until after the Second World War and they were still to be seen on the streets of London in the 1960s. One of them was even brought out of semi-retirement to appear in the Beatles' film *Help*.

Although there was never the same outcry about petrol vans as there was about buses, that didn't mean they were welcome. They 'barked like a dog and stank like a cat,' was one verdict.[25] A clamp-down on fumes and noise could easily have produced the decisive nudge. 'Would the nation as a whole be richer and happier if motor vehicles of all kinds had been absolutely prohibited,' asked the *Economist* in 1911.[26] It was not necessary for regulations to be as radical as that to have far-reaching consequences.

Several German cities imposed strict rules on petrol vehicles. Hamburg banned petrol taxis. When the city council eventually relented it did so in the face of protests about these 'stink bombs'.[27] After initially allowing petrol taxis on its streets Berlin decided not to grant any further licences until the industry had cleaned up its act and removed the 'loud noise and bad odour'.[28] Although the city relaxed its rules in the run-up to the First World War its rigorous licensing regime ensured that electric taxis flourished in Berlin until well into the 1920s.[29]

However, it was the trends in London that had global influence. Britain's attempts at regulation were half-hearted and ineffectual. The turning point came in 1908–09 when the government had two distinct opportunities to establish a regime that favoured electric vehicles. The British approach to environmental control was informed by the doctrine of 'best practicable means', a phrase enshrined in 19th-century legislation established to govern pollution from cement works.[30] Public pressure to tackle motor vehicle noise, and to a lesser extent fumes, was mounting. But instead of establishing rules that favoured electric vehicles, the Home Office sidestepped the issue. In the absence of an objective way of measuring vehicle noise the government decided instead to limit the maximum weight of buses – on the grounds that heavier vehicles were more likely to be noisier than lighter ones.

A second opportunity for decisive action came later in 1909 when the London General Omnibus Company, which now had a near monopoly in the capital after taking over all its main competitors, produced a new type of bus. The bus, which was designed by Searle, was the product of extensive research. However, when the company submitted the bus to Scotland Yard for its approval the police turned it down because it was so noisy. This was a major embarrassment for the London General because it was building several dozen of these buses. It was only after considerable lobbying by the company that the Home Office decided to bend the rules and the police licensed the bus. This decision was critically important because the bus was the forerunner of the standard London bus.[31]

Chapter 23

The first standard London bus, a development of the deafening prototype, was introduced in October 1910. It was the omnibus equivalent of the Ford Model T. Thanks to mass production, the bus cost just £300 – less than half the cost of an electrobus. The new buses had become cheaper to run too, and by 1912 motor buses were cheaper than either horse buses or tramcars.[32] So the government had flunked its chance to curb this environmental nuisance and the advent of cheap motor buses shifted the balance in favour of the malodorous petrol vehicle.

The continuing increase in the number of motor buses brought fresh protests, with the focus moving from smell and noise to accidents. The streets were noisy places, with the clash of iron rims on cobbles from the horse-drawn traffic, punctuated by the sound of street vendors and newspaper sellers trying to shout above the general hubbub. Distracted by the din, pedestrians often failed to notice the danger of an approaching motor vehicle. The combination of poor brakes and a heavy bus could be lethal. The death toll led social reformers Beatrice and Sidney Webb to protest about this 'murderous invasion of our streets'. In October 1912 the latest figures showed that in the previous year motor buses had killed 144 people in London – including 24 children.[33]

Despite the victory of the petrol bus battery-powered commercial vehicles continued to flourish for several years. Part of the reason for this was that electric vehicles although expensive to buy were often cheaper to run. Impartial figures for the cost of operating petrol and electric vehicles are rare. It all depended on who you asked. The manufacturers of electric vehicles claimed they were cheaper, while the makers of petrol vehicles told the opposite story. Their figures were invariably slanted to suit a particular narrative. One of the few reasonably scientific comparisons of costs was carried out over three years between 1911 to 1914 by researchers at the Massachusetts Institute of Technology, in a study financed by the electricity industry.

The researchers studied goods vehicles delivering parcels, coal and beer and moving furniture in the Boston area. They fitted them with primitive tachographs, measured the distance they covered and the time they took and calculated the cost of making their deliveries. Some of the vehicles were electric, some petrol and the rest were horse-drawn.

The results provide the most accurate picture we have of the contemporary balance of costs for running electric and petrol vehicles, at least for the Boston area. It didn't matter whether the vehicles were being used for delivering light parcels or heavy loads of coal, electric vehicles were generally the cheapest method and the most expensive option was the petrol lorry.[34] For most tasks, petrol was about a fifth more expensive than an electric vehicle. The researchers concluded that for short distance work, of less than two miles from base, horses were still the best. But for deliveries of up to ten miles an electric vehicle was the best choice. For customers who lived further afield the practical choice was a petrol lorry because of the battery vehicle's limited range.[35]

This cost advantage meant that electric goods vehicles continued to be popular until well after the First World War. In some places their numbers continued to grow during the 1920s.[36] In Germany, for example, the post office had a large fleet of electric vehicles until the Second World War. In 1930s Berlin the post office's electric parcels vans still outnumbered petrol vans by nearly two to one, with petrol vehicles reserved for deliveries in more remote suburbs.

So why did the electric van cease to flourish? Partly it was a question of the cost of buying new vehicles. Electric vehicles were made in small numbers, while petrol vehicles were increasingly mass produced, especially after the end of the First World War.[37] So although electric vehicles lasted longer and the industry argued that they were cheaper in the long run many companies bought petrol because it was a cheap and easy fix. The durability of electric vehicles was a double-edged sword. It was both an advantage – because it reduced the need for frequent replacements – and a drawback. In an age when modernity was all the rage an electric vehicle soon looked outmoded. Making deliveries in a ten-year-old van didn't project an image of a dynamic go-getting company.[38]

There was also a more subtle reason. The range of an electric vehicle was limited. This didn't matter in towns and cities where most customers lived locally. Nor did it matter for companies with large fleets of delivery vehicles, because like the German post office they could keep petrol vehicles for the longer-distance jobs. But it did matter to smaller companies. A contemporary petrol van could cover nearly five times the area of the electric equivalent so a firm with just one vehicle risked cutting themselves off from their more distant customers if they bought electric. An electric vehicle might be slightly cheaper in the long run, but it was a false economy if it meant abandoning customers.[39]

For smaller companies, buying petrol was a no-brainer: it gave them more flexibility. The economics of the electric van was further undermined by suburban sprawl, the predominant feature of urbanisation in the 20th century. Companies and traders providing services in far-flung suburbs had little option but to buy petrol vehicles.

By the Second World War the electric vehicle was in steep decline all around the world. The widespread adoption of the more efficient diesel engines, especially for commercial vehicles, further undermined the economics of electric vehicles. Even the electricity industry gave up this unequal struggle: the Edison company in Chicago retired its last electric vehicle 'Old Juice Box' in 1947. From time to time someone would design a new electric car. Or a town would try out an electric bus. There would be a flurry of publicity. And then nothing. It was, it seemed, the end of the road for the electric vehicle. Even the most ardent advocate could not have foreseen that within a few years there would be a major revival of battery-powered vehicles.

This comeback was all the more extraordinary because the phenomenon was limited to a single country – Britain. By the mid-1960s, there were 51 000 electric vehicles on Britain's streets, a figure that rivalled the total number of electric vehicles in the world during the golden age before the First World War.[40]

Most of these vehicles were delivery vans and by far the most common type was the humble milk float. These days the emerging electric car industry is keen to distance itself from the image of the milk float. It's easy to see why. The advertising for one electric car emphasises it can accelerate from 0 to 60 miles per hour in just over 7 seconds.[41] The standard jibe about the milk float, which was weighed down with 1.5 tons of lead-acid battery, was that it could accelerate from 0 to 60 in a fortnight.

Electric vehicle technology had stagnated for decades. The technology of the milk float was not much different from that of the electrobus. They both had lead-acid batteries. The heavy battery may have made the milk float seem sluggish but it was extremely well adapted to its job – stopping at one house to deliver the milk (and pick up the empties) and then moving a few yards to repeat the process at the next house.

Delivering the daily pinta was a long-standing tradition in Britain. Refrigerators were rare: in 1948 only 2 per cent of families had a fridge and early morning deliveries were the best way to ensure that the family had fresh milk to go with their breakfast. Originally horse power delivered the milk, but electric milk floats finally ousted the horse after the Second World War.

One of the key reasons for replacing horses with electric vehicles was that they were quiet, so the milkman would not wake his customers when delivering at 5 am. Chloride, the company that made batteries for both milk floats and the electrobus, had no doubt why milk floats were so common. 'Imagine the smell if they all ran on petrol. Not to mention the noise,' said the company. At their peak in the 1970s Britain had 40 000 milk floats.[42]

By the 1980s Britain's fleet of electric vehicles had gone into steep decline. The decline had nothing to do with the deficiencies of electric vehicles and everything to do with wider social, economic and political changes. As more and more people acquired refrigerators – and by the millennium 99 per cent of families had a fridge – people could keep milk for longer, removing the need for daily deliveries. On top of this it became cheaper to buy milk in supermarkets, because a change in the law meant that suppliers could no longer, fix the price of milk. The supermarkets gained a stranglehold on milk supplies and undercut the cost of the doorstep deliveries.[43]

Once one of the most common sights in Britain's suburban streets, the milkman delivering milk and picking up the empties, is now largely a thing of the past. As are glass milk bottles, which were taken back to the dairies, pasteurised and reused. The market that had fostered the electric milk float has now largely vanished.

Chapter 24

A New Tipping Point

In January 2011 United States President Barack Obama used his State of the Union address to launch a presidential initiative to put a million electric vehicles – mostly cars – on the roads by 2015, backing his pledge with cash incentives for consumers and a boost in federal funding for research. 'With more research and incentives, we can break our dependence on oil with biofuels, and become the first country to have a million electric vehicles on the road by 2015,' said Obama.[1]

It was a spectacular headline-grabbing pledge that had its genesis in plans to promote 'clean energy' first announced by Obama's energy secretary Steven Chu at the UN climate change conference in Copenhagen in December 2009. Chu had a track record of promoting renewable sources of energy and nuclear power at the expense of fossil fuel. He was an influential voice at the Copenhagen meeting, partly because of his impressive scientific credentials – he was a joint winner of the Nobel Prize for Physics in 1997.

In July 2010 Chu convened a meeting of energy ministers from the world's major energy users in Washington DC. The meeting came up with a series of measures to reduce air pollution and emissions of greenhouse gases. 'This issue is so important,' Chu told the meeting, 'that it is the defining scientific challenge of today.'[2]

One of a series of measures to emerge from the Washington meeting was that China and the United States agreed to take the lead in promoting electric vehicles, in conjunction with the Paris-based International Energy Agency. The mainstream media concentrated on other measures agreed by the meeting leaving the electric vehicle initiative to be reported in the trade press and specialist environmental outlets. But this often-overlooked initiative has given a tangible boost to electric vehicles.

Hot on the heels of Obama's pledge came China's announcement that it was going to increase its production of plug-in electric vehicles – a term that includes not just pure battery vehicles, but also electric vehicles with a supplementary petrol engine – to 2 million a year by 2020.[3]

Air pollution, alongside climate change, is one of the key challenges of today. Ironically, the internal combustion engine was originally welcomed as a way of reducing air pollution. A hundred years ago London had around 50000 horses in public transport – buses and cabs. Each working horse produced 15 to 35 pounds of manure a day.[4] When it was dry the dung became a powdery dust that blew around in the breeze. When it was wet the mixture spread, forming a thin slippery coating over the surface of the road.

In the last years of the 19th century Tory politician Randolph Churchill complained that he could not find 'denunciatory adjectives' adequate to describe the 'filth and pollution of most West-end streets'. He nevertheless went on to try. 'The nauseating smell, the peculiar character of the dust, coarse polluted with bad acids, which the eyes, nose and mucous membrane of those who perambulate the thoroughfares have to resist.'[5]

We now have a far clearer understanding of how serious a problem modern pollution is. Today one of the most worrying sources of pollution in cities is the diesel exhausts of buses, cars and lorries, which are a potent source of both nitrogen oxides (NO_x) and tiny particles coated with a cocktail of carcinogenic chemicals, known as $PM_{2.5}$ (if their diameter is less than 2.5 micrometres). In London alone nearly 9500 people a year die prematurely largely as a result of breathing in particles and NO_x produced by vehicle exhausts.[6] According to the World Health Organization, outdoor air pollution from all sources is now the world's biggest single cause of death. It kills 3 million people a year, more than malaria.[7]

The United States missed Obama's target and it now says it will not reach its goal of 1 million electric vehicles until 2020.[8] Despite the missed target there has been extraordinary growth in the number of electric vehicles, almost all of it in the 16 countries that signed up to the International Energy Agency's Electric Vehicle Initiative. In 2011 the number of electric vehicles in the world topped 50000, which was claimed to be an all-time high. Growth since then has been spectacular. By the end of 2015 there were 1.25 million electric vehicles around the world.[9]

One country that didn't miss its target is Norway, a nation where 96 per cent of electricity comes from renewable sources, mostly hydropower. The government had been phasing in incentives for drivers to buy electric cars since 1990 and the Norwegian parliament set a goal of putting 50000 electric vehicles on the road by 2018. The incentives have become more and more generous over the years and as a result Norway reached its target three years early in May 2015.

One of the key reasons for the growth in the number of electric vehicles, and particularly the number of electric cars, is that the countries backing the electric vehicle initiative have poured substantial sums of money into promoting them, partly to compensate for a century of technological stagnation.

Surveys have consistently shown that drivers are reluctant to swap their internal combustion engines for electric motors. There are three main reasons.[10] One is unfamiliarity – many motorists simply prefer to stick with the tried and tested. The high cost of buying an electric car is also a major drawback. You would have to be a very keen environmentalist to pay an extra £10000 or more for your car. Finally, there is 'range anxiety' – the fear of finding yourself marooned with a flat battery a long way from home.

The countries that are part of the electric vehicle initiative have adopted a three-pronged strategy to make electric vehicles more attractive. By 2014 they had spent some $7.5 billion on research and development, with the aim of making cheaper and more powerful batteries. These countries have also handed out more than $5 billion in subsidies to buyers of new electric cars. Finally, a further $2.5 billion has been spent on infrastructure, such as public charging points.

These measures are starting to have an impact. When General Motors launched its first electric car in 1996, it still had lead-acid batteries – the same technology that powered the electrobus. Lead-acid batteries were heavy but dependable, short-lived but cheap. Most modern cars now use lithium-ion batteries – similar to those that power your laptop or mobile phone. These batteries are far lighter, giving cars greater range.

The performance and cost of batteries has improved by leaps and bounds. The energy density, the power output per unit of weight, is now three times higher than it was, while the cost of lithium-ion batteries is only a quarter of what it was in 2008. The new batteries are also proving durable and reliable. According to Nissan, engine breakdowns in conventional cars are 25 times more common than battery failure.[11]

For most drivers, range anxiety is largely a question of perception. Most journeys are relatively short. In Britain 96 per cent of car journeys are less than 50 miles. The occasional longer journey is more of a problem and there has been a big push to improve the infrastructure for drivers of electric cars. Drivers of conventional cars expect to be able to top up their tanks – or top up their water – at the nearest service station, and most roads have a service station every few miles.

Five years ago it was rare to see a public charging point for electric vehicles. Drivers of electric cars were, in the phrase that was popularly used to disparage electric cars a hundred years ago, still 'slave to a wire'. Now this is changing. There are more than 12 000 charging points in the Netherlands, compared to 3600 petrol stations. Japan too has more electric charging points than petrol stations.[12]

Of course, there are big differences between a charging point and a petrol station. Charging points may only cater for one vehicle at a time and while it takes only a couple of minutes to fill a petrol tank charging a battery can take eight hours. It is possible to cut the time for a recharge to 30 minutes through the use of rapid charging, although repeated use of this technique reduces battery life.

Most countries that are part of the electric vehicle initiative offer subsidies to people who buy new electric cars. The deals vary from country to country. In Norway the subsidies are on such a scale that it costs no more to buy an electric vehicle than the petrol equivalent. This is a major reason why the country met its target ahead of schedule.

In the past two years the economics of electric vehicles have been hit by a double whammy. Some countries are beginning to rein back on subsidies, while the collapse in the price of oil in 2015 made petrol cheaper.[13] Surprisingly there has been no noticeable impact on growth. The number of electric vehicles continued to rise strongly throughout 2015. Despite this, the number of conventional cars – currently estimated to total 1.2 billion – still dwarfs the number of electrics.

Perhaps the best indicator of long-term trends is the number of models of electric cars, because it reflects the investment made by the motoring industry. If you wanted to buy an electric car in Britain in 2011 you had a choice of just nine models. By 2016 there was a choice of 35.[14]

'The market is approaching a tipping point, where battery power will become as normal as petrol or diesel,' Ian Robertson, BMW's global marketing chief, was quoted as saying in 2014. 'There's no doubt that it's coming and it's coming quickly,' he said.[15] According to analysts at Bloomberg New Energy Finance, the tipping point will come sometime in the next decade, when it will become cheaper to buy and run an electric car than a conventional one even without subsidies. The reason is that the price of vehicle batteries will continue to tumble: Bloomberg's researchers expect the cost of a vehicle battery in the 2020s to be around a third that of today.[16]

There is a tendency to see the evolution of technology as a kind of Darwinian progress. The technology that we see now is the result of the survival of the fittest. This glib assumption underlies many books about the history of technology. But the evidence doesn't always support this notion. 'A technology does not succeed, because it is technologically superior, but it is considered technologically superior, because it has…succeeded, as one specialist in the development of technology has pointed out.'[17] The success of one technology over a rival is at least partly a matter of chance and inferior technologies sometimes gain the upper hand.[18]

Perhaps the best known example of this in recent years was the format wars between the VHS video tape, which was developed by JVC, and the rival Betamax, developed by Sony. Betamax captured pictures and sound better but VHS was cheaper, an advantage that proved decisive among consumers.[19]

Once VHS had edged ahead of Betamax reinforcing feedbacks kicked in, enabling VHS to consolidate its lead. Films began to be released on VHS, but not Betamax. If you wanted to know who was winning the format wars in the late 1980s you only had to walk into your local video rental shop. There was shelf after shelf of different genres, westerns, thrillers, comedies, television programmes and so on. They were all VHS videos. Tucked away in the corner at the back of the shop was a rack marked Betamax with a few dozen titles.[20] As the choice of video titles withered so the number of buyers of Betamax recorders vanished. And so it was that VHS won the format wars.

These feedbacks are crucially important to the success of a developing technology. The early widespread availability of petrol in hardware stores and other shops was the essential underpinning for the growth of the motor car, while the lack of suitable infrastructure for swapping or recharging batteries stymied the electric car. These feedbacks can make or break a technology – or ensure that it is confined to a niche market like the milk float.

For its time the electrobus was among the most technologically advanced and reliable vehicles on the streets. But from conception to death and beyond the electrobus project was riddled with fraud. Such was the scale of the fraud that the bus was doomed to failure. Well engineered as it was, it never stood a chance.

What would have happened if the electrobus had not been in the clutches of a group of swindlers? Any answer must be hypothetical and dozens of different narratives are possible. It could have made a huge difference, it may have made very little. There were a handful of key events in the modern development of transport. One was the advent of the Ford Model T, which set the electric car on the road to extinction. Mass production made petrol cars so cheap that electric cars could not compete.

The story of commercial vehicles is more complex because the fortunes of buses and goods vehicles were so closely tied together. The economic case for buying petrol buses and goods vehicles was far from clear-cut. Electric vehicles often had the edge for making local deliveries because of their lower running costs. But petrol vehicles were becoming increasingly cheaper to buy. Some companies took the long view and bought electric calculating that they would recoup the extra cost of buying electric from the cheaper long-term running costs. For other companies the environmental advantages were a decisive factor, so they continued to buy battery-powered vehicles for delivering goods long after the collapse of the electrobus. Would tougher regulations have tipped the balance in favour of the electric vehicle? In 1908–09 the British government twice failed to grasp the opportunity to control vehicle noise. Consequently the petrol bus gained the ascendancy and ousted its rivals. The battery bus disappeared, as did the steam bus. The electric goods vehicle clung on for a few decades, before it too faltered in the face of the all-conquering motor vehicle.

From the start the public was firmly in favour of electric vehicles and in particular electric buses. But for the bogus patent, the electrobus flotation would almost certainly have been fully subscribed. A successful launch by a financially responsible company could easily have seen hundreds of electric buses on the streets of London, providing tough competition for the petrol bus at exactly the moment when it was most vulnerable. An immediate consequence would have been to cut the cost of manufacturing electric buses and goods vehicles. The electrobus was overpriced anyway, but if a standard electric bus had been produced in sizeable numbers the cost of buying electric would have dropped dramatically. When London eventually adopted a standard petrol bus in 1911, and started making them in their hundreds, the cost of a bus fell by about a half. What might have happened next is a tougher question to answer. There are dozens of ways subsequent events could have unfolded.

One of the more plausible outcomes is that the British government would have deemed the electric vehicle the 'best practicable means' of motor transport. The next logical step – and one that was urged on the government at the time by its own backbenchers – would have been to lay down strict regulations on noise and fumes that vehicles must comply with, using the electric vehicle as the gold standard. Tough controls on noise and pollution would have seen electric buses and vans becoming the normal commercial vehicles on city streets.[21] This sequence of events provides a tantalising glimpse of a completely different future to the one that we're familiar with.

The consequences of such a development could have been enormous with investors backing electric vehicles instead of petrol power. It could have spurred the development of better batteries and perhaps more generally given a boost to other forms of electric transport. Of course, large fleets of electric buses and lorries could not survive without any supporting infrastructure, so the proliferation of electric vehicles would be accompanied by the development of a network of stations for recharging and swapping batteries. This network already existed in embryo a hundred years ago on both sides of the Atlantic but it withered away in the face of a flood of petrol vehicles.

Maybe the owners of charging stations would have tried to attract private motorists as well as delivery vehicles, which in turn could have rekindled public interest in electric cars. This type of feedback would have been a critical step in the transformation of a developing technology into an established one.

There would also be more far-reaching knock-on effects, including a hard-to-predict impact on the development of cities. Would suburban sprawl have been reduced by the more limited range of electric vehicles? Not all the impacts of electric transport would necessarily have been benign. Coal-fired power stations are an important source of pollution in city centres, so the widespread use of electric vehicles could have made urban smogs worse.

One thing is pretty certain: the electric vehicle wouldn't have been stuck in the doldrums for a century and today's electric revival wouldn't have had to start from zero. Our cities could have been a whole lot cleaner, healthier and quieter. The electrobus swindle didn't just impoverish the shareholders of Edwardian England. We were all robbed.

Today we have come full circle. It's hard to escape the echoes of the past. In 2016 Sadiq Khan, mayor of London, announced plans to run 300 electric buses in central London by 2020. If the figure sounds familiar that's because it is. This is precisely the number of buses the London Electrobus Company promised to put on the road 110 years ago. However, today's electric buses are not beset by the same problems that overwhelmed the electrobus.

In September 2016 the first of the modern electric buses started running from Victoria Station on a route that takes them past the old electrobus garage in Horseferry Road. The garage has long since been demolished and the site redeveloped. It is now the headquarters of the government's Department for Transport.[22]

Transport for London is also taking delivery of some new double-deck electric buses, the city's first electric double-deckers in more than a century. The new buses use Chinese battery technology which gives them a range of 190 miles – around five times the range of the old electrobus. In 2017 they are due to start running on a route that last saw an electric bus in 1909, starting their journey in central London and travelling into the north-western suburbs. Their route will take them up the Edgware Road and past the site of the now-demolished Oxford Restaurant.

Figure 16 Look, no exhaust fumes: two electric buses in the same place more than a century apart. An electrobus leaving the garage for Horseferry Road (top) and a modern electric bus (below) in Horseferry Road. The site of the garage has been redeveloped twice in the intervening years. The arch on the right of the modern office block (below), where electrobuses once left the garage to turn into Horseferry Road, is now the entrance to the offices of the Department for Transport.

Epilogue

The outbreak of the First World War proved a watershed for most of the greatest swindlers of the Edwardian era. Ernest Terah Hooley's criminal career had been in terminal decline ever since his unsuccessful prosecution for fraud in 1904. He avoided jail then but couldn't avoid being jailed for more minor frauds in 1912 and again in 1921.

Horatio Bottomley had quite a good war, surrounding himself with the Union flag and using his magazine *John Bull* to stoke up patriotic fervour. The law finally caught up with him after the war when his Victory Bond scheme was exposed as fraudulent. He raised money from the public to invest in the government's Victory Bond but then diverted it to subsidise his extravagant lifestyle. He was jailed for seven years. He briefly met his old friend and fellow fraudster Hooley in Wormwood Scrubs before they went their separate ways – Bottomley to Maidstone and Hooley to Parkhurst.[1]

Harry Lawson was a much diminished figure. Once he had been Lehwess's role model, but now the positions were if anything reversed. Lawson moved into rubber around the same time as Lehwess. Lawson's hopes of regaining his fortune with a rubber company in the Belgian Congo collapsed and his efforts to control the British Blériot aircraft company also fell apart. Both companies collapsed amid accusations of fraud.[2]

At the outbreak of war Edward 'Teddy' Beall was safely locked up in prison and he wasn't released until the end of 1917.[3] Joseph Chansay was last heard of in an Italian jail and the Greek adventurer, Demetrius Delyannis, fled to Greece after Britain got too hot for him. Captain John Taylor went bankrupt. Thomas Garlick became the managing director of a Derbyshire colliery after he emerged from prison and devoted himself to charitable works, according to his obituary.[4] Lehwess continued his career in company promotions, but with mixed results. The common factors in almost all his promotions were duped financiers and disgruntled shareholders, who accused him of misrepresentation, fraud and secretly skimming off the profits.[5]

The Electric Vehicle Company was now Lehwess's main company, but it had less and less to do with electric vehicles. As early as 1910 the company took a stand at the annual air show held at Hendon aerodrome in North London. The 'insuppressible' Lehwess, as one journalist described him, was incongruously peddling something called 'power gas' – a product that had little to do with vehicles, nor electricity.[6]

These activities were plainly lucrative. In the summer of 1911 Lehwess took his mother and his 18-year-old niece on a protracted jaunt to North America where they visited the Niagara Falls and toured Canada and the United States. As ever, Lehwess was mixing business with pleasure. He travelled to Newfoundland with a commission to negotiate timber rights. The burgeoning newspaper industry had a voracious appetite for newsprint and was constantly looking for new sources of wood pulp. According to one garbled report Lehwess was negotiating on behalf of Bottomley.[7]

To make the move into aeronautics more credible the Electric Vehicle Company changed its name for the fourth time – becoming the Mechanical and General Inventions Company in 1913. The following year the company became the British representative for Albatroswerke, one of the foremost German aeroplane manufacturers. As part of the deal Albatroswerke agreed to send its latest biplane to Britain on approval, giving Lehwess not just the option to buy it but also the right to manufacture the aircraft in Britain. The plane won much praise when was exhibited at the 1914 air show. 'The equal of the best of British machines,' was the verdict of the specialist magazine *Flight*.[8]

But the Germans had second thoughts and asked for their plane back. Perhaps the company began to entertain doubts about the wisdom of getting into bed with Lehwess. Under the agreement Lehwess would set up a new £20 000 company to manufacture the plane – a deal uncannily reminiscent of the one Lehwess made with American battery manufacturer Charles Gould. Had someone in Albatroswerke carried out a background check on Lehwess? It certainly opened negotiations with a better established aeronautical company around the same time.

An equally plausible explanation for the change of mind is that with war clouds gathering Germany was sensitive about its cutting-edge military equipment falling into British hands. Britain was lagging behind Germany in the aeronautical arms race, according to the British Committee for Imperial Defence.[9] Under the deal with Lehwess the German company was to provide detailed blueprints of the plane so that it could be manufactured locally. German sensitivity could only have been heightened when Lehwess acquired a new associate – a British army officer with a keen interest in flying – who later joined the board of Mechanical and General Inventions, with the War Office's blessing.[10] Whatever the real explanation, Albatroswerke would never see its plane again.

Lehwess refused to return the biplane and went to court to prevent the Germans getting their hands on it. The case was still pending when war broke out on 4 August 1914. The next day Mechanical and General Inventions wrote to the British government offering to sell them this jewel of German technology. At a meeting between Lehwess, his new chief of staff George

Ractliffe, the elder brother of his private secretary Elsie, and Sefton Brancker of the Royal Flying Corps – later Air Vice-Marshall Sir Sefton Brancker – the government agreed to take the plane, leaving the question of payment to be sorted out later.[11]

In June 1915 Lehwess was finally locked up. But his incarceration had nothing to do with any of his multifarious scams. He was imprisoned simply for being German.

Maybe Lehwess had hoped that handing over the Albatros biplane to the British government would give him some immunity from the general anti-German sentiment. If he did he was mistaken. That year, following the sinking of the transatlantic liner *Lusitania* by a German U-boat, the British government rounded up German civilians living in Britain and interned them. Lehwess was one of thousands of Germans caught up in this indiscriminate trawl. He was interned alongside 20 000 others in Knockaloe camp on the Isle of Man.[12] His 72-year-old mother Jenny was deported to Switzerland. From there she crossed the border into Germany and went to live in Berlin.

Not long after being interned Lehwess was summoned to London to attend the High Court, as part of the continuing litigation surrounding the South Sumatra company. Lehwess realised that it was only a matter of time before the government seized control of the Mechanical and General Inventions Company under emergency wartime legislation which gave it the power to take over German companies and liquidate their assets. So while enjoying his temporary spell of freedom in London, he took the opportunity to visit his offices. He removed some of the company's more incriminating books, including the Electric Vehicle Company's books for 1909 and 1910. They would never be seen again.[13]

Towards the end of the war Lehwess was released from internment – in one of the first batches of civilians to be liberated under a wider repatriation deal agreed between Britain and

Germany. On 23 March 1918 he sailed from Boston in Lincolnshire to the port of Rotterdam in the Netherlands, which was neutral.[14] The number of belongings internees could take was strictly limited, so Lehwess sailed with little more than hand baggage, which was very definitely not his style. Once he reached the Netherlands one of his first moves was to ask for the luggage he had been forced to leave behind.

This was decidedly upmarket baggage, of the kind that could be seen among the first-class cabins of a crack transtlantic liner. There were a dozen pieces, including Gladstone bags, leather suitcases and sea chests mostly bearing his initials. One monogrammed suitcase had silver fittings and contained pearl tie pins and pearl shirt studs.

The British Foreign Office was rather sniffy about Lehwess's request – which was transmitted through the Swiss government – not the least because internees often tried to smuggle out forbidden items, such as money, in hiding places such as trunks with false bottoms. One Foreign Office official noted: 'This man is a rogue. I have heard of him before the war. What reply?'[15] Finally the government grudgingly agreed to let him have his luggage.

The government also wound up hundreds of German-owned companies in Britain. In December 1916 – some six months after Lehwess had removed the incriminating books – the Mechanical and General Inventions Company fell into the hands of the official receiver. The process of liquidating the company would take several years.

Despite 'the absence of the principal books and documents' the official receiver managed to reconstruct a makeshift account of the company's transactions. This process revealed the extent to which Lehwess had used the company's bank account as his own. He owed the company nearly £8000 – a combination of unpaid debts and 88 company cheques that Lehwess had cashed to finance his lavish lifestyle. Lehwess treated the company's bank accounts as his own, observed his private secretary Elsie Ractliffe.[16]

The threat to his company brought a virtuoso display of evasion. Lehwess's first ploy was the debenture dodge. In 1920 one Emmanuel Ginsbourger, who lived in Paris, suddenly turned up clutching £2000 of debentures issued by the Electric Vehicle Company. The company hadn't paid any interest on the bonds and Ginsbourger now had a claim on the company's assets.

This had all the hallmarks of a put-up job, as the official receiver well knew. His discovery a few months later that Ginsbourger was Lehwess's brother-in-law did nothing to dispel his scepticism. In June 1913 Lehwess had married Cecile Ginsbourge and despite the difference in spelling of the surname Cecile and Emmanuel were siblings.[17]

The debentures were issued in mysterious circumstances in January 1910 – precisely the period covered by the missing books – and were subsequently passed around the Lehwess family from Lehwess's mother to his brother-in-law. The company's bank statements from 1910 didn't show a corresponding payment of £2000 – as they should have done – although there was an unexplained receipt for around half this amount. Ten years after the event the bank no longer had any record of who made the payment. The remainder of the purchase price of the debentures, claimed Ginsbourger, was made up by the sale to the company of some second-hand electric cars.[18]

But the clinching factor in Lehwess's campaign to regain control of his company was the Treaty of Versailles. Lehwess always had a penchant for keeping things in the family. The overwhelming majority of shareholders in the Mechanical and General Inventions Company were relatives of Lehwess or his wife.[19] Cecile and her family came from Alsace, which had been German before the war, but now reverted to France under the Treaty of Versailles. Lehwess applied his legal acumen to studying the treaty.

Cecile was now French. And Lehwess himself, as the husband of a Frenchwoman, exercised his right under the treaty to become a French national in September 1920, backdated to Armistice Day – 11 November 1918.[20] And for good measure his mother Jenny Lehwess took advantage of changes in Germany's eastern border and took Polish citizenship – even though she continued to live in Berlin.

At this point the official receiver, whose expertise was in balance sheets and company law, understandably decided to give up grappling with clauses 1 and 2 of sub-section 6 in the Annex referring to Alsace-Lorraine in the Treaty of Versailles. He let Lehwess have his company back.

From his new base in Paris Lehwess now tried to get the British government to pay him for the Albatros biplane. The government was reluctant to pay, not least because Lehwess had never paid for the plane in the first place. Eventually the government gave ground: it agreed to pay Lehwess the notional profit he would have made if he had bought the plane and then sold it to the government – plus interest at 5 per cent. The decision earned Lehwess nearly £800 for risking very little.[21]

Lehwess was the only one of the electrobus swindlers to have a significant career after the war. With a home in Paris he was a familiar figure on the cross-Channel ferries in the 1920s. His main business now was selling a device called the Controlograph – an early version of a tachograph – and he set up companies in both Britain and France. How ironic. Lehwess had several convictions for speeding and had frequently been accused of fraud. He was now selling a tamper-proof spy-in-the-car. His sales pitch was that the Controlograph had two key advantages. First, it recorded vehicle speed, so drivers wouldn't break the speed limit, and second, it recorded mileage – to prevent fraudulent claims for petrol expenses.

Britain introduced a 30 mile-per-hour speed limit in March 1935. Lehwess lobbied Scotland Yard to adopt the device as a way of automatically ensuring that drivers didn't break the speed limit. The police weren't at all keen to deal with him and didn't reply to his initial letter. Undeterred, Lehwess enlisted the support of Linton Thorp, an eminent lawyer, MP and the son of one of the founding shareholders of the Asiatic Bank. Scotland Yard fobbed off Thorp with a non-committal reply. At the bottom of the yard's carbon copy a handwritten warning about Lehwess has been added, showing that the police were well aware of his activities and didn't want to have dealings with him.[22]

Much of the Mechanical and General Inventions Company's business was buying up the rights to inventions, patenting them and developing them.[23] In the summer of 1928 Lehwess once again took the ferry to England to meet Sir Herbert Austin, the head of the Austin Motor Company. The two men had known each other since the turn of the century when they were both members of what was now the Royal Automobile Club. Lehwess had a new invention, which he thought Austin would be interested in – a sunshine roof for motor cars. He had applied for a patent for the sunshine roof in May, but the patent wouldn't be granted for another six months.

Austin was very interested. Other manufacturers had played around with the idea for several years but their designs were prone to leak. Lehwess gave Austin a test drive in a car fitted with his sunshine roof and showed him the plans, which were still unprotected by patent. But instead of licensing the invention Austin patented his own sunshine roof. Lehwess accused Austin of cheating, saying that he had ripped off the key principles of a sunshine roof when he had examined Lehwess's patent. There was no record of the meeting and Austin denied everything.

The 'sunshine roof case' as it was known became one of the most celebrated and costly legal actions of the 1930s. Austin accused Lehwess of blackmail – saying he was hoping Austin would pay up rather than be dragged through the courts. Lehwess was evasive when he gave evidence. Austin's lawyers said he only told the truth when 'there was a document staring him in the face'.[24] So who was cheating whom? The courts found it hard to decide. The verdict went first one way, then the other and finally back again.

Lehwess was represented by one of the most eminent KCs of the day, Sir Stafford Cripps, who went on to become Chancellor of the Exchequer in the post-Second-World-War Labour government. Lehwess's rather chequered career remained firmly buried and Cripps successfully exploited Austin's vague recollection of events that had taken place five years before. After a 14-day hearing costing a record £10-a-minute the jury awarded Lehwess nearly £100 000 in damages.[25]

Austin appealed and the appeal judges sided with him, awarding Lehwess just £2 on a technicality. The case was once again front-page news. Lehwess in turn appealed and the case was heard in the House of Lords, the highest court in the land. In 1935 the Law Lords partially restored the original damages, awarding Lehwess £35 000, the equivalent of £10 million today.[26]

Lehwess passed his final years in Paris. From time to time he still employed de Martigny, who now called himself a journalist. He still had a network of interlinked companies based in Britain and France. The Mechanical and General Inventions Company rented an office address in London from William Longman, who had recently become bankrupt after pulling the dodgy underwriting scam once too often in the promotion of a company that was building a greyhound racing stadium.

Lehwess set up companies in France and Britain to exploit his sunshine roof patent. The British company was Solcar Sunshine Roof Patents. In addition to Lehwess, the other directors were familiar faces: William Longman and Arthur Riding, the man who had been the last company secretary of the London Electrobus Company.[27]

However, a number of other car manufacturers were now making sunshine roofs and Lehwess's patent had become virtually worthless. The French counterpart, Brevets Solcar, diversified and was renamed Omnium Financiers pour L'Industrie et Commerce.[28] By the outbreak of the Second World War its chief asset was a cinema on the Champs Elysées. Lehwess lived round the corner in a flat near Porte Maillot. He died in a clinic specialising in cancer treatment on 13 January 1941. He was 69.[29]

Notes and References

Introduction

1 *Pageant of the Century*, Odham's Press, 1933, p. 150.
2 John R Day, *The Story of the London Bus*, London Transport Executive, 1973, p. 45.
3 Theodore (T C) Barker and Michael Robbins, *A History of London Transport*, vol. 2, George Allen and Unwin, 1974, pp. 132, 120–21.
4 *Tramway and Railway World*, 10 February 1910, p. 12.
5 German Prisoners, the National Archives, FO 383/441, No. 92207, 24 May 1918.
6 *Economist*, online version: economist.com, 10 July 2007, print version: *Economist Technology Quarterly*, 8 September 2007, p. 8.
7 This was Lehwess's private secretary, Elsie Ractliffe, she died in 1986 at the age of 98.
8 George Robb, *White-Collar Crime in Modern England*, Cambridge University Press, 1992, p. 6; Mihir Bose and Cathy Gunn, *Fraud*, Unwin Hyman, 1989, p. xi; Michael Levi, *The Phantom Capitalists*, Heinemann, 1981, p. 163.
9 According to his bankruptcy hearings Ernest Terah Hooley gave bribes to editors of the *Empire*, the *Rialto*, the wife of the editor of the *Financial Times*, a leader writer on the *Financial News* and the *Pall Mall Gazette*, while an unnamed intermediary kept the evening papers sweet. *Financial Times*, 28 July 1898, p. 5; *Times*, 8 November 1898, p. 12.
10 Charles Duguid, *How to Read the Money Article*, Effingham Wilson, 1901.
11 *Statist*, 9 April 1887, p. 389; *Contemporary Review*, August 1898, p. 197; Robb, p. 117. See also John Hill Jr, *Gold Bricks of Speculation*, Lincoln Book Concern, 1904, p. 193, for the reptile press in North America.
12 'The Ties That Bind Us', BBC television series *Hustle*, first broadcast 24 March 2006.
13 This description of Hooley comes from Norman Birkett (later Baron Birkett) and is quoted in Martin Gilbert, *Fraudsters*, Constable, 1986, p. 10.
14 For Edward Beall hiring a burglar to steal incriminating documents see the *Daily Mirror*, 15 January 1904, p. 4. For the allegations against Hooley see the *Financial Times*, 21 June 1904, p. 5. The boxer's name was Howard or Horner, see letter from Detective Inspector William Burch, dated 9 February 1912, the National Archives, MEPO 3/163.

15 Tenax (pseudonym for Edward Bell), *The Gentle Art of Exploiting Gullibility*, David Weir, 1923, p. 214, says Edward 'Eddie' Guerin and Darby (or Derby) Sabini were two violent criminals used by Bottomley. There are various accounts of Guerin's criminal career, see, for example, the *Times*, 26 July 1907, p. 14. Chicago May's real name was May Vivienne Churchill. Sabini, born Ottavio but also called Charles, had his own Home Office file, Racecourse ruffians, the National Archives, HO 144/10430. Edward Bell was one of those who received death threats, Sidney Theodore Felstead, *Horatio Bottomley*, John Murray, 1936, p. 244. See also Sidney Theodore Felstead and Lady Muir, *Sir Richard Muir*, John Lane, 1927, pp. 318–23.

16 The electrobus isn't even mentioned in one of the earliest histories of the London bus: Vernon Sommerfield, *London's Buses*, St Catherine Press, 1933.

Chapter 1: The First Electrobus

1 Thanks to Sarah Holland in the Met Office press office for this.
2 *Daily Mirror*, 13 April 1906, p. 4.
3 *Times*, 18 April 1906, p. 7. The editorial was prompted by a letter (p. 4) from Sidney Colvin, who was an eminent art and literary critic.
4 *Morning Post*, 19 April 1906, p. 2.
5 Some sources say he was introduced as a Count, see *Rialto*, 2 May 1906, p. 4.
6 Martigny was talking to a foreign news agency; he is quoted in several foreign newspapers including the *Star*, of Canterbury, New Zealand, 26 June 1906, p. 2.
7 The London Electrobus Company, the National Archives, BT 31/17731/88381 and RAIL 1078/14. The prospectus lists the bullet points.
8 Public Carriage Office report for 1906, quoted in Charles Klapper, *The Golden Age of Buses*, Routledge and Kegan Paul, 1984, p. 69; the *Star*, 16 April 1906, p. 3, has a report of the Scottish bus explosion; three days later a bus in Birmingham was destroyed by fire, *Daily News*, 20 April, p. 8, followed by another one in London, *Daily News*, 23 April, p. 9.
9 Evidence of Frank Searle, of the London and General Omnibus Company, to House of Commons select committee on cabs and omnibuses, HC 295, 1906.
10 *Daily Express*, 18 April 1906, p. 5.
11 *Star* (Christchurch, New Zealand), 26 June 1906, p. 2.
12 *Star*, 18 April 1906, p. 3.
13 *Daily Chronicle*, 19 April 1906, p. 5; *San Francisco Call*, 27 May 1906, p. 19; *Standard*, 19 April 1906, p. 5.
14 *Daily Mirror*, 13 April 1906, p. 4.
15 *Daily Mirror*, 24 April 1906, p. 11.
16 *Times*, 21 April 1906, p. 6; *Daily Mail*, 21 April 1906, p. 3.
17 It was not until October 1910 that the number of petrol buses exceeded the number of horse buses, Charles Lee, *The Early Motor Bus*, London Transport, 1974, p. 25.

18 Theodore (T C) Barker and Michael Robbins, *A History of London Transport*, vol. 2, George Allen and Unwin, 1974, pp. 129–30.

19 *Financial Times*, 20 April 1906, p. 3.

20 *Tribune*, 19 April 1906, p. 4; *Daily News*, 19 April 1906, p. 12; (see also *Daily News*, 18 April, p. 12); *Evening News*, 23 April 1906, p3.

21 London Electrobus Company, the National Archives, BT 31/17731/88381 and RAIL 1078/14. National newspapers also published the prospectus.

22 Stanley Spooner went on to found *Flight International*. There is an obituary in *Flight International*, 11 April 1940, p. 333.

23 *Automotor Journal*, 5 May 1906, p. 546. The letter was published by the *Times*, 24 April 1906, p. 10. The *Financial Times, Financial News, Tribune, Morning Post, Daily Express* and the *Daily Mirror* also published the letter or referred to it in news articles.

24 The company was Scott Stirling & Co, then the third largest supplier of petrol buses in London, *Daily Express*, 23 April 1906, p. 5; *Daily News*, 24 April 1906, p. 8.

25 *Times*, 28 April 1906, p. 15. The original report by Henry Joel, dated 26 April 1906, is in the Guildhall Library, Ms 18000/108B/0058.

Chapter 2: A Bogus Patent

1 Charles Duguid, *How to Read the Money Article*, Isaac Pitman and Sons, 1936, (seventh edition), p. 55.

2 *Daily Mirror*, 23 April 1906, p. 6.

3 Patent 3653 of 1902, the modern patent number on the European Patent Office website is GB190203653A.

4 The rights only covered the area within 15 miles of Charing Cross.

5 The patent does make a number of references to an electric motor and to an electric controller, but these were covered by a separate patent, which the London Electrobus Company was not buying.

6 Motor Car Emporium, the National Archives, BT 31/15868/54970.

7 *Financial Times*, 24 April 1906, p. 5; *Morning Leader*, 24 April, p. 8; *Star*, 24 April, p. 3.

8 Rebecca Longman, the owner of the debenture bond, was William Longman's wife. Securities Exchange, the National Archives, BT 31/16786/73034.

9 *Rialto*, 2 May 1906, p. 4.

10 *Financial Times*, 25 April 1906, p. 4; *Morning Leader*, 25 April, p. 8.

11 *Electrical Review*, 27 April 1906, p. 687. The engineer, William Crampton, was appointed on 17 April.

12 *Daily Mirror*, 28 April 1906, p. 7.

13 *Daily Mirror*, 26 April 1906, p. 4.

14 *Morning Leader*, 1 May 1906, p. 2.

15 *Daily Mirror*, 7 May 1906, p. 6.

16 *Rialto*, 25 April 1906, p. 5. The magazine's coverage is very anti-Semitic. Lehwess was also fingered as the real promoter in a letter in the *Financial Times*, 4 May 1906, p. 5.

17 *Daily Mirror*, 25 April 1906, p. 5.
18 Richard Nelsson, 'Nostalgia for Press Cuttings', the *Guardian*, www.theguardian.com/commentisfree/2013/feb/10/nostalgia-press-cuttings, retrieved 26 January 2017.
19 The cuttings included ones from *Candid Friend*, 11 January 1902, p. 412, and *Autocar*, 27 September 1902, p. 338.
20 *Daily Mirror*, 23 June 1904, p. 5.

Chapter 3: The Lure Of Siberian Gold

1 *Autocar*, 3 May 1902, p. 486. Lehwess gave an interview to the *Daily News*, 25 April 1902, p. 9, before setting off.
2 Edward Lehwess, 'About Myself', *Candid Friend*, 11 January 1902, pp. 412–13.
3 *Jewish Chronicle*, 17 April 1896, p. 14; Edvard E Lehwess, *Rechtsfragen bei der Verheirathung einer Regierenden, Insbesondere einer Deutschen Fürstin mit einem Auswärtigen, Bezw. Ausländischer Prinzen*, Freiburg, 1897.
4 *Candid Friend*, 11 January 1902, p. 412.
5 Dan H Laurence, *Bernard Shaw: Collected Letters*, Max Reinhart, 1972, pp. 656-57. According to Laurence Lehwess was a friend of the Webbs.
6 *Daily News*, 19 June 1899, p. 5; *Times*, same date, p. 9.
7 *Daily Mail*, 13 September 1899, p. 3.
8 'One hundred years of the Tour de France', *Motor Sport Magazine*, July 1999, p. 58.
9 *Daily Mail*, 13 September 1899, p. 3.
10 *Automobile*, May 1900, p. 149.
11 *Evening News*, 9 November 1901, p. 1.
12 Frank Harris, *My Life and Loves*, originally published 1922–27 in Paris, also Corgi Books, 1967. Harris gives his date of birth as 1855, some biographers say 1856.
13 Hugh Kingsmill (pen name of Hugh Kingsmill Lunn), *Frank Harris*, John Lehmann, 1949, pp. 91–94.
14 *Financial Times*, 3 November 1898, p. 3. The identity of the blackmailer isn't known for sure, but Hooley later said he was being blackmailed by Edward Beall.
15 H G Wells, *Experiment in Autobiography*, Gollancz, 1934, p. 524. See also Philippa Pullar, *Frank Harris*, Penguin, 2001, p. 175; Kingsmill, p. 93.
16 John Sutherland Harvey, the proprietor of *Candid Friend*, was also involved in these meetings. He initially intended to go on the trip. *Candid Friend*, 21 December 1901, p. 292; *Autocar*, 19 April 1902, p. 418.
17 *Daily Mail*, 17 January 1902, p. 6.
18 *Candid Friend*, 21 December 1901, p. 292.
19 *Candid Friend*, 21 December 1901, p. 292, and 28 December, p. 338; *Autocar*, 29 March 1902, cover.
20 Patrick Collinson, 'Bricks are worth their weight in gold', *Guardian*, 8 December 1999, *G2*, p. 2. Most houses in 1900 were either sold leasehold or buy to let.

Notes to Pages 32-37

21 *Candid Friend,* 1 February 1902, p. 557.
22 *Le Matin,* 11 April 1902, p. 2.
23 The details of the trip and the car, with some minor embellishments, appear in a number of books. The earliest, written by someone who was closely associated with Lawson and knew Lehwess well, is Herbert O Duncan, *The World on Wheels,* privately published, Paris, 1923, pp. 1060–63. See also Alan Hess, *Wheels Round the World,* Newman Neame, 1951, pp. 11–15; Timothy R Nicholson, *The Trailblazers,* Cassell, 1958, pp. 1–10, and Timothy R Nicholson, *The Wild Roads,* Jarrolds, 1969, pp. 79–81.
24 Pullar, p. 215.
25 *Autocar,* 3 May 1902, pp. 486–87.
26 *Candid Friend,* 1901, p. 920.
27 Siberian Goldfields Development Company, the National Archives, BT 31/8928/65838.
28 *Economist,* 12 January 1901, p. 45. See also Hubert A Meredith, *The Drama of Making Money,* Sampson Low Marston, 1931, pp. 163–68, and Sidney Theodore Felstead and Lady Muir, *Sir Richard Muir,* John Lane, 1927, p. 164.
29 Ernest Terah Hooley, *Hooley's Confessions,* Simkin Marshall, 1925, p. 186.
30 *Statist,* 17 September 1904, p. 476. The exposé continues in subsequent issues, 24 September, p. 520, and 1 October, p. 560.
31 The Asiatic Banking and Trading Corporation, Guernsey Registry. The bank was registered on 19 March 1902. The founding shareholders (subscribers) were: Edward Lehwess, 10 000 shares, Jenny Lehwess, 1000 shares, Max Cudell of Berlin, 10 000 shares, Frederick Frentzel, 1000 shares, John Sutherland Harvey, 1000 shares, Louis Macrory, 1000 shares and Frederick W T Thorp, 1000 shares. The Asiatic Banking and Trading Corporation Gesellschaft mit beschränkter Haftung was registered in Berlin on 9 December 1901, *Börsen Zeitung,* 19 December 1901, p. 12.
32 *Standard,* 24 April 1902, p. 3; *Times,* 2 October 1902, p. 4.
33 *Autocar,* 3 May 1902, p. 487.
34 Robert W Paul, *Catalogue of Selected Animated Photograph Films,* London, 1906–7, p. 66. The film was 90 feet long. Three films were due to be shown at the Automobile Club of America dinner at New York on 24 May 1902: 'Leaving London for Trip Around the World', 'Running at High Speed on Rotten Row' and 'Repairing Breakdown to Dr Lehwess' Car', *Brooklyn Eagle,* 23 May 1902, p. 13.
35 *Evening Telegraph* (Angus), 16 May 1902, p. 3.
36 *Autocar,* 27 September 1902, p. 338.
37 Press Limited, the National Archives, J 13/3288. Press Limited was the publisher of *Candid Friend.* In February 1902 J Morris Catton, a dodgy company promoter and associate of Frank Harris, tried to bankrupt the magazine after he and Harris fell out. See Pullar, p. 216; A I Tobin and Elmer Gertz, *Frank Harris,* Haskill House, 1970, p. 198.
38 *Manchester Guardian,* 25 June 1902, p. 3.

39 *Autocar,* 27 September 1902, p. 338.
40 *La Vie au Grand Air,* 29 November 1902, pp. 804–06.
41 The chef's departure is mentioned in the report of a later court case, *Standard,* 1 April 1903, p. 9.
42 *Autocar,* 18 October 1902, p. 408.
43 *Daily Express,* 14 January 1903, p. 8; *Motor Car Journal,* 24 January 1903, p. 898.
44 *Westminster Budget,* 27 February 1903, p. 24. Friswell became the first motoring knight in 1909.
45 Duncan, p. 1063; *Autocar,* 27 May 1905, p. 725.

Chapter 4: Two Criminal Convictions

1 Obituary of Frank Froest, *Times,* 8 January 1930, p. 14.
2 *Evening News,* 10 May 1904, p. 3; *Financial Times,* 11 May 1904, p. 5; *Standard,* same date, p. 5.
3 *Motor Car Journal,* 12 May 1899, p. 147.
4 *Times,* 16 November 1896, p. 7.
5 Peter Thorold, *The Motoring Age 1896–1939,* Profile Books, 2003, p. 5.
6 Club advert in the *Autocar,* 18 July 1896; William Plowden, *The Motor Car and Politics in Britain,* Penguin, 1973, p. 14; Carlton Reid, *Roads Were Not Built for Cars,* Island Press, 2015, p. 277.
7 *Economist,* 2 October 1897, pp. 1392–93; Herbert O Duncan, *The World on Wheels,* privately published, Paris, 1923, p. 672. Duncan was closely associated with Lawson. See also Thorold, pp. 68–70.
8 Motorists led by John Douglas-Scott-Montagu MP – later Lord Montagu of Beaulieu – campaigned to overturn the patents. For background on the patents see the *Engineer,* 11 December 1896, pp. 587–88. The scheme fell apart after a decisive court case in 1901, *Financial Times,* 31 July 1901, p. 4.
9 Automobile Association Ltd, the National Archives, BT 31/8078/58240. The company was registered on 16 July 1898.
10 *Automotor and Horseless Vehicles Journal,* September 1898, pp. 462–72.
11 The absence of any court proceedings to force the Automobile Association to pay royalties points to a deal between the two men. Furthermore, when the car dealers set up an association to fight the patents – the Automotive Mutual Protection Association – Lehwess did not join it.
12 *Standard,* 14 February 1900, p. 7; 5 May, p. 8; *Times,* 14 February 1900, p. 14; 4 May, p. 15; 5 May, p. 17. Lehwess prosecuted one director, Sydney Atkins, for embezzlement. The other, Hans Conrad Zacharias, resigned. Zacharias and Lehwess had been students together in Zurich and they shared a house in Notting Hill Gate. See *London Gazette,* 1 January 1901, p. 48.
13 There was a curious postscript to this liquidation. Today the Automobile Association is best known for providing a rescue service to members whose cars have broken down. This Automobile Association had originally been set up in by motorists in 1905, principally to establish a system of patrols to warn

its members of police speed traps. Lehwess sold the rights to use the name to the association for £100. Automobile Association Ltd, the National Archives, BT 34/1490/58240. The liquidators' accounts, 9 May 1907, show a receipt of £100 from the Motor Users' Proprietary, the corporate name used by the AA and a corresponding payment of £100 to 'staff'.

14 The tip-off came from a Yorkshire engineer who was familiar with the new system of numbering cars. For the Motor Car Act 1903, see Plowden, p. 18. The emporium was set up a few months before the Automobile Association but didn't become active until after the Automobile Association went into liquidation. The Motor Car Emporium, the National Archives, BT 31/15868/54970.

15 *Kensington News*, 3 June 1904, p. 3.

16 *Standard*, 28 May, p. 8; 6 June, p. 9; 23 June, p. 3; *Times*, 28 May 1904, p. 6; 6 June, p. 3; 23 June, p. 9; *Kensington News*, 3 June 1904, p. 3; *Daily Telegraph*, 6 June 1904, p. 11; 23 June, p. 6; *Yorkshire Evening Post*, 22 June 1904, p. 4; *Daily News*, 23 June 1904, p. 9.

17 Provincial Carriers, the National Archives, BT 31/10299/77389. Clark was a director, Lehwess a shareholder. See also *Commercial Motor*, 7 September 1905, p. 500. For the description of Clark see Elsa A Nystrom, *Mad for Speed*, McFarland, 2013, p. 95.

18 *Daily News*, 23 June 1904, p. 9.

19 *Times*, 23 June 1904, p. 14.

20 This was the *Daily Mirror*, 23 June 1904, p. 5.

21 Automobile Club minute book, 8 August 1904, p. 102.

22 Piers Brendon, *The Motoring Century: The Story of the Royal Automobile Club*, Bloomsbury, 1997, p. 42. Additional information from Jessica Bueno De Mesquita at the RAC archives.

23 *Financial Times*, 25 January 1899, p. 2. The official receiver's report was so sensational that it was leaked to the *Sunday Special*. The company was the Beeston Tyre Company.

24 There is a list of these front sheeters in Ernest Terah Hooley, *The Hooley Book*, John Dicks, 1904. The Earl de la Warr was paid £25 000 to adorn the prospectus of the Dunlop company. The normal cash bribe for editors was £100 or £200 but it could be a lot more. See 'The Art of Blackmail', *Contemporary Review*, August 1898, pp. 196–204, and George Robb, *White-Collar Crime in Modern England*, Cambridge University Press, 1992, p. 117.

25 The National Archives, MEPO 3/163, letter dated 12 August 1903.

26 *Sheffield and Rotherham Independent*, 1 June 1899, p. 4.

27 Anthony Trollope, *The Way We Live Now*, Chapman Hall, 1875, p. 330.

28 The National Archives, MEPO 3/163 has the statement of the publican (Alfred Paine). See also the *Financial Times*, 11 May 1904, p. 5. The story is mostly taken from Richard Muir's opening speech at Bow Street. The shares were in Siberian Goldfields Development Company and the S G Syndicate.

29 *Financial Times*, 23 September 1901, pp. 3–4. Almost identical articles appeared on the same date in the *Financier*, pp. 5–6; *Financial News*, p. 4, and the *Statist* on 28 September 1901, pp. 578–80.

30 *Financial Times*, 2 June 1904, p. 6.
31 *Financial Times*, 11 May 1904, p. 5.
32 Evidence of Charles Coop, a journalist on the *Statist*, on 1 December 1904 at the Old Bailey. Old Bailey Proceedings Online (www.oldbaileyonline.org, November 1904, trial of Ernest Terah Hooley and Henry John Lawson).
33 The National Archives, CRIM 1/94.
34 Plowden, p. 482. In March 1905 there were 15 895 motor vehicles on Britain's roads. By March 1907 there were 32 451 vehicles. The number of motor buses in London was 15 or 20 in January 1905. Two years later there were 800 of them.
35 Colin Buchanan, *Mixed Blessing*, Leonard Hill, 1958, p. 9, gives the number of private cars on the roads of Britain in March 1914 as 132 000 compared to 133 000 buses, taxis and goods vehicles.
36 Charles Lee, *The Early Motor Bus*, London Transport, 1974, p. 9.
37 Statement by George Cawston (an associate of Hooley and Lawson), the National Archives, CRIM 1/94. Cawston said both the London General Omnibus Company and the London Road Car Company had agreed to buy German Daimler buses from Lawson.
38 *Autocar*, 5 July 1902, p. 19.
39 In August 1902 Lehwess, while he was apparently in Berlin, entered two Dürkopp vehicles in trials in Welbeck in Cambridgeshire, *Motor Car Journal*, 9 August 1902, p. 473.
40 *Hackney Express*, 9 May 1903, p. 2; *Westminster Budget*, 15 May 1903, p. 14. Lehwess registered the Dürkopp Motoren Gesellschaft Ltd on 11 May 1903, the National Archives, BT 31/10293/77320. Lehwess was the managing director, the company never traded. The annual Stock Exchange walk to Brighton continued until 2003.
41 The National Archives, RAIL/1078/45. The analyst is anonymous, but is virtually certain to have been retained by the London Road Car Company. Many of the files in the series RAIL/1078 were evidently collected by this bus company. A confidential report addressed to the London Road Car secretary survives in RAIL 1078/32. Files RAIL/1078/14, RAIL/1078/20 and RAIL/1078/32 all contain press clippings collected by agencies naming the client as the London Road Car Company, while a report in RAIL/1078/24 has the client's name as a typed header.
42 Anthony Trollope, *The Way We Live Now*, Chapman and Hall, 1875, p. 61.
43 *Daily Mail*, 19 May 1906, p. 3. The piece in the Chat on 'Change column was probably penned by Charles Duguid. Duguid was the *Daily Mail*'s city editor from 1906 to 1911 and the pre-eminent financial journalist of his day. He started his Fleet Street career on the *Economist* and he subsequently worked for the *Pall Mall Gazette*, the *Morning Post* and the *Observer*. His concern was echoed in the trade press, see *Motor Traction*, 2 February 1907, p. 112.
44 Lehwess signed two contracts in October and November 1905 with De Dion Bouton Ltd, one of Lawson's companies, while Lawson was in prison, and others after he had been released. See De Dion Bouton (1907) prospectus,

Times, 11 March 1907, p. 14. The effect of these contracts was to give Lehwess a monopoly on De Dion Bouton buses. *Commercial Motor*, 4 April 1907, p. 115.

45 *Commercial Motor*, 23 March 1905, p. 40; 13 April, p. 111; 27 April, p. 152; 11 May, p. 191. The magazine also reported that the emporium was importing 200 bus chassis, 30 November, p. 240.

46 According to Scotland Yard's engineering adviser William Worby Beaumont, the leading motor engineer of his day, *Financial News*, 22 April 1909, p. 6.

47 *Automotor Journal*, 7 December 1907, p. 1781.

Chapter 5: A Most Deliberate Swindle

1 *Daily Mirror*, 1 May 1906, p. 4.

2 *Daily Mirror*, 1 May 1906, p. 4.

3 *Daily Mirror*, 26 April 1906, p. 4.

4 *Financial Times*, 27 April 1906, p. 6.

5 London Electrobus Company, listing application, Guildhall Library, Ms 18000/108B/0058.

6 *Daily Mail*, 27 April 1906, p. 7; 30 April, p. 5; *Daily Mirror*, 28 April 1906, p. 4.

7 *Daily Mirror*, 4 May 1906, p. 11.

8 *Daily Mirror*, 7 May 1906, p. 6.

9 *Financial Times*, 7 May 1906, p. 5.

10 The address was 17 Cockspur Street. Over the years Lehwess rented a number of offices in 14 to 17 Cockspur Street.

11 The first sighting of Improved Electric Traction was when it exhibited an electric van at the Commercial Vehicle Motor Show in March 1906. Its stand was next door to that of the Motor Car Emporium, *Commercial Motor*, 29 March 1906, p. 77.

12 *Financial Times*, 7 May 1906, p. 3.

13 *Financial Times*, 24 April 1906, p. 5. Herbert James Rowbottom was born in Islington in 1874, his elder brother (Charles) Ernest Rowbottom in 1872.

14 *Rialto*, 25 April 1906, p. 5. The magazine calculated that if the London Electrobus Company was as profitable as the prospectus claimed Lehwess would pocket 35 per cent of the profits. See also the *Rialto*, 2 May 1906, p. 4.

15 *Times*, 19 May 1906, p. 10; London Electrobus Company, the National Archives, BT 31/17731/88381.

16 *Daily Mirror*, 9 May 1906, p. 11.

17 London Electrobus Company listing application, Guildhall Library, Ms 18000/108B/0058, circular of 16 May 1906. See also the *Daily Mirror*, 18 May 1906, p. 11.

18 Extract of a report by Robert Lacau, of Paris, and the complete report by Frank Broadbent are in the electrobus listing application, Guildhall Library, Ms 18000/108B/0058.

19 *Financial Times*, 29 June 1906, p. 4.

20 London Electrobus Company, the National Archives, BT 31/17731/88381.
21 *Rialto*, 25 April 1906, p. 5; 2 May, p. 4.
22 See *Truth*, 6 March 1907, p. 583, and C J Scotter, *Lost in a Bucket Shop*, Field and Tuer, 1890, quoted by Dilwyn Porter, 'Speciousness is the Bucketeer's Watchword and Outrageous Effrontery his Capital', in *Cultures of Selling*, edited by John Benson and Laura Ugolini, Ashgate, 2006, p. 113. On one deal the odds of Longman winning (and the client losing) were put at 5000 to 1, *Irish Times*, 3 November 1900, p. 9.
23 Quoted in Sidney Theodore Felstead and Lady Muir, *Sir Richard Muir*, John Lane, 1927, p. 161.
24 *Critic*, 1 December 1900, p. 16.
25 *Critic*, 5 October 1901, p. 15.
26 *Financial Times*, 28 January 1902, p. 3; 29 January, p. 4.
27 *Rialto*, 2 May 1906, p. 4.
28 *Standard*, 30 August 1906, p. 3; London Electrobus Company Annual Report, 1906–7, Guildhall Library, Tramway and Omnibus reports, box 981.
29 *Financial Times*, 31 August 1906, p. 2.
30 Cyril Martyr to secretary of Stock Exchange, 5 September 1906, Guildhall Library, Ms 18000/108B/0058.
31 London Electrobus Company, decision of application for settlement, 20 February 1907, Guildhall Library, Ms 18000/108B/0058.
32 This list of shareholders seems to date from early 1907, Guildhall Library, Ms 18000/108B/0058.
33 Securities Exchange, the National Archives, BT 31/16786/73034; *Motor Finance*, 18 September 1907, p. 529; Longman v. Longman, the National Archives, Divorce Court file, J 77/1014/773.
34 Annual Report, London Electrobus Company 1906–7, Guildhall Library, Tramway and Omnibus reports, box 981. The accounts up to 17 August 1906 show a payment of £5750 for preliminary expenses, including underwriting. A further £6000 was paid in advance for electrobuses, presumably to the Motor Car Emporium.
35 The Birmingham, Liverpool, Nottingham, Lancashire, Yorkshire, Scottish and Provincial Electrobus Companies were all registered on 26 April 1906. None of these companies ever ran a bus. See the National Archives, BT 31/11494/88539, BT 31/11494/88547, BT 31/11494/88548, BT 31/11494/88549, BT 31/11495/88552, BT 31/11495/88556 and BT 31/11501/88617.
36 *Automotor Journal*, 7 December 1907, p. 1781; *Commercial Motor*, 7 November 1907, p. 225.
37 First World War service records, the National Archives, WO 372/21/6686.
38 1901 Census, the National Archives, RG 13 /369.
39 *Era*, 17 March 1900, p. 14, has an announcement of Martigny's marriage. His wife was Julia White, a musical hall vocalist whose stage name was Maude Wight.
40 *Era*, 5 May 1900, p. 30; 12 May, p. 7; 10 November, p. 23. Martigny also managed Irene Szilassy's comic opera company.

Chapter 6: The Dress Rehearsal

1 *Times*, 21 April 1909, p. 3; *Scotsman*, 22 April 1909, p. 10; *Manchester Guardian*, 23 April 1909, p. 8.
2 Edinburgh and District Motor Omnibus Company, the National Archives, BT 31/11403/87535.
3 Edinburgh and District Motor Omnibus Company, Stock Exchange listing applications, London Guildhall Library, Ms 18000/106B/0528. The minimum subscription was £25 000.
4 Edinburgh and District Motor Omnibus Company, the National Archives, BT 31/11403/87535.
5 *London Gazette*, 17 December 1909, p. 9626.
6 Edinburgh and District Motor Omnibus Company, the National Archives, BT 31/11403/87535.
7 *Motor Finance*, 17 April 1907, p. 258, quotes a letter from Longman. Longman lent Orr the money to promote the company.
8 The figure of £12 000 was given by Ernest Rowbottom, the emporium's manager, *Financial News*, 22 April 1909, p. 6. The company only ever ran a couple of charabancs on excursions.
9 These were the Edinburgh and District Motor Omnibus Company's figures, *John Bull*, 9 March 1907, p. 222. Similar figures appear in the *Financial News*, 21 April 1909, p. 5. Scottish Motor Traction was another victim of the emporium's erratic deliveries. It sued the emporium for failing to deliver buses on time, *Scotsman*, 26 April 1906, p. 6.
10 This was Edward Beall's *Motor Finance*.
11 *Scotsman*, 21 April 1909, p. 11.
12 *Pall Mall Gazette*, 16 March 1912, p. 11. The league's manifesto appears in Alfred Mayhew, *Mayhew's What's What in the City*, Mayhew's Financial Publications, 1913, pp. 65–66. Alfred Hercules Mayhew died on 11 October 1913. He was 70.
13 These figures come from Board of Trade reports, Mayhew, p. 44.
14 Mayhew, p. 44.
15 One of these associates was Samuel Habgood, a photographer based in Wimbledon, who had 20 shares in the Edinburgh company. Mayhew had 100 shares. Edinburgh and District Motor Omnibus Company, the National Archives, BT 31/11403/87535.
16 *Scotsman*, 21 March 1907, p. 3.
17 He lived at Alltrees, Shipley, near Horsham.
18 *Rubber and Oil*, 15 November 1911, p. 302.
19 *Financial Times*, 2 November 1911, p. 7.
20 *Scotsman*, 21 March 1907, p. 3, and *Motor Finance*, 27 March 1907, p. 228. Packing meetings was a common corporate tactic, see Charles Duguid, *How to Read the Money Article*, (seventh edition), Isaac Pitman and Sons, 1936, p. 123.
21 *Manchester Guardian*, 4 April 1907, p. 8; *Scotsman*, 4 April 1907, p. 3.

22 *Motor Finance*, 10 April 1907, p. 239.
23 *Scotsman*, 5 April 1907, p. 9.
24 Macdonald was in touch with another dissident shareholder, Hugo Schultess Young, a barrister who was helping Mayhew and Habgood, *Motor Finance*, 24 April 1907, p. 273.
25 *Scotsman*, 15 May 1907, p. 6.
26 Edinburgh and District Motor Omnibus Company, the National Archives, BT 34/2073/87535. The company that bought the buses was called the Motor House, the National Archives, BT 31/17776/88989. The links with Lawson are detailed in *Motor Finance*, 1 July 1908, pp. 247–48; 2 September 1908, p. 289.
27 *Scotsman*, 21 April 1909, p. 11.
28 According to figures given to the Edinburgh shareholders the initial order from the emporium was for 30 buses, *Scotsman*, 25 May 1906, p. 2. This was worth £300 to Macdonald.
29 According to Francis Gore-Brown KC, who represented Macdonald's fellow directors, *Financial Times*, 25 October 1909, p. 2.
30 *Times*, 21 April 1909, p. 3; *Scotsman*, 21 April 1909, p. 11; 22 April, p. 10; *Manchester Guardian*, 23 April 1909, p. 8. The *Financial Times* did mention the deal six months later in its report of the appeal case, 25 October 1909, p. 2.
31 Macdonald was also a director of other companies, such as the short-lived London Power Omnibus Company. Macdonald, who died in 1951, was a key primary source for some historians.

Chapter 7: Post Office Motors

1 Motor Coach Syndicate, the National Archives, BT 31/11364/87098, has Frank Harris, no occupation, living at 54 Acacia Road, near Regents Park in a return dated 12 January 1906. This is probably one of the secret addresses referred to in Philippa Pullar, *Frank Harris*, Penguin, 2011, p. 227. The Electoral Roll for 1906–07 has Mrs Nellie Harris, Frank's wife, living at the same address (Frank is not listed).
2 Harris's biographer refers to his interest in a coach company, Pullar, p. 245. Harris was also a backer of the New Motor Bus Syndicate, which promoted one of the bus companies that became part of the Vanguard group.
3 The magazine was to be called the *Automobile Review*, Pullar, p. 229. The editorial offices were at 12–13 Henrietta Street, Covent Garden, the same address as *Candid Friend*.
4 *Motorist and Traveller*, the first issue appeared in January 1905.
5 *Motorist and Traveller*, 1 April 1905 had a Motor Car Emporium advert about the sale of 51 buses to the London Road Car Company. The emporium also advertised in subsequent issues.
6 *Daily News*, 13 February 1905, p. 8. The Postal Museum has a report of the first motor van on 9–10 May 1905, POST/10/349.
7 Motor Coach Syndicate, the National Archives, BT 31/11364/87098.

8 Motor Coach Syndicate, the National Archives, BT 34/2065/87098 includes a £70 expenses claim from Harris for inspecting chassis in Paris in June. Reliance Motor Transit, the National Archives, BT 31/11437/87926 has letter dated 25 June 1906 saying Lehwess and the secretary were indisposed. Lehwess was in France looking at taximeters, he sailed for New York with them in September; see *Automobile* (New York), 18 October 1906, p. 521.

9 Motor Coach Syndicate, the National Archives, BT 34/2065/87098. The syndicate paid Harris £60 for an article in the *Times* in August 1906, and a further £150 for unspecified articles in October and November.

10 *John Bull*, 29 September 1906, p. 400.

11 National Motor Mail Coach Company, the National Archives, BT 31/11459/88150.

12 *John Bull*, 1 June 1907, p. 511.

13 *John Bull*, 22 June 1907, p. 598.

14 Affidavit from Robert Bolton, a City solicitor, on 5 March 1908, National Motor Mail Coach Company, the National Archives, J 13/4585. See also the *Financial Times*, 14 April 1908, p. 7; *Commercial Motor*, 23 April 1908, p. 214.

15 One of Longman's last forays into underwriting was Associated Greyhound Racecourses. The share issue wasn't a success. Longman defaulted and was successfully sued, *Financial Times*, 28 June 1928, p. 12. He subsequently went bankrupt.

16 Modern Traffic Development Corporation, the National Archives, BT 31/11811/91692.

17 George Robb, *White-Collar Crime in Modern England*, Cambridge University Press, 1992, p. 95.

18 *Commercial Motor*, 23 April 1908, p. 214.

19 Petition from Bernard du Sautoy Anstis, dated 18 October 1907, National Motor Mail Coach Company, the National Archives, J 13/4585; *Financial News*, 30 October 1907, p. 7; *Financial Times*, 30 October 1907, p. 4.

20 Modern Traffic Development Corporation, the National Archives, BT 31/11811/91692.

21 The retired naval commander was du Sautoy Anstis, the National Archives, J 13/4585.

22 *Financial Times*, 30 October 1907, p. 4.

23 Lehwess tried to recoup his losses by suing the company for the cost of registering it, *Financial Times*, 13 May 1908, p. 9. The National Motor Mail Coach Company, Clinton's claim, is still a leading case in company law. See Denis J Keenan, *Smith & Keenan's Company Law*, Pearson Longman, 2005, p. 53. The principle is that a company can't run up expenses before it exists.

24 National Motor Mail Coach Company, the National Archives, BT 34/2083/88150.

Chapter 8: A Transatlantic Con

1 *New York Times*, 29 May 1902, p. 5. See also Michael Brian Schiffer, *Taking Charge*, Smithsonian Books, 1994, p. 78.

2 The batteries for the prototype electrobus were supplied by Emil Laurence Oppermann of the X Electric Accumulator Company, see *Financial Times*, 7 May 1906, p. 5; X Electric Accumulator Company, the National Archives, BT 31/11165/85174. The battery was patented in 1904, British Patent 25902 (modern numbering GB190425902).

3 See, for example, *San Francisco Call*, 10 September 1906, p. 9. The earliest use of the word 'electrobus' seems to have been in the correspondence columns of the *Times*, 12 April 1890, p. 8.

4 Provincial Carriers paid the rates until 31 March 1906, Westminster City Council rate books for 45 Horseferry Road. The garage had previously been part of John Broadwood's piano factory.

5 The two chief shareholders in Reliance Motor Transit were Lehwess and William Longman, the National Archives, BT 31/11437/87926. Among the other companies that Lehwess had an interest in were the Rocket Motor Omnibus Company, Rapid Road Transit and its replacement the London and Westminster Motor Omnibus Company.

6 It continued to pay the rates on the Horseferry Road garage until the electrobuses began running in July 1907, Westminster City Council, rate books, March 1906, September 1906, March 1907 and September 1907.

7 *Argus* (Melbourne), 17 July 1883, p. 10; *Age* (Melbourne), 6 November 1906, p. 8; 9 November 1906, p. 13; *Financial Times*, 6 September 1906, p. 2; *Daily News*, 6 September 1906, p. 9. Li Hongzhang is the modern transliteration of Li Hung Chang.

8 Westminster City Council rate books for 45 Horseferry Road. Reliance Motor Transit left owing money for rates which were due for the period up to 30 September 1906. On 31 March 1907 the new ratepayers were the Motor Car Emporium and the London Electrobus Company.

9 Reliance Motor Transit, the National Archives, BT 31/11437/87926; *Argus* (Melbourne), 8 September 1906, p. 19; 11 September, p. 9; 9 November 1907, p. 19; *Age* (Melbourne), 9 November 1907, p. 13; *Advertiser* (Adelaide), 14 January 1908, p. 7.

10 US Immigration records show Longman entering the country from Mexico at the frontier station of Laredo on 21 July 1906.

11 *Times*, 2 May 1908, p. 5; *Financial Times*, 2 May 1908, p. 6; 9 July 1908, p. 9. The promoter was George Cuddon: he was convicted of forgery in connection with this fraud.

12 *Financial Times*, 7 August 1907, p. 8.

13 Passenger list for *Kronprinz Wilhelm*, available on a number of online databases, including Ancestry.co.uk. For twin purpose of visit see *Automobile*, 18 October 1906, p. 521.

14 This was the United States Taxameter Company. See *New York Times*, 24 October 1906, p. 13.

15 *History of Gould Electronics*, http://www.fundinguniverse.com/company-histories/gould-electronics-inc-history/ retrieved 16 May 2015.

16 *Financial News*, 19 May 1909, p. 7; *Financial Times*, 19 May 1909, p. 7.

17 *Financial News*, 19 May 1909, p. 7; 21 May, p. 6; *Financial Times*, 19 May 1909, p. 7; 21 May, p. 8.

18 *Financial News*, 20 May 1909, p. 7; *Financial Times*, 20 May 1909, p. 3.

19 Gould Storage Battery Company, the National Archives, BT 31/11727/90877.

20 *Automotor Journal*, 28 March 1908, p. 411, highlights the close involvement of the battery manufacturers in helping to make the electrobus a success.

21 *Commercial Motor*, 17 January 1907, p. 437; *Motor Traction*, 20 January 1907, p. 74; *Financial Times*, 22 January 1907, p. 6; *Manchester Guardian*, 1 February 1907, p. 4.

22 Passenger and Crew Lists of Vessels arriving at New York, New York, 1897–1957, the National Archives and Records Administration. Lehwess paid for Rowbottom's passage.

23 *Investors' Guardian*, 18 March 1905, p. 273. The Motor Omnibus and Waggon Company (company number 83 846) was registered on 8 March.

24 *Commercial Motor*, 28 February 1907, p. 579; *Financial Times*, 8 March 1907, p. 8.

25 *Commercial Motor*, 27 August 1908, p. 590.

26 *Commercial Motor*, 14 March 1907, p. 11; *Motor Traction*, 16 March 1907, pp. 302–03.

27 Motoring reporters from the national press had been given a preview earlier in the year, *Manchester Guardian*, 1 February 1907, p. 4.

28 *Electrical Engineer*, 22 February 1907, p. 271.

29 *Electrical Engineer*, 22 February 1907, p. 271.

Chapter 9: A Fresh Start

1 *Commercial Motor*, 18 July 1907, p. 481; *Daily Express*, 18 July 1907, p. 5.

2 *Daily News*, 17 July 1907, p. 9.

3 *Evening Telegraph* (Dundee), 16 July 1907, p. 5; *Commercial Motor*, 18 July 1907, p. 481.

4 *Automotor Journal*, 20 July 1907, p. 1012. This critique was repeated virtually word for word in *Motor Finance*, 24 July 1907, p. 465.

5 *Electrical Review*, 20 December 1907, p. 999.

6 Today the site of the electrobus garage is occupied by the Department for Transport.

7 *Westminster Gazette*, 17 July 1906, p. 4. Dewar was the Fullerian Professor of Chemistry at the Royal Institution. He died in 1923. See also *Daily News*, 24 July 1906, p. 8.

8 *Times*, 14 November 1906, p. 2.

9 *Commercial Motor*, 20 December 1906, p. 349.

10 William Plowden, *The Motor Car and Politics in Britain*, Penguin, 1973, p. 228.

11 *Times*, 18 April 1906, p. 4; Motor Bus Noise, the National Archives, HO 45/10323/129649.

12 *Truth*, 25 April 1906, p. 969.

13 *Times*, 14 July 1906, p. 6.

14 Motor Bus Noise, the National Archives, HO 45/10323/129649.

15 *Times*, 16 July 1906, p. 4; 23 July, p. 6.

16 *Pall Mall Gazette*, 20 August 1906, p. 8.

17 *Times*, 25 January 1907, p. 6.

18 *Truth*, 22 January 1903, p. 202.

19 Street Noise Abatement, the National Archives, HO 45/9999/A48242.

20 Motor Bus Noise, the National Archives, HO 45/10323/129649. The Home Office file on the deputation (178149) hasn't survived.

21 *Manchester Guardian*, 17 August 1906, p. 10; 9 October, p. 12.

22 *Westminster Gazette* 13 July 1906, p. 9; *Daily News*, 13 July 1906, p. 7; *Daily Chronicle*, 13 July 1906, pp. 5–6.

23 The 'expert' was Bertram Blount, a chemist and motorist, *Westminster Gazette*, 17 July 1906, p. 3. He was also quoted in the *Spectator*, 21 July 1906, p. 9.

24 Herbert Gladstone papers, British Library, Ms 46096, ff. 162, 167. The other reports were for leaking oil (2100), defective brakes (900), defective steering (360) and smoky exhausts (200). In 1906 and the first four months of 1907 the police refused to relicense 158 buses.

25 Charles Klapper, *The Golden Age of Buses*, Routledge and Kegan Paul, p. 69. See also *Commercial Motor*, 1 November 1906, front cover, for industry protests about 'police extremism'.

26 *Daily Mail*, 31 August 1907, p. 3.

27 See Klapper, p. 67. The Vanguard company was a merger of four companies: the London Motor Omnibus Company, the London and District Motor Bus Company, the London and Provincial Motor Bus and Traction Company and the Motor Bus Company. See *Financial News*, 25 June 1907, p. 2; *Financial Times*, 25 June 1907, p. 3.

28 Klapper, p. 65; *Times*, 29 July 1907, p. 3. The fourth largest bus company was the London Power Omnibus Company. Norman D Macdonald was a director.

29 Theodore (T C) Barker and Michael Robbins, *A History of London Transport*, vol. 2, George Allen and Unwin, 1974, p. 127.

30 *Economist*, 7 September 1907, p. 1495.

31 Klapper, p. 69. The bus companies were the Star (23 buses), Pat Hearn (nine buses) and Victoria Omnibus (nine buses). Birch Brothers scrapped a further 14 motor buses in November. See *Commercial Motor*'s fortnightly bus censuses.

32 *Automotor Journal*, 27 July 1907, p. 1052.

33 *Commercial Motor*, 30 September 1909, p. 74.

34 *Times*, 23 July 1907, p. 11.

35 Accounts from June 1906 to 15 July 1907, London Electrobus Company, the National Archives, BT 31/17731/88381.

36 Statistical Abstract for London 1912–13, London County Council. The wholesale price of oats increased steadily from 17 shillings per quarter (28 lb) in 1904 to 20 shillings by 1911.

Chapter 10: A Brawl In The Edgware Road

1 The account of the brawl is a synthesis of newspaper reports of the court case. The witnesses gave different versions of events. The best accounts are in the local papers: *Marylebone Times*, 13 September, 1907, p. 4; 20 September, p. 8; *Paddington Times*, 13 September, p. 4; 20 September, p. 8; 11 October, p. 8; *Advertiser: A Weekly Newspaper for Marylebone, St John's Wood, Paddington and Surrounding Districts*, 14 September, p. 3; 21 September, p. 9; *Marylebone Mercury*, 14 September 1907, p. 5; 21 September, p. 5; 12 October, p. 7. Of the dailies the *Times* on 11 and 16 September and 5 October, and the *Daily Telegraph*, 16 September have detailed reports. The story also appears in the *Evening Standard*, 10 September, the *Daily Express*, the *Daily Mail*, the *Standard*, 11 September, the *Daily Mail*, the *Daily Mirror* and the *Standard* on 16 September and 6 October, the *Evening News*, 5 October. *Lloyd's Weekly News* covered the case on 15 September and 6 October. All of the reports spell Colatto's name with a single 't'. Colatto spelled his name with two 't's in the 1911 Census, and in his subsequent business ventures.
2 Canadian Passenger Lists. Locock and his wife arrived in Vancouver from Hong Kong on 11 October 1905 on the *Princess Victoria*.
3 *Candid Friend*, 8 March 1902. There is a picture of Captain Locock in the same issue, p. 753.
4 They included Florence Roze, the wife of the conductor at the Covent Garden Opera House. Petition of Margaret Barbenson Locock, 23 December 1902, the National Archives, Divorce Court file, J 77/773/3523.
5 Petition of Margaret Barbenson Locock, 14 February 1911, the National Archives, Divorce Court file, J 77/1032/1290.
6 *London Gazette*, 8 July 1910, p. 4890. The agency went on to become one of the most reputable in London. The partnership was dissolved in June 1910, shortly before Sawer got married.
7 International Motor Traffic Syndicate, the National Archives, BT 31/12112/94860. Lehwess later admitted that the International Motor Traffic Syndicate was his trading name, *Financial News*, 21 May 1909, p. 6.
8 Nathaniel Newnham-Davis, *Dinners and Diners: Where and How to Dine in London*, Grant Richards, 1901, p. 375.
9 See Sidney Theodore Felstead and Lady Muir, *Sir Richard Muir*, John Lane, 1927, p. 185.
10 The Asiatic Banking and Trading Corporation, Guernsey Registry, ledger of unnumbered companies registered in 1902, p. 734. One of the seven founding subscribers to the corporation, with 1000 shares, was Louis Macrory MD, of Battersea. Lists of electrobus shareholders are in the Guildhall Library, Ms 18000/108B/0058, and the National Archives, BT 31/17731/88381. At the time the bank held 25 000 shares out of a total of 46 000 shares issued by the London Electrobus Company.

11 *Evening News*, 4 October 1907, p. 3.
12 *Lloyd's Weekly News*, 6 October 1907, p. 10.

Chapter 11: Enter The Black Prince

1 *Financial News*, 14 November 1907, p. 2; *Financial Times*, 14 November 1907, p. 2; *Financier*, 14 November 1907, p. 2; *Rialto*, 20 November 1907, p. 10; London Electrobus Company, the National Archives, BT 31/17731/88381.
2 *Motor Finance*, 13 November 1907, pp. 596–98.
3 *Financial News*, 19 March 1914, p. 9. 'The Adventure of Charles Augustus Milverton', Arthur Conan Doyle, *Strand Magazine*, April 1904.
4 *Financial Times*, 29 January 1914, p. 3. Teresa Grimshaw, the typist, knew Beall as 'Clement' or Clements.
5 Edward Marjoribanks, *The Life of Sir Edward Marshall Hall*, Victor Gollancz, 1930, p. 125; David Kynaston, *The City of London*, vol. 2, Pimlico, 1995, pp. 77–78.
6 Ernest Nicholls, *Crime within the Square Mile*, John Long, 1935, p. 134; *Financial News*, 19 March 1914, p. 9.
7 *Critic*, 8 April 1899, p. 33.
8 *Lloyd's Weekly Newspaper*, 28 December 1879, p. 10.
9 By 1899 Beall had been responsible for 200 company swindles, *Critic*, 8 April 1899, p. 33.
10 *Economist*, 19 July 1884, p. 874.
11 *Echo*, 1 August 1898, p. 3; *Financial Times*, 2 August 1898, p. 3.
12 *Financial Times*, 13 April 1892, p. 3.
13 A F Baker, *Banks and Banking*, London, 1892. Baker is an alias for Charles Singleton. See also *Financial Times*, 11 December 1894, p. 2.
14 Nicholls, p. 136.
15 Trial of Edward Beall, Charles Singleton and others, Old Bailey Proceedings Online, evidence on 8 November 1899.
16 Old Bailey Proceedings Online, evidence on 3 November 1899.
17 *Daily Mail*, 19 July 1899, p. 8; 2 November, p. 6; *Financial Times*, 4 November 1899, p. 4; Old Bailey Proceedings Online, evidence on 1 November 1899.
18 *Financial Times*, 11 December 1894, p. 3; 3 November 1899, p. 2; Old Bailey Proceedings Online, evidence of Henry Norris, 2 November 1899 and Frederick John Baker, 6 and 7 November.
19 *Critic*, 14 July 1900, p. 6. See also Alfred Mayhew, *Mayhew's What's What in the City*, Mayhew's Financial Publications, 1913, p. 36, and Robert (R A) Haldane, *With Intent to Deceive*, William Blackwood, 1970, p. 78.
20 *Financial Times*, 24 June 1899, p. 2.
21 *Financial Times*, 11 December 1894, p. 3.
22 *Financial Times*, 27 February 1895, p. 5; 22 March 1899, p. 3.
23 *Financial Times*, 23 March 1899, p. 5.
24 *Financial Times*, 20 November 1899, p. 3.
25 1901 Census, the National Archives, RG 13/1022.

26 Habitual Criminals Register 1902, the National Archives, MEPO 6/13.
27 *Truth*, 1 February 1906, p. 271; 8 February, p. 332; *Truth* Stock Exchange supplement, 26 June 1907.
28 *Financial News*, 19 March 1914, p. 9.
29 Contract dated 7 May 1906 in British Motor and Engineering Company, the National Archives, BT 31/11236/85824. See also the British Duplex Motor Engine Syndicate BT 31/17791/89176, list of directors, 1 May 1909. For the connoisseur of false names there are more in British Motor Engineering Company (1907) BT 31/12041/94097; the Roto-Motor Syndicate BT 31/11527/88847; the Dustless and Non-slip Road Manufacturing Company BT 31/11644/90016 and Dustroy BT 31/11644/90017.
30 Sidney Theodore Felstead and Lady Muir, *Sir Richard Muir*, John Lane, 1927, pp. 203, 205.
31 See Kynaston, p. 467. Kynaston calls Edge a 'semi-villain'.
32 *Motor Finance*, 20 February 1907, p. 153; 13 March, p. 197; 27 March, p. 228; 10 April, p. 236; 17 April, p. 258; 24 April, p. 272; 29 May, p. 340; 5 June, p. 356; 12 June, p. 377; 7 August, pp. 483, 489; 18 September, p. 529, and 2 October, p. ii.
33 *Motor Finance*, 24 July 1907, p. 465.
34 *Motor Finance*, 16 October 1907, back cover.
35 *Motor Finance*, 13 November 1907, pp. 596–98.
36 *Motor Finance*, 27 November 1907, p. 612.
37 London Electrobus Company, the National Archives, BT 31/17731/88381.
38 *Daily Mail*, 2 December 1907, p. 3.
39 *Daily Mail*, 25 February 1908, p. 2.

Chapter 12: The Other Brighton Run

1 *Standard*, 20 April 1908, p. 6; *Times*, 20 April 1908, p. 4; *Financial Times*, 21 April 1908, p. 7; *Brighton Herald*, 25 April 1908, p. 7.
2 *Winning Post*, 15 July 1911, p. 2; *Financial Times*, 27 September 1911, p. 7.
3 *Brighton Herald*, 25 April 1908, p. 7; *Automobile Owner and Steam and Electric Car Review*, May 1908, p. 176.
4 *Standard*, 20 April 1908, p. 6; *Times*, 20 April 1908, p. 4; 21 April, p. 4; David Kaye, *British Battery Electric Buses*, Oakwood Press, 1976, caption following p. 10 and Colin Morris, *Southdown*, vol. 1, Venture Publications, 1994, p. 15.
5 *Commercial Motor*, 23 April 1908, p. 206. The magazine says that the electrobus did not arrive until the next day. The local papers suggest it arrived after lunch.
6 This included the borough accountant of Eastbourne, Eastbourne Borough Council, motor omnibus committee minutes, 25 May 1908, East Sussex Record Office DE/A/21/1.
7 *Electrician*, 6 December 1907, pp. 282–84; *Electrical Review*, 20 December 1907, p. 999.
8 *Commercial Motor*, 28 November 1907, p. 290; *Automotor Journal*, 28 March 1908, pp. 399, 411–12.

9 *Motor Finance*, 29 January 1908, p. 40; 12 February, p. 66; 26 February, pp. 70, 72–73; 25 March, pp. 109–10.
10 *Motor Finance*, 22 April 1908, pp. 146–49.
11 The company was 'no longer a hopeless venture' according to the *Automotor Journal*, 2 May 1908, p. 570. *Motor Traction* was more sceptical, 2 May 1908, p. 467.
12 London Electrobus Company, the National Archives, RAIL/1078/14. Another copy is in Les Archives Nationales du Monde du Travail (Roubaix), 65 AQ Q 279.
13 See also *Electrical Review*, 1 May 1908, p. 746.
14 Dering's other directorships included Maxim's Ltd. From 1910 he became a director of a number of companies controlled by Joseph Chansay, including Aywara Rubber and Cotton Estates, Ceylon Travancore Rubber & Tea Estates, Esmeralda Consolidated Mines (Mexico), Essequibo Rubber and Tobacco Estates and Rubber and Oil Consolidated Investments.
15 London Electrobus Company memorandum of association, p. 30, Guildhall Library, Ms 18000/108B/0058.
16 *Economist*, 25 April 1908, p. 893.
17 *Daily Mail*, 27 April 1908, p. 3.
18 *Commercial Motor*, 30 April 1908, p. 221.
19 *Electrical Review*, 1 May 1908, p. 746.
20 London Electrobus Company, the National Archives, BT 31/17731/88381. The Asiatic Banking and Trading Corporation received 990 shares, the International Motor Traffic Syndicate 250, Lehwess 172, his mother 111, and Thomas Bradley Collins, in name at least editor of *Motor Finance*, received five.
21 *Motor Finance*, 8 April 1908, front cover. The Motor Share and Investment Trust has a full page advert offering 'special dealings in London electrobus shares' and claiming to buy them at a premium.
22 *Daily Mail*, 27 April 1908, p. 3.
23 *Daily Mail*, 28 April 1908, p. 2; 29 April, p. 2; 1 May, p. 2.
24 This figure is inflated by £5000 of shares registered in the name of the Asiatic Banking and Trading Corporation.

Chapter 13: The French Sailors

1 *Daily News*, 28 May 1908, pp. 8, 11; *Times*, 26 May 1908, p. 8; 28 May, p. 9; *Dover Express and East Kent News*, 29 May 1908, p. 3; *Electrician*, 29 May 1908, p. 269.
2 *Commercial Motor*, 26 April 1906, p. 162, says the first electrobus had a 14 horsepower French Thomson-Houston motor. Westminster City Council rate book for September 1907 shows that the Compagnie Générale d'Electricité paid the rates for six months on the Earl Street offices used by the electrobus company.
3 *L'Echo de Paris*, 28 April 1907, p. 3; *Financial Times*, 14 November 1907, p. 2; *Commercial Motor* 2 May 1907, p. 223; *Motor Traction*, 11 May 1907, p. 583;

Compagnie Générale des Omnibus, Les Archives Nationales du Monde du Travail (Roubaix), 65 AQ Q 368.

4 See Frank Searle in *Commercial Motor*, 16 March 1926, p. 148.

5 The other director was a 25-year old engineer called Jack Darwen.

6 *Cheltenham Chronicle*, 11 July 1908, p. 8; 18 July, p. 8, has sympathetic articles about the electrobus. See also *Commercial Motor*, 6 August 1908, p. 530. The *Cheltenham Looker-on*, 25 July 1908, p. 19, lists Lehwess and Darwen among the guests at the Queen's Hotel. Also a Mr Longman.

7 *Oxford Chronicle*, 31 July 1908, p. 6. The electrobus tour was not entirely successful. It failed to climb one steep hill, see *Oxford Times*, 1 August 1908, pp. 7, 9.

8 *Yorkshire Evening Press*, 1 August 1908; *Yorkshire Herald*, 1 August 1908. The address was a lodging house in the 1901 Census.

9 The letters to Cambridge are in the Cambridgeshire Archives, CB/2/CL/7/52/2. The other towns that were approached included Aberdeen, Barry, Bath, Blackpool, Burnley, Cardiff, Glasgow, Harrogate, Loughborough, Southport and Torquay.

10 *Eastbourne Chronicle*, 11 July 1908, p. 2; clipping in East Sussex Record Office, DE/A/40/2.

11 Eastbourne Borough Council, minutes of motor omnibus committee, 23 December 1907, East Sussex Record Office, DE/A/21/1.

12 Eastbourne Borough Council, motor omnibus committee, 25 May 1908, East Sussex Record Office, DE/A/21/1. The borough accountant says four electrobuses would require nine sets of batteries, which would cost £1395. See also *Commercial Motor*, 26 November 1908, p. 231.

13 Bath asked to test an electrobus, Loughborough approved an electrobus service on 21 September, Salisbury also wanted electrobuses. None of this happened. The company didn't reply to Salisbury's enquiries, see *Salisbury Times*, 4 December 1908, p. 8.

14 Torquay's steam buses ceased running on 8 October; see *Commercial Motor*, 15 October 1908, p. 105.

15 Torquay Council's improvement and licensing committee (minute 9823c) approved the application on 15 October 1908. The London Electrobus Company told the council on 19 November that arrangements to run the electrobuses were in progress. And there the correspondence ends.

16 Grace's Guide, http://www.gracesguide.co.uk/Brotherhood-Crocker_Motors, retrieved 29 May 2015. The company is last listed in the 1906–07 London telephone directory.

17 *Commercial Motor*, 28 November 1907, pp. 289–90; 18 June 1908, p. 381; *Hackney Mercury*, 7 December 1907, p. 4.

18 London Transport Museum, *Reinohl Collection of Ephemera*, vol. 11, p. 145.

19 *Times*, 2 September 1908, p. 14, quoting T Graham Gribble, an associate of Douglas Fox.

20 *Standard*, 27 March 1908, p. 10.

21 *Daily Mirror*, 30 November 1908, p. 5; *Times*, 30 November 1908, p. 12; *Commercial Motor*, 3 December 1908, p. 255; *Tramway and Railway World*, 3 December 1908, p. 504; *Electrical Engineer*, 4 December 1908, p. 818.

22 *Automotor Journal*, 28 November 1908, p. 1584.

23 Quotes from the letter appear in a number of local newspapers as well as the London Electrobus Company prospectus of April 1908. See *Leamington Spa Courier*, 6 March 1908, p. 7.

24 *Motor Finance*, Motor Share and Investment Trust advertising supplement, 3 June 1908 quotes from this letter. The full letter hasn't survived, but was dated 29 February according to the *Times*, 6 April 1908, p. 8.

25 *Electrician*, 26 June 1908, p. 425.

26 *Financial Times*, 23 June 1908, p. 7; *Daily Mail*, 24 June 1908, p. 5; *Commercial Motor*, 25 June 1908, p. 403.

27 *Cosmopolitan Financier*, 11 July 1908, p. 821, has an article by Bowden Green containing the full text of the motion.

28 *Times*, 3 July 1908, p. 23.

29 *Daily Mirror*, 1 June 1908, p. 3.

30 *Times*, 6 July 1908, p. 13; 8 July, p. 11.

31 Herbert Gladstone papers, British Library, Add Ms 46096, ff. 164–65.

32 *Cheltenham Chronicle*, 18 July 1908, p. 8.

33 *Electrician*, 11 September 1908, p. 832–34, and 18 September, pp. 869–73, reprints the full paper. See also: *Electrical Engineer*, 11 September 1908, p. 374; *Light Railway and Tramway Journal*, 11 September 1908, p. 183; *Times*, 16 September 1908, p. 16.

34 *Daily News*, 10 December 1908, p. 9; *Devon and Exeter Gazette*, 26 December 1908, p. 6.

Chapter 14: A Black Hole

1 See, for example, *Critic*, 2 May 1908, p. 313.

2 Charles Duguid, *How to Read the Money Article*, (seventh edition), Isaac Pitman and Sons, 1936, p. 126.

3 Benny Green, *The Streets of London*, Pavilion Books, 1983, p. 77.

4 *Commercial Motor*, 30 April 1908, p. 225.

5 *Commercial Motor*, 2 July 1908, p. 423.

6 Theodore (T C) Barker and Michael Robbins, *A History of London Transport*, vol. 2, George Allen and Unwin, 1974, p. 127, quote £450-£650 for a chassis, plus £100 for the body.

7 *Commercial Motor*, 26 November 1908, p. 231.

8 *Commercial Motor*, fortnightly bus censuses; Metropolitan Steam Omnibus Company, the National Archives, BT 31/11794/91540.

9 The early electrobuses had a drive shaft. This proved to be unreliable and from 1908 onwards the buses were built with a chain drive and the earlier ones converted.

10 London Electrobus Company, the National Archives, BT 34/3229/88381.

11 *Daily Mail,* 16 November 1908, p. 3.
12 *Commercial Motor,* 26 November 1908, p. 231.
13 London Electrobus Company, annual report, 18 December 1908, Guildhall Library, Tramway and Omnibus reports, box 1028.
14 Musgrave resigned on 18 September 1908 and Lehwess joined the board. Lehwess resigned on 3 December 1908.
15 Ernest Evan Spicer, *Practical Auditing,* H Foulks Lynch, 1911, p. 15.
16 *Motor Finance,* 12 February 1908, pp. 57–59; *Financial Times,* 19 January 1909, p. 2.
17 *Automotor Journal,* 5 December 1908, p. 1600.
18 Roland Huntford, *Shackleton,* Hodder and Stoughton, 1985, p. 358. See also the *Financial Times,* 14 February 1913, p. 3; 10 April, p. 5; 15 April, p. 10. The company was the City of Monte Video Public Works Corporation, the National Archives, BT 31/18958/104435.
19 Steele Lockhart, the National Archives, BT 31/12522/99693.
20 *Financial Times,* 26 May 1909, p. 8.
21 *Financial Times,* 10 April 1913, p. 5. Garlick wrote a cheque for £15,000, he took the shares, but the company never cashed the cheque.

Chapter 15: The Sell-Off

1 Letter from Motor Share and Investment Trust, dated 3 June 1908, London Electrobus Company, the National Archives, RAIL/1078/14.
2 *Rubber and Oil,* 27 April 1910, front page.
3 *Motor Finance,* 3 June 1908, p. 201.
4 *Commercial Motor,* 18 June 1908, p. 381; 25 June 1908, p. 401; *Motor Finance,* advertising supplement, 3 June 1908; the National Archives, RAIL/1078/14.
5 London Electrobus Company, the National Archives, BT 31/17731/88381, register of shareholders, 11 January 1909. Most of the sales were made by Thomas Bradley Collins, the editor of *Motor Finance,* and H W Blackburn, the secretary of the Motor Share and Investment Trust. These names may be fictitious.
6 *Mainly about People,* 20 June 1908, p. 608.
7 *Daily Mail,* 17 June 1908, p. 3. This was an offer to sell deferred shares. The article doesn't name the firm of 'stockbrokers'.
8 *Motor Finance,* 25 March 1908, p. 110; London Electrobus Company, the National Archives, BT 31/17731/88381. The register of shareholders shows that the International Motor Traffic Syndicate held 14600 shares on 11 January 1909, the Asiatic Banking and Trading Corporation 5000 and Jenny Lehwess 3250. Lehwess held 5959 shares in his own name.
9 Petition of Securities Exchange, 14 July 1909, Motor Share and Investment Trust, the National Archives, J 13/5224.
10 *Daily Mail,* 5 November 1907, p. 5.
11 *Daily Mirror,* 4 December 1908, p. 4.

12 The last issue of *Motor Finance* was 2 September 1908. The office was at Goschen House, 12–13 Henrietta Street. Two of Beall's companies also used the same address. Frank Harris and *Candid Friend* were previously based at the same address. Albert Edwin Griesbach was listed as a lowly stockbroker's clerk in the 1911 Census.

13 *Financial Times*, 15 April 1909, p. 4.

14 *Truth*, 31 March 1909, p. 775.

15 Record of verbal contract dated 24 June 1909 suggests Lehwess had 22 000 shares left, International Motor Traffic Syndicate, the National Archives, BT 31/12112/94860.

Chapter 16: A Veil Of Secrecy

1 Gould Storage Battery Company, the National Archives, BT 31/11727/90877. The Inland Revenue was owed £45, and more nebulously Locock was claiming £80 for rent and there was a £50 debenture.

2 *London Gazette*, 29 September 1908, pp. 7053, 7054, 7055–56.

3 *Financial News*, 19 May 1909, p. 7; 20 May, p. 7; 21 May, p. 6; 26 May, p. 7; *Financial Times*, 19 May 1909, p. 7; 20 May, p. 3; 21 May, p. 8; 26 May, p. 8.

4 The judge was Walter Phillimore, later Baron Phillimore.

5 International Motor Traffic Syndicate, the National Archives, BT 31/12112/94860.

6 *Automotor Journal*, 28 May 1908, p. 412. The Gould batteries performed well for the first 5000 miles. The engineers expected them to last 8000 to 10 000 miles before they would need new plates.

7 International Motor Traffic Syndicate, the National Archives, BT 31/12112/94860.

8 *Financial Times*, 11 December 1909, p. 8; 16 December, p. 9; 9 November 1910, p. 8; 10 November, p. 7; 11 November, p. 11; 12 November, p. 7; 15 November, p. 5.

9 Gould Storage Battery Company, the National Archives, BT 31/11727/90877, letter dated 10 January 1910.

10 Mechanical and General Inventions Company, the National Archives, J 13/8025. Affidavit of Elsie Ractliffe, 18 July 1918. Will of Jenny Lehwess, 16 December 1920, probate granted 11 January 1924. Another instance of Lehwess's light-fingered approach was given during the Motor Car Emporium's bankruptcy hearing. The emporium had paid £400 to set up the Electric Vehicle Company. In January 1907 the Electric Vehicle Company issued a cheque to repay the emporium. Lehwess cashed it. See *Automotor Journal*, 7 December 1907, p. 1781.

11 London Electrobus Company, the National Archives, BT 34/3229/88381. The company had issued debentures to the value of £11 935. For Lehwess's holdings see *Cosmopolitan Financier*, 13 November 1909, p. 1236. Trial of Saxby, William Charles Hart, Old Bailey Proceedings

Online, evidence of William Saxby, 10 June 1910. The transcripts spell his name Saxeby.

Chapter 17: The Greek Adventurer

1 *Financial Times*, 17 July 1909, p. 5, has the full text of the circular.
2 *Truth*, 21 July 1909, p. 156.
3 *Truth Cautionary List for 1912*, Truth Publishing Company, 1913, p. 77. There are similar entries in other editions of the list.
4 *Financial Times*, 22 July 1909, p. 9. The battery hire company was Pritchetts and Gold, the National Archives, BT 31/16607/69517.
5 *Cosmopolitan Financier*, 22 January 1910, p. 69; Reorganisation and Control Syndicate, the National Archives, J 13/6386, petition of Michie Fraser and others, 15 January 1912. The lease of the garage was originally held by the Motor Car Emporium; it was inherited by Improved Electric Traction.
6 Theodoros Delyannis was assassinated in June 1905. The Greek surname is Δηλιγιάννης. There are several transliterations.
7 Trial of Saxby, William Charles Hart, Old Bailey Proceedings Online, evidence of Michael Theodosius, of the Greek Consulate, 14 June 1910.
8 Atlas Banking Corporation, the National Archives, BT 31/18110/93536.
9 *Cosmopolitan Financier*, 1 September 1907, p. 122.
10 *Wheel of Fortune*, April 1908, p. iii.
11 *Cosmopolitan Financier*, 2 April 1910, front cover.
12 *Cosmopolitan Financier*, 12 December 1908, p. 1469.
13 Anglo-Continental Investment Syndicate, the National Archives, BT 31/12223/96080 and J 13/4989; *Truth*, 23 June 1909, p. 1522.
14 *Truth*, 21 October 1908, p. 963.
15 *Truth*, 21 April 1909, p. 931; 29 June, pp. 1698–700.
16 Reorganisation and Control Syndicate, the National Archives, BT 31/18940/104157. The syndicate was registered on 21 July 1909. Receivers were called in at the London Electrobus Company on 22 July. Delyannis's announcement was reported in the *Daily Mail*, 19 July 1909, p. 2.
17 *Daily Mail*, 26 July 1909, p. 2; *Cosmopolitan Financier*, 31 July 1909, p. 854.
18 There are discrepancies in the precise number of electrobuses owned by the London Electrobus Company. According to *Commercial Motor*'s fortnightly censuses the company had 20 buses between October and the end of December 1908. David Kaye, *British Battery Electric Buses*, Oakwood Press, 1976, says registration plates were issued to 21 London electrobuses. Delyannis in his 1909 circular claimed the company has 24 buses. According to the *Financial News*, 7 March 1911 p. 6, the Reorganisation and Control Syndicate bought 22 electrobuses from the London Electrobus Company.
19 Almost the last piece of positive publicity from the electrobus company was reported in the *Daily Mail*, 8 April 1909, p. 3. The government was considering introducing compulsory engine governors to prevent speeding. The electrobus company claimed it would only cost £5 to adapt an electrobus.

20 One magazine that continued to laud the electrobus was the *Automobile Owner and Steam and Electric Car Review*, September 1909, p. 272.

21 *Cosmopolitan Financier*, 4 September 1909, p. 994.

22 *Cosmopolitan Financier*, 7 August 1909, inside front cover.

23 *Cosmopolitan Financier*, 27 November 1909, p. 1269; *Financial Times*, 10 December 1909, p. 6.

24 *Cosmopolitan Financier*, 13 November 1909, p. 1235.

25 *Cosmopolitan Financier*, 18 September 1909, p. 1043.

26 Reorganisation and Control Syndicate, the National Archives, BT 31/18940/104157.

27 *Cosmopolitan Financier*, 30 May 1908, p. 604; 11 July, p. 821. The edition of 13 Feb 1909, p. 219, has a brief plug for the electrobus.

28 *Financial Times*, 31 July 1909, p. 5; *Truth*, 4 August 1909, p. 281.

29 Atlas Banking Corporation, the National Archives, J 13/5002.

30 *Times*, 15 January 1910, p. 3; *Truth*, 19 January 1910, p. 142.

31 *Financial Times*, 10 December 1909, p. 6.

32 London Electrobus Company, the National Archives, BT 31/17731/88381.

33 Hove Borough Council, minutes of watch committee, 13 December 1909, East Sussex Record Office, DO/A/17/5, p. 206.

34 *Financial Times*, 25 October 1913, p. 10.

Chapter 18: The Whistleblower

1 This is the most likely date for the end of the London electrobuses. The electrobus receivers' accounts finish on 8 January 1910 (the National Archives, BT 31/17731/88381). There is no evidence of any income from fares after this. The petition of Michie Fraser, 15 January 1912 (Reorganisation and Control Syndicate, the National Archives, J 13/6386) says the syndicate purchased the buses on 3 January 1910. The Reinohl Collection at the London Transport Museum suggests the bus service stopped at the end of 1909.

2 Four-page supplement to *Cosmopolitan Financier*, 8 January 1910.

3 *Cosmopolitan Financier*, 13 November 1909, p. 1236.

4 *Daily Mail*, 26 June 1909, p. 2.

5 *Daily Mail*, 13 January 1910, p. 4. Roberts was backed by Ernest Polden, a theatrical impresario who had been a director of Hooley's Siberian Goldfields Development Company.

6 *Cosmopolitan Financier*, 22 January 1910, p. 69.

7 The new company was to be called the London Electro Autobus Company. No such company was registered.

8 Possibly because of an out-of-court settlement. *Financial Times*, 29 January 1910, p. 5; 26 February, p. 3; *Financial News*, 26 February, p. 5. See also *Cosmopolitan Financier*, 19 March 1910, p. 193.

9 *Cosmopolitan Financier*, 19 March 1910, p. 193.

10 Reorganisation and Control Syndicate, the National Archives, J 13/6386, petition of Michie Fraser.

11 *Tramway and Railway World*, 10 February 1910, p. 12.
12 *Financial News*, 15 January 1910, p. 4; *Daily Mail*, 17 January 1910, p. 2.
13 Cosmopolitan Publications, the National Archives, BT 31/12416/98350 and J 13/5470; *Truth* 27 April 1910, p. 1086. The receivers sold the *Cosmopolitan Financier* to new owners in July 1910. On 6 April 1910 the Reorganisation and Control Syndicate increased its registered capital to £40 000, in preparation for a fresh attempt to sell more shares. Nothing ever happened. Delyannis was the moving spirit behind Rubber and Oil Consolidated Investments, which was registered on 4 April 1910, the National Archives, BT 31/32056/108594.
14 The sources for this story are reports in the *Times*, 5 March 1910, p. 3; 9 June, p. 4; 11 June, p. 4; 13 June, p. 3; 14 June, p. 4; 15 June, p. 4; 16 June, p. 4; *Financial Times*, 9 June 1910, p. 9; 11 June, p. 8; 13 June, p. 8; 14 June, p. 8; 15 June, p. 11; 16 June, p. 13; *Standard*, 9 June 1910, p. 10; 11 June, p. 9; 13 June, p. 10; 14 June, p. 10; 15 June, p. 11; 16 June, p. 11; *Saturday Review*, 18 June 1910, p. 781 and the Old Bailey transcripts of the trial of William Charles Hart Saxby.
15 The receivers' accounts were circulated at the meeting. The six-monthly accounts are in the London Electrobus Company, the National Archives, BT 31/17731/88381.
16 This article appeared in *Cosmopolitan Financier*, 13 November 1909, pp. 1235–36.
17 *Truth*, 29 June 1910, pp. 1698–99.
18 *Financial Times*, 4 June 1910, p. 7.

Chapter 19: A Franchise In Fraud

1 Reorganisation and Control Syndicate, the National Archives, J 13/6386, petition of Michie Fraser, pp. 8–9 quotes the letter sent to Semple. Semple's name has been redacted in the court papers, but not very well. Only one shareholder with fifty shares has a six-letter surname with descenders and ascenders in the right place. Semple was also one of the shareholders supporting the petition. See also *London Gazette*, 19 January 1912, p. 472.
2 The two syndicates had a curiously complicated relationship. The International Motor Traffic Syndicate was the third largest shareholder in the Reorganisation and Control Syndicate, with a stake of £250. In preparation for the launch of the Reorganisation and Control Syndicate Lehwess transferred all his electrobus shares – some 22 000 of them – plus sundry other assets to the International Motor Traffic Syndicate and mortgaged these assets for £250 – which he promptly invested in the Reorganisation and Control Syndicate.
3 *Financial Times*, 25 April 1911, p. 8; *Electrical Review*, 28 April 1911, p. 672.
4 *Sussex Daily News*, 14 February 1911, p. 3; *Brighton Gazette*, 15 February 1911, p. 8.
5 *Electrical Review*, 10 February 1911, p. 215; *Financial News*, 28 February 1911, p. 6; 7 March, p. 6.
6 *Financial News*, 8 February 1911, p. 8; *Financial Times*, 8 February 1911, p. 12. The Reorganisation and Control Syndicate had paid the rates, Westminster

City Council rate books for March 1910. The landlord was Improved Electric Traction, see *Electrical Review*, 10 February 1911, p. 215.

7 Rubber and Oil Consolidated Investments, the National Archives, BT 31/32056/108594.

8 *Truth*, 3 August 1910, pp. 287–88.

9 *Financial Times*, 9 April 1913, p. 5; 1 January 1914, p. 3.

10 The magazine was *Financial Outlook*. The bucket shop was Metropolitan and Counties Investors, its name in pre-Chansay days was Redway, Furness. Metropolitan and Counties Investors, the National Archives, BT 31/19493/109840. For criticism see *Financial Times*, 4 January 1912, p. 4. See also *Truth Cautionary List for 1911*, Truth Publishing, 1912, p. 65.

11 The office block was Salisbury House, in Finsbury Circus. It still survives.

12 *Commercial Motor*, 30 June 1910, p. 354, reports the attempted injunction. In a related action the Reorganisation Syndicate also sued Improved Electric Traction, *Times*, 12 October 1910, p. 3; *Standard*, 5 November 1910, p. 10. Improved Electric Traction then retaliated by suing the Reorganisation and Control Syndicate, *Standard*, 24 March 1911, p. 12. None of these actions seems to have been reported.

13 *Financial News*, 8 February 1911, p. 8.

14 *Financial News*, 28 February 1911, p. 6; 7 March, p. 6.

15 *Times*, 13 July 1911, p. 21. The falsified article appeared in *Cosmopolitan Financier*, 13 November 1909, p. 1235.

16 *Truth Cautionary List for 1911*, Truth Publishing, 1912, p. 70; *Truth*, 17 January 1912, p. 139.

17 *Times*, 13 July 1911, p. 21.

18 Reorganisation and Control Syndicate, the National Archives, BT 31/18940/104157.

19 *Truth*, 17 July 1912, p. 157.

20 *Truth*, 18 June 1913, p. 1546. The case was reported in *Financial Times*, 11 June 1913, p. 12. It was overturned on appeal.

21 *Financial Times*, 20 September 1899, p. 3; see also 2 October 1899, p. 3.

22 A receiver was appointed 28 April 1910. Cosmopolitan Publications, the National Archives, BT 31/12416/98350.

23 Samuel Habgood, the photographer from Wimbledon who was closely associated with Mayhew in the clean-up the City campaign, bought a small shareholding in the electrobus company in late 1907. He converted this into an investment in the Reorganisation and Control Syndicate and would doubtless have supported any legal action. Reorganisation and Control Syndicate, the National Archives, J 13/6386.

24 *Electrical Review*, 5 April 1912, p. 541.

25 *Financial Times*, 16 April 1912, p. 3.

26 *Financial Times*, 23 May 1913, p. 9; *Times*, 23 May 1913, p. 13. The company was the Ceylon Travancore Rubber and Tea Estates, the National Archives BT 31/19765/107836 and J 13/6151. The director was Sir William Hudson. Dering was also on the board.

27 Rubber and Oil Consolidated Investments prospectus, *Financial Times*, 6 April 1910, p. 13.

28 The National Archives has the Companies House files for Mamia River Estates, BT 31/13219/109183; Ceylon Travancore Rubber and Tea Estates, BT 31/19265/107836; Aywara Rubber and Cotton Estates, BT 31/19448/109401; Anglo-Cuban Oil Bitumen and Asphalt, BT 31/32088/114028.

29 Aywara Rubber and Cotton Estates, the National Archives, BT 31/19448/109401.

30 Rubber and Oil Consolidated Investments, the National Archives, BT 31/332056/108594 and J 13/6720.

31 Anglo-European Bank, the National Archives, J 13/6477, report of official receiver, E C Bliss, 20 December 1913.

32 *Truth*, 2 July 1913, p. 31; 16 July, p. 157; 3 December, p. 1319.

33 *Financial Times*, 25 April 1914, p. 5.

34 *Financial Times*, 16 May 1914, p. 5; 23 June, p. 3.

Chapter 20: The Battle Of The Buses

1 *Commercial Motor*, 5 May 1910, p. 174.

2 Ken Fines, *A History of Brighton and Hove*, Phillimore, 2002, p. 88.

3 regencysociety-jamesgray.com/volume26/source/jg_26_155.html, retrieved 1 July 2015.

4 See, for example, a report in the *Morning Post*, 27 November 1883, p. 5, of activities of the West End Tramways Opposition Association. See also Roy Porter, *London: A Social History*, Penguin Books, 2000, pp. 271–73; Geoffrey Wilson, *London United Tramways*, George Allen & Unwin, 1971, p. 21. Lady Chichester was opposing a horse tramway in Twickenham.

5 *Truth*, 25 April 1906, p. 969.

6 Hove Borough Council watch committee minutes, East Sussex Record Office, DO/A/17/4, p. 326; Brighton Borough Council watch committee minutes, 6 December 1907, East Sussex Record Office, DB/B/12/24.

7 Hove Borough Council watch committee minutes, East Sussex Record Office, DO/A/17/5, p. 14. The letter from Horace Thornton representing an unnamed syndicate was received on 25 February 1908. Thornton was a director of both the International Motor Traffic Syndicate and Improved Electric Traction. He had previously headed an attempt to introduce American-made Fischer hybrid buses in London.

8 Hove Borough Council watch committee minutes, East Sussex Record Office, DO/A/17/5, p. 62.

9 The bus company confusingly often referred to its five hybrids as electric buses – or even electrobuses: see the *Electrical Times*, 9 July 1914, pp. 34–35.

10 US Department of Energy, Argonne National Laboratory, *Electric Buses Energize Downtown Chattanooga*, August 1997.

11 Hove Borough Council watch committee minutes, East Sussex Record Office, DO/A/17/5, p. 99.

12 25 Montague Place was made a grade II listed building by Historic England on 11 May 2015. The original building plans are in the East Sussex Record Office, DB/D7/6364a.
13 *Electrician*, 25 June 1909, pp. 421–23; *Electrical Times*, 9 July 1914, pp. 34–35.
14 Hove Borough Council watch committee minutes, East Sussex Record Office, DO/A/17/5, pp. 187–89; Brighton Borough Council watch committee, East Sussex Record Office, DB/B/12/26 pp. 71–77.
15 Brighton Borough Council watch committee minutes, East Sussex Record Office, DB/B/12/26, pp. 71–72.
16 Hove Borough Council watch committee minutes, East Sussex Record Office, DO/A/17/6, letter of 13 September 1911.
17 *Brighton Herald*, 12 June 1909, p. 2; Brighton Borough Council watch committee minutes, East Sussex Record Office, DB/B/12/30, p. 240.
18 Hove Borough Council watch committee minutes, East Sussex Record Office, DO/A/17/6, report of chief constable 30 April 1913. There were also 13 complaints about hybrid buses: Brighton Borough Council watch committee, East Sussex Record Office, DB/B/12/26, p. 75.
19 Canon Flynn was based at St John the Baptist Church, Palmeira Square, Hove.
20 Thomas Tilling started out providing horses and carriages before diversifying into motor transport. See Peter Thorold, *The Motoring Age 1896–1939*, Profile Books, 2003, p. 62.
21 *Electrical Times*, 9 July 1914, pp. 34–35.
22 *Commercial Motor*, 28 December 1916, p. 374.
23 *Electrical Engineer*, 16 June 1911, p. 677. See letter from the United's secretary Frank Smith, dated 15 April 1915, Brighton Borough Council watch committee, East Sussex Record Office, DB/B/12/30, p. 241. The United was paying 1.9d a unit. In 1907 the London Electrobus Company was paying 1d a unit, *Electrical Review*, 20 December 1907, p. 999. The *Electrician*, 21 January 1916, p. 579, says Brighton's municipal trams were paying 1.35d a unit in 1915.
24 *Commercial Motor*, 28 December 1916, p. 374; Colin Morris, *Southdown*, vol. 1, Venture Publications, 1994, pp. 15, 16.
25 Brighton Borough Council watch committee, East Sussex Record Office, DB/B/12/31.
26 Letter from Thomas Tilling, dated 31 May 1917, Brighton Borough watch committee minutes, 30 June 1917, East Sussex Record Office, DB/B/12/31.
27 Inquest papers, 26 January 1917, East Sussex Record Office, COR 1/3/445.

Chapter 21: Boom, Bounce And Bust

1 David Kynaston, *The City of London*, vol. 2, Pimlico, 1995, p. 520; Hubert A Meredith, *The Drama of Making Money*, Sampson Low Marston, 1931, p. 214; *Rubber and Oil*, 27 April 1910, cover.
2 *Financial Times*, 23 March 1910, p. 6.
3 Meredith, pp. 210–11.
4 Meredith, p. 213.

5 Kynaston, p. 521. See also *Truth*, 30 March 1910, p. 792.
6 *Financial Times*, 7 June 1910, p. 3.
7 Lee Syndicate, the National Archives, BT 31/19238/107610; Victoria (Malaya) Rubber Estates, BT 31/19259/107800.
8 *Truth*, 9 March 1910, p. 576.
9 *Financial Times*, 7 June 1910, p. 3; Victoria (Malaya) Rubber Estates, Stock Exchange listing application, correspondence with Stock Exchange, 18 May 1910, Guildhall Library, Ms 18000/128B/0059.
10 *Financial Times*, 5 April 1911, p. 4; 8 April, p. 5.
11 *Rubber and Oil*, 18 October 1911, p. 267.
12 Lee Syndicate, the National Archives, J 13/6290, petition dated 20 June 1912.
13 The first issue of *Rubber and Oil* was 20 April 1910.
14 *Rubber and Oil*, 4 January 1911, cover.
15 *Rubber and Oil*, 18 October 1911, p. 267.
16 *Financial Times*, 7 December 1911, p. 2; 8 December, p. 2; 9 December, p. 2; 11 December, p. 2.
17 Improved Electric Traction, the National Archives, BT 31/11428/87822 and BT 34/2077/87822, letters dated 2 July 1912 and 3 January 1913.
18 *Financial News*, 4 January 1912, p. 10; *Financial Times*, 4 January 1912, p. 3; *Financier*, 4 January 1912, p. 6.
19 The fullest report of the meeting is in the *Financial Times*, 4 January 1912, p. 3.
20 *Rubber and Oil*, 13 January 1912, pp. 23, 2.
21 I know of no evidence that Beall was linked to the South Sumatra, but any link would have been carefully concealed.
22 The promoter was a shell company called the Commercial and Financial Agency, the National Archives, BT 31/19373/108717.
23 *Financial Times* carried a series of letters: 20 February 1911, p. 2; 22 February, p. 2; 1 May, p. 2; 19 July, p. 2; 21 July, p. 2.
24 *Financial Times*, 7 November 1911, p. 3; *Straits Times*, 23 April 1912, p. 10.
25 *New York Daily Tribune*, 17 March 1912, p. 4.
26 *Financial Times*, 19 April 1912, p. 5.
27 *Financial Times*, 8 May 1912, p. 3.
28 *Financial Times*, 6 June 1912, p. 10.
29 *Financial News*, 6 June 1912, p. 9; *Financial Times*, 6 June 1912, p. 10.
30 *Financial Times*, 12 December 1912, p. 11.
31 'Former Plantation Workers Compensated after 16 Years', *Star online*, 13 August 2012 http://www.thestar.com.my/news/nation/2012/08/13/former-plantation-workers-compensated-after-16-years/thestar.com.my, retrieved 28 May 2016.

Chapter 22: The Master Blackmailer

1 *Critic*, 24 March 1914, pp. 115–16.
2 Sidney Theodore Felstead and Lady Muir, *Sir Richard Muir*, John Lane, 1927, p. 205. The cover price of *Rubber and Oil* was 1d.

3 *Financial Times*, 4 December 1913, p. 5.
4 Webb took over the *Critic* in November 1905. Hess was jailed for fraud in January 1909. He got 12 months, despite having a previously unblemished character, *Times*, 27 January 1909, p. 4.
5 *Daily Telegraph*, 10 March 1914, p. 4.
6 *Rubber and Oil*, 1 November 1913, p. 8.
7 *Financial Times*, 15 January 1914, p. 3; 10 March, p. 3; *Financial News*, 7 March 1914, p. 5. In November 1913 Roumanian Consolidated shares were worth around 21 shillings.
8 *Financial News*, 15 January 1914, p. 9; *Financial Times*, 15 January 1914, p. 3.
9 *Times*, 29 January 1914, p. 2, has the best report of what Willis heard.
10 *Financial News*, 15 January 1914, p. 9; *Financial Times*, 15 January 1914, p. 3.
11 Sidney Theodore Felstead and Lady Muir, *Sir Richard Muir*, John Lane, 1927, p. 205.
12 *Financial Times*, 7 March 1914, p. 10.
13 *Times*, 29 January 1914, p. 2. The weight of 1000 sovereigns was almost 8 kilograms, or 17 lb.
14 Felstead and Muir, p. 205. The book is based on Muir's case notes.
15 *Financial Times*, 15 January 1914, p. 7. Before working on *Rubber and Oil* Robinson worked on the Chansay organ *Financial Outlook*. See also *Financial News*, 7 November 1912, p. 9.
16 *Financial News*, 1 January 1914, p. 9; *Financial Times*, 1 January 1914, p. 3; *Financier* 1 January 1914, p. 7.
17 *Financial News*, 22 January 1914, p. 9; *Financial Times*, 22 January 1914, p. 3.
18 *Financial Times*, 22 January 1914, p. 3; 29 January, p. 3; *Daily Telegraph*, 11 March 1914, p. 4.
19 Rubber and Oil, the National Archives, BT 31/13173/108684; Rubber and Oil Trust & Investment Corporation, BT 31/13186/108827; Motor Share and Investment Trust, BT 31/12190/95700.
20 *Daily Telegraph*, 11 March 1914, p. 4; *Financier*, 11 March 1914, p. 4.
21 *Daily Telegraph*, 11 March 1914, p. 4.
22 *Financial Times*, 19 March 1914, p. 11.
23 *Financial News*, 19 March 1914, p. 9.
24 *Critic*, 24 March 1914, p. 115.
25 *Financial Times*, 19 March 1914, p. 6.
26 *Critic*, 12 May 1914, p. 175. The solicitor that Merchant used for his appeal was Percy R Gibbs, who had become the main solicitor used by Lehwess.

Chapter 23: The Trendsetter

1 H G Wells, *Tono-Bungay*, Macmillan, 1909, p. 109.
2 Gijs Mom, *The Electric Vehicle*, Johns Hopkins University Press, 2004, p. 182.
3 *Power Wagon*, July 1912, pp. 17–22. Only 54 of these double-deck buses were in service, the rest were in reserve or being repaired.

4 About 40 per cent of the vehicles in the United States were steam cars, 38 per cent electric cars, with petrol bringing up the rear on 22 per cent, *Encyclopedia Brittanica*, 15th edition, vol. 2, p. 518, Chicago, 1978.

5 Arthur H Beavan, *Tube, Train, Tram and Car*, George Routledge, 1903, introduction by Llewellyn Preece, p. xiv.

6 See 'Motoring's Bicycling Beginnings', chapter 13 of Carlton Reid, *Roads Were Not Built for Cars*, Island Press, 2015.

7 Thomas D Murphy, *British Highways and Byways from a Motor Car*, L C Page, 1908, p. 44.

8 *Electrical World*, July 1902, quoted in Michael Brian Schiffer, *Taking Charge*, Smithsonian Books, 1994, p. 85.

9 Advert for the Columbus Electric in the *Literary Digest*, 19 February 1910, reproduced in Schiffer, p. 126.

10 Schiffer, p. 169.

11 Jean-Louis Loubet, *L'Histoire de l'Automobile Française*, Editions du Seuil, 2001, p. 20.

12 'The Unimportance of Touring Ability', *Electric Vehicles*, August 1916, quoted in David A Kirsch, *The Electric Vehicle and the Burden of History*, Rutgers University Press, 2000, p. 186.

13 John Keats, *The Insolent Chariots*, J P Lippincott, 1958, p. 186.

14 Schiffer, *Taking Charge*, p. 171.

15 The Electromobile Company in Britain is said to have made electric cars until 1921; it was listed in the London telephone book until 1929.

16 Electric Van Wagon and Omnibus Company full page advert, *Motor Finance*, 1 January 1908. It was the question of the moment: the *Daily Mail*'s headline on the launch of the electrobus was 'Petrol, Steam or Electricity?', 24 April 1906, p. 7.

17 The chassis used by Thomas Tilling when it won the Brighton parcel van contract in 1905 was identical to the one used on its buses, *Daily News*, 13 February 1905, p. 8. See also *Encyclopaedia Britannica*, 1911, vol 18, p. 922.

18 *Observer*, 7 June 1908, p. 8. Searle said that the scope for the electrobus was limited because of the difficulty it had climbing hills.

19 *Economist*, 9 December 1911, p. 1203.

20 An article in the *Automobile Owner and Steam and Electric Car Review* September 1909, p. 272, says the Vanguard company converted some petrol buses to electric for a trial. The *Daily Mail*, 14 April 1909, p. 8, reports that the London General was experimenting with an electric bus. See also *Motor Finance*, 3 June 1908, p. 201; *Commercial Motor*, 8 April 1909, p. 93; David Kaye, *British Battery Electric Buses*, Oakwood Press, 1976, p. 9.

21 Compagnie Générale des Omnibus, Les Archives Nationales du Monde de Travail (Roubaix), 65 AQ Q 368.

22 Report of the London Traffic Branch of the Board of Trade, Cd 4379, 1908, p. 24.

23 *Scientific American*, 6 January 1912, p. 5. Engineers believed electric vehicles had a bright future, but the public should be better educated about how to treat batteries. See the *Journal of the Institution of Electrical Engineers*, 15 April 1914, p. 32; Schiffer, p. 163.

24 The number of electric delivery vehicles hit a peak of 12000 in the United States at the start of 1915, *Automobile*, 21 January 1915, p. 127. Quoted in Judy Anderson and Curtis Anderson, *Electric and Hybrid Cars*, McFarland & Co, 2005, p. 129.

25 Philip Bagwell, *The Transport Revolution from 1770*, Batsford, 1974, p. 222.

26 *Economist*, 7 October 1911, p. 703.

27 Mom, p. 149.

28 Mom, p. 150; *Cosmopolitan Financier*, 13 February 1909, p. 219.

29 Mom, p. 151.

30 The phrase occurs in the Alkali Act of 1874 and is repeated frequently in the Royal Commission on Noxious Vapours, C 2159, 1878. See also *New Scientist*, 9 May 1974, p. 290.

31 Frank Searle, *Commercial Motor*, 16 March 1926, pp. 149–50.

32 John R Day, *The Story of the London Bus*, London Transport Executive, 1973, p. 46. For running costs see Anthony Bird, *Roads & Vehicles*, Arrow Books, 1973, p. 141.

33 *Financial Times*, 30 October 1912, p. 9; Beatrice and Sidney Webb, *The Story of the King's Highway* (*English Local Government from the Revolution to the Municipal Corporations Act*, vol. 5), Longmans Green, 1913, p. 254.

34 *Scientific American*, 22 June 1912, p. 561.

35 *Commercial Vehicle*, 1 November 1915, p. 26, quoted in Kirsch, p. 149.

36 Mom, p. 265.

37 Bagwell, p. 209.

38 See Schiffer, p. 165.

39 Kirsch, p. 145, gives some figures. A petrol truck could cover about five times the area that an electric van could.

40 *Commercial Motor*, 27 May 1966, p. 79. The source of these figures is a press release issued by the Electric Vehicle Association of Great Britain.

41 This is the BMW i3.

42 *Financial Times*, Chloride Battery advert, 13 July 1973, p. 9. There are similar figures in the House of Lords select committee on science and technology report on electric vehicles, HL 352, 1979.

43 Andrew Rosen, *The Transformation of British Life 1950 to 2000*, Manchester University Press, 2003, p. 14. The Milk Marketing Board, which had guaranteed a minimum price for milk, was effectively wound up in 1994.

Chapter 24: A New Tipping Point

1 'Remarks by the President in State of Union Address', The White House, Press Release, 25 January 2011.

2 http://www.cleanenergyministerial.org/Resource-Center/Ministerials/ CEM1-Resources. An excerpt from Chu's closing remarks is on YouTube. https://www.youtube.com/watch?v=8mAi-U8I7mg&feature=youtu.be, retrieved 5 November 2016.

3 http://www.gov.cn/zwgk/2012-07/09/content_2179032.htm, retrieved 17 March 2015.

4 Martin Melosi, *Garbage in the Cities*, Texas A&M University Press, 1981, p. 20.

5 *Times*, 1 June 1894, p. 14.

6 *Guardian*, 16 July 2015, p. 4.

7 *Nature*, 17 September 2015, p. 367. Traffic accounts for at least 5 per cent of the pollution deaths globally.

8 David Shepardson, Reuters, 21 January 2016.

9 *Global EV Outlook 2016*, International Energy Agency, 2016, p. 4.

10 *Wired Magazine*, August 2010; Transport Research Laboratory Report PPR668, TRL, July 2013.

11 'Nissan LEAF Battery Reliably Outperforms Cynics, Critics and Alternatives', Nissan Europe press release, 23 March 2015, id:131218. The company says only 3 out of 35 000 cars in Europe have had battery failure.

12 http://phys.org/news/2015-02-electric-car-japan-gas-stations.html, retrieved 24 March 2015.

13 Political developments in 2016 may also affect the future of electric vehicles. According to Britain's business secretary Greg Clark, electric vehicles will be at the heart of the country's post-Brexit industrial strategy, *Guardian*, 25 November 2016. On the other hand the new American president has said he will axe the tax breaks for electric vehicles, which is likely to slow growth. See https://www.bloomberg.com/gadfly/articles/2016-11-16/donald-trump-and-fuel-efficiency-electric-cars-will-survive.

14 http://www.nextgreencar.com/electric-cars/buying-guide/, retrieved 18 October 2016.

15 John Vidal, 'Electric Car Sales Speed Up', *Observer*, 3 May 2014.

16 Bloomberg New Energy Finance, press release, 25 February 2016.

17 Werner Rammert, quoted in Gijs Mom, *The Electric Vehicle*, Johns Hopkins University Press, 2004, p. 1.

18 W Brian Arthur, *The Nature of Technology: What It Is and How It Evolves*, Allen Lane, 2009, p. 104.

19 Barry Fox, *New Scientist*, 31 March 1983, p. 891.

20 This is a description of what used to be my local shop, Video City. There was also a handful of Video 2000 tapes. The shop closed in June 2015: http:// videocitylondon.com/, retrieved 1 August 2015.

21 Alternatively motor manufacturers might have been prompted to make petrol vehicles that were as quiet and clean as electric vehicles.

22 'Mayor Unveils First Fully Electric Bus Routes for Central London', press releases from Transport for London and the Mayor of London, dated 9 September 2016.

Epilogue

1 Sidney Theodore Felstead, *Horatio Bottomley*, John Murray, 1936, p. 289.
2 Congo Rubber Plantations, the National Archives, J 13/6162; *Financial Times*, 20 January 1916, p. 3.
3 Habitual Criminals Register 1917, the National Archives, MEPO 6/29. After he emerged from prison Beall was placed under the supervision of the Central Association for Aid of Discharged Convicts.
4 *Derbyshire Times*, 9 January 1942, p. 4.
5 Among the companies linked to Lehwess were the Asia Caoutchouc Trust (promoted by the Commercial and Financial Agency); Rubber and Petroleum Trust; Lombiry; Marovoay Rice Lands and the Newfoundland Exploration Syndicate.
6 *Commercial Motor*, 31 March 1910, p. 75. The motor show of November 1910 was one of the last times the Electric Vehicle Company exhibited electric vehicles, the *Times*, 12 November 1910, p. 18.
7 *Rubber and Oil*, 23 August 1911, p. 213. The report (which repeats an article in an unnamed Canadian paper) wrongly says Bottomley owned the *Financial News*.
8 *Flight*, 4 April 1914, pp. 358–62.
9 http://www.rafmuseum.org.uk/research/online-exhibitions/rfc_centenary/british-military-aviation-1862-1912/war-clouds-gather.aspx, retrieved 23 July 2015. The committee report was dated December 1911.
10 Mechanical and General Inventions Ltd, the National Archives, J 13/8025, affidavit of Henry (Harry) Retallack-Moloney, 18 July 1918. He formally joined the board in October 1914. It is possible that the War Office wanted to keep tabs on this German with ambitions to manufacture military aircraft.
11 Aeronautical Supplies, the National Archives, MUN 4/6460. The Royal Naval Air Service took over the plane three days after the outbreak of war.
12 http://encyclopedia.1914-1918-online.net/article/prisoners_of_war_and_internees_great_britain, retrieved 24 July 2015.
13 Mechanical and General Inventions Ltd, the National Archives, J 13/8025, affidavits of Elsie Ractliffe, 11 July 1918, and George Esden from the official receiver, 24 June 1921. On 6 December 1915 Lehwess was ordered to appear in court in London, South Sumatra Rubber Estates, the National Archives, J 13/6051.
14 For more details of this controversial agreement see John C Bird, *Control of Enemy Alien Civilians in Great Britain, 1914-1918*, Garland, 1986.
15 Luggage of Dr Edward E Lehwess, 24 May 1918, German prisoners, the National Archives, FO 383/441.
16 Petition of the Board of Trade, dated 18 April 1918; affidavit of Elsie Ractliffe, 11 July 1918, Mechanical and General Inventions Ltd, the National Archives, J 13/8025.

17 Affidavit of Emmanuel Ginsbourger, 30 April 1921, and George Esden, 21 June 1921, Mechanical and General Inventions Ltd, the National Archives, J 13/8025. Cecile Ginsbourge married Lehwess on 26 June 1913. One of the witnesses was Robert Asch. The spelling of the surname varies: among the other variants are Ginsburger and Gintzburger.

18 Affidavit of Emmanuel Ginsbourger, 30 April 1921. The debentures were originally issued to Robert F Tochtermann and then passed on to Jenny Lehwess. Tochtermann was a director of Lehwess's US company, the United States Taxameter Company.

19 Affidavit of Elsie Ractliffe, 11 July 1918.

20 Affidavit of Edward Ernest Lehwess, dated 6 July 1922, Mechanical and General Inventions Ltd, the National Archives, J 13/8025.

21 Aeronautical Supplies, the National Archives, MUN 4/6460. See note from treasury solicitor, 29 March 1926. Lehwess had previously successfully sued Albatroswerke for compensation. The company had been reconstructed and the successor company denied liability and refused to pay up.

22 Various devices for recording speed, the National Archives, Metropolitan Police, MEPO 2/3883. Linton Thorp, KC, MP (1884–1950) who wrote in support of Lehwess was the son of Frederick Thorp, one of the founders and directors of the Asiatic Banking and Trading Corporation. Linton Thorp's obituary is in the *Times*, 8 July 1950, p. 6.

23 Mechanical and General Inventions Ltd, the National Archives, J 13/8025, petition of the Board of Trade, dated 18 April 1918.

24 *Daily Mirror*, 23 October 1933, p. 5; *Times*, 25 October 1933, p. 4.

25 *Daily Mirror*, 8 November 1933, p. 1.

26 *Daily Mirror*, 15 March 1935, p. 15; *Times*, 15 March 1935, p. 4. The case is mentioned briefly in Eric Estorick, *Stafford Cripps*, William Heinemann, 1949, p. 60. There are various court papers in Mechanical and General Inventions Ltd, the National Archives, J 13/14233.

27 *Financial Times*, 1 April 1935, p. 1. Arthur Riding was the company secretary of the electrobus company. The existence of the two companies led to a further successful legal action by the Austin Motor Company.

28 L'Omnium Financiers pour L'Industrie et Commerce, Les Archives Nationales (Paris), AJ 40/741, 1914. La Société Anonyme des Brevets Solcar & Aerable Monobloc changed its name in June 1934.

29 National Probate Calendar for 1947, p. 270. His British assets amounted to slightly less than £5000. His wife, Cecile, was denounced for being Jewish in *Au Pilori*. Not long afterwards she disappeared and the French police were unable to trace her. Dossier Lehwess, rapport de la SEC, 9 mars 1943, Les Archives Nationales (Paris), AJ 38 177 and L'Omnium Financiers pour L'Industrie et Commerce, AJ 40/741, 1914.

Select Bibliography

Arthur, W Brian, *The Nature of Technology: What It Is and How It Evolves*, Allen Lane, 2009.

Bagwell, Philip, *The Transport Revolution from 1770*, Batsford, 1974.

Barker, Theodore (T C) and Michael Robbins, *A History of London Transport*, vol. 2, George Allen and Unwin, 1974.

Bose, Mihir and Cathy Gunn, *Fraud*, Unwin Hyman, 1989.

Brendon, Piers, *The Motoring Century: The Story of the Royal Automobile Club*, Bloomsbury, 1997.

Buchanan, Colin, *Mixed Blessing*, Leonard Hill, 1958.

Day, John R, *The Story of the London Bus*, London Transport Executive, 1973.

Duguid, Charles, *How to Read the Money Article*, Effingham Wilson, 1901; seventh edition, Isaac Pitman and Sons, 1936.

Duncan, Herbert O, *The World on Wheels*, privately published, Paris, 1926.

Felstead, Sidney Theodore, *Horatio Bottomley*, John Murray, 1936.

Felstead, Sidney Theodore and Lady Muir, *Sir Richard Muir*, John Lane, 1927.

Fines, Ken, *A History of Brighton and Hove*, Phillimore, 2002.

Green, Benny, *The Streets of London*, Pavilion Books, 1983.

Harris, Frank, *My Life and Loves*, originally published in Paris, 1922–27, Corgi Books, 1967.

Hess, Alan, *Wheels Round the World*, Newman Neame, 1951.

Hooley, Ernest Terah, *Hooley's Confessions*, Simkin Marshall, 1925.

Select Bibliography

Huntford, Roland, *Shackleton*, Hodder and Stoughton, 1985.

Kaye, David, *British Battery Electric Buses*, Oakwood Press, 1976.

Keats, John, *The Insolent Chariots*, J P Lippincott, 1958.

Kingsmill, Hugh (pen name of Hugh Kingsmill Lunn), *Frank Harris*, John Lehmann, 1949.

Kirsch, David A, *The Electric Vehicle and the Burden of History*, Rutgers University Press, 2000.

Klapper, Charles, *The Golden Age of Buses*, Routledge and Kegan Paul, 1984.

Kynaston, David, *The City of London*, vol. 2, Pimlico, 1995.

Lee, Charles, *The Early Motor Bus*, London Transport, 1974.

Marjoribanks, Edward, *The Life of Sir Edward Marshall Hall*, Victor Gollancz, 1930.

Mayhew, Alfred, *Mayhew's What's What in the City*, Mayhew's Financial Publications, 1913.

Meredith, Hubert A, *The Drama of Making Money*, Sampson Low Marston, 1931.

Mom, Gijs, *The Electric Vehicle*, Johns Hopkins University Press, 2004.

Murphy, Thomas D, *British Highways and Byways from a Motor Car*, L C Page, 1908.

Nicholls, Ernest, *Crime within the Square Mile*, John Long, 1935.

Nicholson, Timothy R, *The Trailblazers*, Cassell, 1958.

Nystrom, Elsa A, *Mad for Speed*, McFarland, 2013.

Pageant of the Century, Odham's Press, 1933.

Plowden, William, *The Motor Car and Politics in Britain*, Penguin, 1973.

Porter, Dilwyn, 'Speciousness is the Bucketeer's Watchword and Outrageous Effrontery his Capital', in *Cultures of Selling*, edited by John Benson and Laura Ugolini, Ashgate, 2006.

Porter, Dilwyn, 'A Trusted Guide of the Investing Public', in *Speculators and Patriots*, edited by R P T Davenport-Hines, Frank Cass, 1986.

Pullar, Philippa, *Frank Harris*, Penguin, 2001.

Reid, Carlton, *Roads Were Not Built for Cars*, Island Press, 2015.

Robb, George, *White-Collar Crime in Modern England*, Cambridge University Press, 1992.

Schiffer, Michael Brian, *Taking Charge*, Smithsonian Books, 1994.

Symons, Julian, *Horatio Bottomley*, House of Stratus, 2001.

Tenax (pseudonym for Edward Bell), *The Gentle Art of Exploiting Gullibility*, David Weir, 1923.

Thorold, Peter, *The Motoring Age 1896–1939*, Profile Books, 2003.

Tobin, A I and Elmer Gertz, *Frank Harris*, Haskill House, 1970.

Trollope, Anthony, *The Way We Live Now*, Chapman and Hall, 1875.

Wells, H G, *Experiment in Autobiography*, Gollancz, 1934.

Wells, H G, *Tono-Bungay*, Macmillan, 1909.

A fuller bibliography and notes on other sources can be found at www.mostdeliberateswindle.com

Acknowledgements

The research for this book has been carried out at a large number of archives and libraries. I owe a big debt to all their staff, people who know their collections inside out and generously nudge enquirers in the right direction.

My thanks in particular go to Joe Le Page of the Guernsey Registry, who scoured the registry's dusty basement and found the records of an enigmatic unnumbered company in a long-forgotten ledger, and also to Jessica Bueno De Mesquita at the RAC Archives, who chased down the references to Lehwess in the club's archives.

Vic Bristoll and the staff at the wonderful newspaper library at Colindale also had an inexhaustible fund of knowledge about the papers and periodicals in their care. The library, which closed in November 2013, was an irreplaceable resource. Almost all the country's newspapers and even the most obscure reptile journals were available to be read at half-an-hour's notice.

I'd also like to thank the staff of the British Library (and especially the news room – Colindale's replacement), City of Westminster Archives, the libraries at the Institution of Electrical Engineers and the Institution of Mechanical Engineers, Les Archives Nationales in Paris and Les Archives Nationales du Monde du Travail at Roubaix, the London Transport Museum Archives, the National Archives and the University of Sussex Library.

A host of other archivists have diligently and helpfully answered my queries, including Patrick Collins at the Motoring

Reference Library (part of the National Motor Museum), Debra Lyons at the Cambridgeshire Archives, Shona Milton at the East Sussex Record Office, Mark Pool at Torquay Library, Tim Reid at Royal Borough of Kensington and Chelsea Archives, Peter Ross at the Guildhall Library, Jeremy Smith at the London Metropolitan Archives, Kate Swann at the National Army Museum and Glynn Wilton at the Tramway Museum Archives. I am particularly grateful to Colette Whitfield and her colleagues in Brighton and Hove's inter-library loan service. Their pièce de résistance was finding a vanishingly rare booklet, *Half-Forgotten Frauds*, that was not in any of the copyright libraries. They must have wondered about my esoteric reading tastes.

A large number of friends and colleagues have helped over the years, including Alison Goddard and Adam Goff. In the early stages of my research Ian Yearsley's encyclopedic knowledge of early motor transport was particularly helpful while Alan Felton gave me useful pointers on researching Edwardian music hall artists. I'd also like to thank Carol Dyhouse, who read an early draft, for her helpful suggestions. It is almost inevitable that over the ten years' research that has gone into this book I will have forgotten to acknowledge someone's contribution. I apologise in advance, but if you jog my memory I will make amends on the book's website: www.mostdeliberateswindle.com.

Finally I owe an enormous debt to my partner Stephanie Pain. She has not only put up with my obsessive pursuit of this story but also been an invaluable in-house editor.

List of Illustrations

List of Illustrations

Index

Index

Index

Horseferry Road garage 74-75, 79, 85-86, 120, 171, 240
Horses replace motor buses 92-93, 194
Hotel Cecil 9, 10, 12, 45, 81, 116, 117, 133, 139, 144-47
Hove, motor bus noise 191-95
Hybrid buses 192, 193, 195
Improved Electric Traction 52, 80, 163, 181, 202
International Motor Traffic Syndicate 19, 52, 95, 97-98, 130, 154, 157, 158, 180, 183
John Bull 67-68, 242
Khan, Sadiq, mayor of London 239
Lawson, Harry J 44-47, 64, 111
   Arrest of 39
   Relations with Lehwess 39-41, 49, 242
Lee Syndicate 199-201, 203, 207
Lehwess, Dr Edward Ernest 2-3, 24-25, 40-42, 52-57, 144-45, 180-81, 243-51
   Company promotions 59-61, 66-72, 204-05
   Court appearances 43-44, 154-59, 183-84, 205-07, 249-50
   In brawl 95-104
   Relations with Beall 111-13, 124, 150-52, 199-204, 208
   Relations with Delyannis 163, 167, 170, 173-74, 176-78
   Round the world drive 26-38
   Talks with Gould 73-81
Lehwess, Jenny 26, 34, 57, 158-59, 245, 248
Locock, Captain Edward Ainslie 69-71, 79, 80, 95-104, 155, 158
London bus, standard 225-26
London Electrobus Company 9, 52, 55-56, 94, 160, 168, 170, 172
   Debentures issue 142, 144, 159, 167, 173, 176, 178
   General meetings 105, 139-40, 142-44

Returns investors' money 51, 53-54
Share issues 13-16, 17-25, 113-14, 121-25
Shortage of electrobuses 140-44
London General Omnibus Company 14, 92-93, 151, 197, 223, 225
London Motor Omnibus Company 14
London Road Car Company 48, 57, 92
London to Brighton
   Car (emancipation) run 40, 116
   Electrobus run 116-17, 119-20
   Parcels van service 67
London, motor bus boom 48-49, 59, 75, 86, 92, 220
Longman, William 55-56, 60-63, 69-70, 73-77, 111-13, 115, 150-51, 250
Loughborough, electrobus visit 129
Macdonald, Norman D 59, 63-65
Macrory, Louis 102
Mansion House meeting 134-36
Martigny, Baron de 10-11, 17, 19-20, 52-53, 57-58, 81, 250
Martin, Sir Theodore 86-90
Massachusetts Institute of Technology 226-27
Maxim's, Parisian restaurant 32, 145
Mayhew, Alfred Hercules 61-62, 64-65, 186
McIver, Lewis, MP 135-36
Mechanical and General Inventions Company 243-47, 249-50
Merchant, James 110-11, 204, 213, 215-18
Metropolitan Steam Omnibus Company 141
Milk floats 229-30
Modern Traffic Development Corporation 69-71
Montagu, John Douglas-Scott 28
Motor bus
   Breakdowns 11, 121, 223
   Fires 11
   Noise 14, 86, 91, 93, 130, 134-36, 191, 194

Index

Index

Trams 11, 96, 120, 129-30, 137, 190-91, 196

Tree, Herbert Beerbohm 137

Truth 5, 89-90, 152, 161, 166, 169, 178, 182, 185, 188, 191

VHS and Betamax video tapes 236-37

Victoria (Malaya) Rubber Estates 199-200

Vincent, Helier Alexandre 184-85, 187-89

Webb, Beatrice and Sidney 27, 226

Webb, Thomas, of the *Critic* 208-13, 218

Wells, H G 6, 30, 31, 219

Wilkinson Sword 13, 144

Yelverton, Roger 178, 180, 184

York, electrobus visit 129-30

About the Author

Mick Hamer has been a freelance journalist for more than 35 years, writing for news-stand magazines and Fleet Street papers. For most of this time he was *New Scientist*'s transport consultant. In 2001 he was short-listed in the Syngenta science writing awards.

Transport has been the focus of much of his journalism. He covered the public inquiries into the King's Cross Fire, the Clapham rail crash and the Zeebrugge ferry disaster for several national media organisations.

Before carving out his career as a freelance journalist Mick Hamer worked for Friends of the Earth. In 1977 he became the first director of Transport 2000. He later worked on transport research at University College, London.

He lives in Brighton and has another life moonlighting as a jazz pianist.